P9-CKS-724

The Quest for Permanence

The Quest for Permanence

The Symbolism of Wordsworth

Shelley and Keats

821.71
P419q

David Perkins

112903

LIBRARY ST. MARY'S COLLEGE

HARVARD UNIVERSITY PRESS

Cambridge, Massachusetts

WITHDRAWN

Permission has been received from the following publishers and copyright holders to quote passages from the following publications:
From "Burnt Norton" in *Four Quartets,* copyright, 1943, by T. S. Eliot. Reprinted by permission of Faber and Faber, Ltd., and Harcourt, Brace and Company, Inc.
From *A Witness Tree* by Robert Frost, copyright, 1942, by Robert Frost. Reprinted by permission of Henry Holt and Company, Inc., and Jonathan Cape, Ltd.
From *Collected Poems* by Thomas Hardy. Reprinted by permission of Macmillan and Company, Ltd., London; The Macmillan Company, New York; and St. Martin's Press.
From *Collected Poems* by W. B. Yeats. Reprinted by permission of Mrs. W. B. Yeats, Macmillan and Company, Ltd., London; The Macmillan Company of Canada, Ltd.; and The Macmillan Company, New York.

This book has been aided by a grant from the
Ford Foundation

© Copyright, 1959, by the President and Fellows of Harvard College
Distributed in Great Britain by Oxford University Press, London

Third Printing, 1969
Library of Congress Catalog Card Number 59–11515
Printed in the United States of America

To the memory of Miriam Williams

Preface

The concern of this study, as described in the opening chapter, is the way in which an urgent preoccupation has simultaneously controlled both theme and style, or form, in the work of three individual poets. It tries to concentrate on a leading characteristic of poetry since the romantic age: the need and development of symbols in a context (an organic conception of nature openly, even militantly espoused) that both stimulated and at the same time frustrated the attempt. With the loss of conventions familiar since the Renaissance, the English romantic poets were confronted with a dilemma in expression, and they tried to resolve it through a new exploration into the use of poetic symbols. The intention here is to consider Wordsworth, Shelley, and Keats as they open three different approaches which have since been extended and refined. Any attempt to catch poetry in the process of one of its large historical transitions must have the pious hope of drawing whatever range of implication it may have from fidelity to what is individual in the particular writer. It is partly for this reason that the critical method varies somewhat with each of the three romantic poets, and, in particular, that the final chapters on Keats focus more on specific poems. The smaller bulk of Keats's output, of course, more readily permits such an approach; but the important consideration is that his mode of expression demands it. Compared with Wordsworth or Shelley, he is likely to build more qualifications and contrary tendencies into a given poem, and his method is also more dramatic, so that his personal beliefs do not always stand on the surface of his expression.

My obligations to previous critical writing are too large to list piecemeal. I am especially indebted to the fine interpretive studies of Professors Carlos Baker, Douglas Bush, R. D. Havens, Clarence Thorpe, Earl Wasserman, and Newman White. I am also grateful to many friends and students for criticism — both constructive and destructive — of my notions, and should especially mention Mrs. Gabriella Schlesinger. To Professors Douglas Bush, W. J. Bate, and Hyder Rollins, who have taught, prompted, and corrected me for many years, I owe more than I can say.

D. P.

Cambridge, Massachusetts
August 1959

CONTENTS

The Quest for Permanence

❦ I ❦

WORDSWORTH

The Isolation of the Human Mind

Unquestionably, poetry during the last century and a half has been passing through one of its major transitions. There is no reason to suppose that this transition has come to an end; but we may at least have reached a point where we can view it in one long perspective. It would seem less startling now than twenty years ago to say that Wordsworth, Arnold, and Eliot, for example, have more in common with each other than with Blake, Shelley, or Yeats. The younger Eliot may have spoken slightingly of the "ruminative" verse of the nineteenth century, but the *Four Quartets* are in the Wordsworthian vein of introspective meditation which Keats generously praised as a new means of "thinking into the human heart." Yeats, though he descends more through another line, willingly proclaimed himself to be one of the "last romantics." We are less eager than we used to be to deprive him of that claim (except that we might discount his word "last" as natural bravado). At the same time it is obvious that all of these writers share preoccupations, anxieties, and resources in making poetry which distinguish them from previous writers, and which permit us, if we are not lost in local variegations, to discuss them as a unit.

If we take the late eighteenth and early nineteenth centuries as a watershed, as a period in which new themes

1

created new opportunities and challenges still urgent today, it will follow that our contemporary poetry has its main source in the great romantic writers. It is true that the romantics themselves turned to the past, or to certain selected pasts, for aid and reassurance. But the habitual images and symbolic assertions of their poetry, where perhaps we tap a deeper level of feeling, do not suggest a comfortable repose on the past. Where the neoclassic poet often tended to picture himself as a later Horace fingering in his garden or rural retreat the modes of a long and mellow tradition, the romantic writer, in his usual metaphors of the poet, expressed his sense of breaking through to new areas. It is not that the romantics deliberately sought novelty for its own sake. But the "cloud of mind," as Shelley said, was "discharging its collected lightning." [1] They found in themselves certain urgent notions, impressions, and way of feeling which had not previously been exploited in poetry, and hence they had to create some relatively new technical means to accommodate them. Partly for these reasons, they tended to represent the poet in the image of the discoverer, a man isolated in some difficult exploration or quest. It is a figure which aroused a mingled anxiety and pride, and it is one which has a certain historical justice. They were explorers and pioneers, and they have been followed by settlers and squatters who have both carried further and domesticated their discoveries. Periods of intense intellectual exploration are often followed by years of codification and cataloguing, when the new "points and resting places in reasoning," as Keats called them, are pursued, refined, fitted together, and organized into system. From one point of view, this process

1. Preface to *Prometheus Unbound*, p. 202. Unless otherwise noted, all citations of poetry and miscellaneous prose by Wordsworth, Shelley, and Keats are from the Oxford Standard Authors editions: Wordsworth (1936), Shelley (1935), Keats (1956).

of refining describes what has been taking place in the literary history of the modern world. We are still living in the comet's tail of the early nineteenth century. Hence the romantic writers have an interest and a relevance for us which is more than merely historical without necessarily being universal. They faced circumstances basically similar to our own, and as a result they shared many of our hopes. Yet at the same time they mustered a confidence and inventive vigor which, like all large achievements, offers the most salutary reassurance to those who live within a similar context and must find a way to deal with it.

It would be tedious and ultimately impossible to specify all the ways in which the romantic context resembled our own. The present study will be concerned with a human tendency or need which, for the sake of brevity, could be called a quest for permanence. The phrase, like any other, is only suggestive, applying equally to the search for the objectively permanent and also to states of mind — confidence, calm, security, and the like — associated with the experience of certitude. One aspect, for example, is typified by romantic transcendentalism or romantic Platonism, except that here they are discussed in terms of emotional response, of need and desire, where they turn into poetry rather than abstraction, and where often they are too idiosyncratic to be pinned down in a formula. It is as much a reaction against immediate circumstances as a quest, or rather the two impulses are inextricably one: the romantic poets, like most people, possessed a clearer image of what they did not like than of what they would put in its place. It is rather difficult to blanket such different writers in any generalization, but in one way or another they were all haunted by the instability, the uncertainty, the jostle and constant change which seemed to them the leading principles both of their own psychology

3

and of the life around them (though not always, in the case of Wordsworth, of the natural world). At times, and this is especially true of Keats, they attempted to find meaning in the flux; but more often they simply turned away, yearning for a different reality, more stable and more suited to the needs of the heart. The theme is an inevitable, always renewed quest on which, rightly or wrongly, human nature is led. In developing it, we shall have to refer to the compulsions which underlie their search, to their different resolutions of it, and, with Wordsworth and, more tentatively, with Keats, to what finally led them to abandon it.

Of course, the search for what may seem stable and permanent is something innate in the human psyche, but in the modern world the search seems to have been intensified, or at least to have become more conscious and articulate. One obvious consideration is the breakup of a widely held religious view of life. It is worth remembering that the great romantic poets were seldom orthodox in their opinions. Although "Daddy Wordsworth," as Edward Fitzgerald called the aging poet, was a stern defender of the church, it was possible for Coleridge, in 1796, to refer to him as "at least, a *semi*-atheist." Shelley, of course, was banished from Oxford after writing his pamphlet on the *Necessity of Atheism,* and during the proliferation of his subsequent opinions he never came to terms with traditional Christianity. Keats, in so far as one can judge from his letters and poems, maintained a youthful and brilliant agnosticism. But the absence of religious faith does not bring about an escape from the needs religion serves. It simply means that something else must be put in its place, and the question, for all of these poets, was what. A second large factor which affects poetry from the romantics to the present time is the intuition of an organic universe.

4

Where the organic view of nature is held as a belief or presumption, it demands of the perceiving mind, if we would see things as they are, a certain "unity of being," to borrow Yeats's phrase. And if, in the modern world, the sense of the organic interconnection of things is not always present as an actual belief, it at least works strongly as a hope or idea. Hence when poets start to dwell on the fragmentation of experience, they do so with a distaste and dissatisfaction. There is, so to speak, a tendency to self-blame, or an extension and projection of self-blame. Thus the atomization of experience, when it becomes a theme, is not always asserted to be intrinsic in nature. Rather it is described as the result of our own inadequate sensibility, perhaps forced upon us by conditions peculiar to our own time. But if we start with a context where organic interconnection and process is assumed, and where the process is seen as infinitely extensive, how, in such a world, is the natural desire for permanence and stability to find an answer? And how is the answer to be anything more than a kind of outcry? Furthermore, if the assumption of an organic universe is not common to all poets, there is an always shared sense of the almost impossible multiplicity of experience. What any man must sift and take account of has piled to overwhelming proportions. Of course, there is always the possibility of a retreat in which, in one way or another, the actual complexity of human experience is largely denied. Here, as in other ways, the romantics were prototypes for modern poetry; for there was a temptation to withdraw into some form of aestheticism, or else into one or another variety of stoicism. Finally, one must take into account the fact that reality is seldom conceived as a body of stable fact unmodified by the perceiving mind. Rather, as the romantics knew only too well, the mind itself makes its own contribution.

5

The problem then is to find an expression which contains that additional complication without slipping back into a sort of desperate, step-by-step literalism in an attempt to be sure of our ground.

— 2 —

The quest for permanence, in so far as it becomes a paramount concern, inevitably becomes a leading theme of poetry. In other words, it is a dilemma from which poetry will be made. But the same factors which intensify the search for permanence also make it more difficult to write poetry. On the whole, poetry since the decline of neo-classicism seems to have devised and refined upon two ways of dealing with the modern context. One involves a step-by-step literalism. This is a poetry of naked statement, intensified, of course, by passion, but basically expository or descriptive of the poet's dilemma. We see an attraction towards this way of writing in such diverse figures as Wordsworth, Yeats, and Eliot, not to mention poets in between. On the other hand, poets, often the same ones, have also moved towards a way of writing which seems to permit condensation, suggestion, and a more sharply focused synthesis — in short, towards the use of symbol. It is on this second, more consciously innovational use of language that the present study will concentrate.

The tendency to rely on symbols in modern literature is an offshoot of the romantic movement. Not that the romantic poets themselves are used as models, though that may often be true. What is certainly true is that the romantics shared with later writers an urgent need for symbolic expression, and that they used symbols in analogous ways. In talking about symbols it is all too possible to complicate thought without advancing it. Hence throughout the discussion I

6

shall try to be closely empirical. For the present purpose it is sufficient to describe a symbol in literature as a key image which taps and summarizes a dense and often fluid complex of doubts, intuitions, emotions, preoccupations, and the like. As such it may appear through the body of a poet's work as a recurrent metaphor extending and deepening its significance from context to context. Or it may appear as the organizing principle of a particular poem — the Grecian urn in Keats's ode, for example. In such cases one can distinguish a symbol when the image used calls for a weight of response beyond what we should ordinarily be expected to grant and, secondly, when the image is elaborated at some length without much overt metaphoric reference. In other words, the second term of the comparison is not made obvious, either because it is not fully possessed by the writer or because its metaphoric reach is too complex and many-faceted.

Of course, poetic expression always involves the use of symbols, and speech itself can hardly be carried on without them. Yet when we turn to our own time, we find a number of factors which complicate the situation. For one thing, writers work within a context of critical utterance about symbols, beginning in England more or less with Coleridge, which makes them more aware of what they are doing. One of the effects of this increased sophistication is that the modern writer may be more willing to let the symbol speak for itself. He has, perhaps, more confidence in the symbol as a means of effective communication, and does not think it necessary to append detailed elucidations. Whether this confidence is completely justified is another question. Furthermore, the conscious need for symbols has imposed itself upon writers more at some times than at others, and seldom more urgently than at present. This is a large factor in the contemporary dilemma simply because our possible modes of experiencing have multiplied in the modern world. More roads are open to the human spirit, with the result that there is less agreement even on fundamentals. Now any artist whose total work merits consideration will be found pledged to a basic sincerity. He wants to tell the truth, or at least truth in a form appropriate to art. But in the absence of agreed interpretations this yearning for sincerity becomes very difficult to satisfy. In man's controversy with reality or truth, perhaps the heart of the struggle for wisdom is how to retain the urge toward honesty and yet not let it lock itself into a fixed mania for certainty and so become, in the long run, dishonest. Certainly there is the danger that the compulsion for certainty may create fatigue or despair, and, at the least, fritter away effort. For a writer, however, it is precisely this dilemma which symbolic expression can help to bypass. It keeps him from overtly committing himself. *Moby Dick* is an example. Ultimate issues are explored but nothing is ex cathedra, and notions of truth and falsehood are not an immediate consideration. A second point is that when society with the intellectual syntheses it supports is more diverse than homogenous, those writers uncommitted to a creed can be sure of little more than their own personal experience. Each must speak for himself and trust that he thus speaks for other men as well. But to the extent that he writes out of feelings which are intimate and private, he may tend to become inaccessible to his readers unless he provides a tedious length of commentary and exposition. Thus the problem becomes to put a large nexus of relatively personal concern in a way that is condensed, concrete, and referred to something objective; and the method of symbolism offers an answer.

I have been speaking of what are, in a broad sense, technical advantages which the use of symbols offers to a writer. The main advantage is that it permits him to remain in a state of what Keats called *"Negative Capability,* that is when man is capable of being in uncertainties, Mysteries, doubts, without any irritable reaching after" certainty. But, as Keats himself recognized, few men can be content for very long in this attitude. The fullest release of our energies ordinarily requires a confidence that they can be made to serve some of our most urgent needs. If it is thought that poetry is mainly amusement, or even that it can hope only to offer "a fine isolated verisimilitude caught from the Penetralium of mystery," [2] we would not expect a major poetic achievement. There must be a belief that poetry can do more, that it can be a means of discovering and communicating important truth. In this connection, we should not forget that romantic and later poets have lived in obvious competition with analytic thought and science; and the prestige of science has, of course, sharpened the need that poetry should arrogate to itself functions that science cannot fulfill. Hence the nineteenth- and twentieth-century defense of poetry has stressed synthesis and totality of impression. Poetry can give us, as Wordsworth, Coleridge, and Shelley explicitly said, a distilled version of totality, in which qualitative value (versus quantitative measurement) is included. Some version of this always appears in later English criticism, in Continental criticism since Kant's *Critique of Judgement,* and in the general modern defense of the humanities. We are touching, in other words, on the romantic doctrine of the imagination.

Whatever else may be involved, the word "imagination" always suggested to the romantics a power to make sense of the multitudinous glimpses of the phenomenal world. More than that, it is a process of insight and understanding which

2. To George and Tom Keats, 21 December 1817, *The Letters of John Keats,* ed. H. E. Rollins (Cambridge, Mass., 1958), I, 193–194.

9

reaches, in its highest function, to some ultimate vision of truth. As such, it is partially analogous to what in previous centuries had been called "reason." Indeed, Wordsworth at least once remarked that "Imagination" is simply "Reason in her most exalted mood" (*Prelude,* XIV, 192). But the word "reason" had been appropriated by scientific analysis, and the romantics needed another word to suggest the cognitive process they had in mind. Key words, however, never fail to react upon the conceptions they express, and the word "imagination" — especially when used in opposition to "reason" — had or developed implications rather different from those emphasized in the term "reason." For one thing, as reason throughout the eighteenth century came to denote analysis, imagination was conceived as a process of coalescing and synthesizing. Furthermore, it suggested an insight that was absolute, unverifiable by reason or any other process of mind. It stressed that the insight was immediate and spontaneous, and also that it was irrational and arose from unconscious sources. Moreover, the word "imagination," always retaining a residue of its previous meaning, continued to suggest a faculty that creates images. Hence in the romantics, thought itself, when it is of much value, is usually conceived as proceeding by means of images rather than in disembodied abstraction. The relevance of this to the justification of poetry is obvious. Finally, this exalted conception of the imagination gave dignity and importance, by a kind of spread and infiltration, to all mental processes which could be described as imaginative. As a result, purely visionary and dream-like elaborations were also felt to have a certain validity. Thus the romantic account of the imagination included most of the notions which, in more special applications, have served as a ground of hope and confidence for writers since. This has a major relevance to our discussion of symbolism; for the symbol can be viewed as a technical equivalent or result of the trust in imagination. As the romantics sometimes explicitly said, the imagination can give "birth to a system of symbols, harmonious in themselves, and consubstantial with the truths of which they are the conductors." [3] In using the symbol, stemming as it does, according to various formulations, from the imagination, the subconscious, the world-memory, or the distilled traditional wisdom of the human race, the modern writer intends to tap a mode of expression which can be trusted as a more limited and abstract, not to say willed, utterance can not.

But if in the modern world the need for symbolic expression is both more urgently felt and more openly acknowledged, it is also complicated by an additional factor. As we take up the more specific theme of this study, the quest for permanence as it shows itself in three poets, we find that one large aspect of this quest involves the search for adequate symbols. But to speak of "search" implies a certain lack. It is plain that the use of symbols in art has, in the past, tended to rest on the fact that certain attitudes or ways of feeling, being widely shared, had worked themselves into a conventional pattern of symbols. This pattern was, of course, equally available to the writer and his readers. But where such an agreement is lacking, the pressure towards representational, directly imitative art often seems to get stronger. At this point one can borrow a suggestive remark from Freudian psychology to the effect that directly representational or literal dreams show, in a particular person, that he has not yet become reconciled to his life; whereas plainly symbolic dreams suggest that some kind of an inner settlement has occurred. Now romanticism, as compared with the Renais-

3. S. T. Coleridge, *Statesman's Manual, Works,* ed. H. N. Coleridge (1839), p. 229.

LIBRARY ST. MARY'S COLLEGE

sance and the neoclassicism that capped the Renaissance, especially grew up in a state of unsettlement. This is even truer of the last half century; yet the unsettlement has been accompanied by a desire for symbolic expression. Hence the modern poet has been forced to find or create his own symbols, with all the concomitant dangers of seeming merely capricious or obscure.

Because they worked in a similar context which generated similar preoccupations, and because they developed technical means of expression which later poets have adopted and refined, the romantics can be regarded as prototypes for contemporary poetry. Or rather, since, despite common roots, they all vary in approach and method, they can be regarded as a number of prototypes, offering local harmonies and resolutions of the larger themes of poetry since the early nineteenth century. Specifically in Wordsworth, Shelley, and Keats, we find three different ways of making poetry of the quest for permanence or, to highlight another facet, three different resolutions of the anxieties created by the need for permanence.

— 3 —

What is written largest in Wordsworth as a prototype for modern poetry is not his solution (if it is a solution). Rather it is his sense of the gulf between human nature, with all of its greedy demands, its turbulent assertions, its often chaotic passions, and the rest of nature. Few critics have paid much attention to this side of Wordsworth,[4] for Wordsworth differs from most modern poets in that he does not accept the split as final or necessary. Hence there has been a natural tend-

4. Sir Herbert Read, *Wordsworth* (London, 1930), p. 183, remarks that "The distinction between the life of Nature and the life of Man is perhaps the most important point to remember in considering Wordsworth's poetry," but he does not develop the point.

ency to follow Wordsworth himself, and to stress his hope that the human mind can be formatively infused with the life of nature. But if one asks what motivates and gives urgency to this hope, and if one turns to Wordsworth's poetry without being controlled by his own overt emphasis, one finds that he was seeking to ease a suffocating, almost panicky fear that man is doomed to isolation from the healthful influence of his natural surroundings. In the poetry, this fear expresses itself, first of all, in situations where man is pictured as an actual intruder, whose "restless thoughts" and impulsive actions violate the harmonious "calm of nature."

In one instance the *Prelude* speaks of a "month of calm and glassy days" spent on an island during the war with France. "Each evening, pacing by the still sea-shore," Wordsworth heard the "monitory sound" of the "sunset cannon" (X, 320–325). While the sun

> went down
> In the tranquillity of nature, came
> That voice, ill requiem! seldom heard by me
> Without a spirit overcast by dark
> Imaginations, sense of woes to come,
> Sorrow for human kind, and pain of heart. (X, 325–330)

A key word here is the preposition "in." It implies that the sun went down in accordance with the tranquil order of nature proceeding without relation to human activities. But it also suggests that the cannon breaks in upon the "tranquillity of nature," shattering its "glassy" calm, or at least the calm it momentarily imposes on the human observer. The cannon calls to mind the bloody passions associated with war, and the dark imaginations it evokes suggest that the observer himself is all too precarious in his composure. He seems fearfuly receptive to the "voice" of the cannon, and as it intrudes it vitiates his response to the natural scene.

13

Another example would be the poem "Nutting," which describes a boyhood trip to the woods to gather hazelnuts. The child came to a nook which had not previously been visited. Here

> the hazels rose
> Tall and erect, with tempting clusters hung,
> A virgin scene!   (lines 19–21)

He stood still for a while

> Breathing with such suppression of the heart
> As joy delights in; and with wise restraint
> Voluptuous, fearless of a rival, eyed
> The banquet.   (lines 22–25)

After dallying beneath the tree, he rose

> And dragged to earth both branch and bough, with crash
> And merciless ravage; and the shady nook
> Of hazels, and the green and mossy bower,
> Deformed and sullied, patiently gave up
> Their quiet being.   (lines 44–48)

As he turned away from "the mutilated bower," he was "Exulting, rich beyond, the wealth of kings"; yet he also "felt a sense of pain when" he "beheld/ The silent trees." In this poem, the phrasing carries obvious sexual implications, and the emotions expressed — the joy of anticipated possession, the dallying, the "merciless ravage" and the remorse — affirm the root metaphor. To have felt and described the experience in these terms suggests not only how strongly he was affected but why. For although the remorse, which may be directly related to the patience of nature in enduring the attack, implies some chastening of the child's feelings, the incident revealed a chasm separating nature from the mind and habits of man. The shady nook does not infuse its calm into the human soul. The state of mind in which the grove is entered is the opposite of receptive. Guilty and assertive feeling blots out almost all sensitivity to the scene except the "voluptuous" temptation to take and mar. In other words, we do not discover here an approach to nature with the receptivity Wordsworth would have conceived formative. Instead, it is a misuse, an onslaught; and the place is accordingly left "deformed and sullied."

"Nutting" provides something of a prototype for recurring episodes in the *Prelude*. Among the most marked is the account of stealing out at night, as a child, to snare woodcocks:

> Through half the night,
> Scudding away from snare to snare, I plied
> That anxious visitation; — moon and stars
> Were shining o'er my head. I was alone,
> And seemed to be a trouble to the peace
>
> (*Prelude,* I, 312–316)

of the surroundings. A passage from an earlier version had related

> How my heart
> Panted among the scattered yew-trees, and the crags
> That look'd upon me, how my bosom beat
> With expectation.[5]

Both versions then relate how "strong desire/ O'erpowered" him and he took a bird from someone else's snare:

> and when the deed was done
> I heard among the solitary hills
> Low breathings coming after me, and sounds
> Of undistinguishable motion, steps
> Almost as silent as the turf they trod. (*Prelude,* I, 321–325)

5. *The Prelude,* ed. Ernest de Selincourt (London, 1926), p. 506n. The lines quoted appear in ms. V. According to De Selincourt, V "is the earliest extant draft of any considerable part of *The Prelude,* and . . . should probably be dated 1799–1800" (p. xxii).

As in "Nutting," there is at first a strange, excited expectation. There is also a sense of guilt projected in the "low breathings" and "steps" he hears. But the guilt does not arise primarily from the theft. Significantly, he felt it before he took the bird "Which was the captive of another's toil." As soon as he came among the mountains he felt himself "to be a trouble to the peace/ That dwelt among them," and a sense of guilt objectified itself in his consciousness of the "crags/ That look'd upon" him. Like Gulliver among the Houyhnhnms, he was the only passionate, desiring intelligence in a harmonious and tranquil world. Similarly, when Wordsworth and his companions came as "plunderers" among the rocks or when he took the boat, "an act of stealth/ And troubled pleasure," and rowed swiftly out on the "silent lake," the experience is again construed as guilty desire amid the surrounding tranquillity (I, 326–400).

Boyhood episodes which involve his own personal acts provide particularly clear-cut illustrations of the sense of man as intruder, and the association of this intrusion with guilt. But analogous feelings appear in a reaction to other people — a reaction which may be less immediately vivid but which goes further in explaining the alternating blandness and deep uneasy disturbance with which Wordsworth's poetry treats actual human beings encountered within the setting of nature. Here one must not think of poems with an openly didactic theme, like *Peter Bell*, which is concerned with human beings who are unresponsive to nature, and who are automatically supposed to be guilty. This can be taken for granted. Less obvious, but more general and disturbing, is the feeling that the mere presence of human beings may bring a certain stain, an uneasy ripple, upon the calm surface of nature. A singularly apt example occurs in an episode in the *Prelude* (V, 435 ff.) where the body of a

16

drowned man is recovered from a lake. The setting as a whole is one of complete tranquillity. The man himself, as he rises "bolt upright" with a "ghastly face" is dead. In a real sense, the drowned man has about as much or more repose than human nature would ever wish. But the point is that Wordsworth tacks on to the incident a rather prosaic statement that he was able to tamp down his reaction to it, that it did not unduly affect him. There is surely some significance in this need to reassure himself. It is also suggestive that the actual presentation of the occurrence is far more impressive than the attempt to state that he was capable of taking it in his stride. The "anxious crowd" that huddles in the twilight about the lake, the people in the boat, "sounding with grappling irons," are not themselves an intrusion. They are associations brought in as mere planetary actions gravitating about the rising of the human corpse. What does intrude is the corpse itself, "ghastly" and "bolt upright" in the very midst of the tranquil lake — "mid that beauteous scene/ Of trees and hills and water." It is "a spectre shape/ Of terror," frightening in itself and possibly the more disturbing because it symbolizes the poet's own fears concerning human nature. And the very violence of these fears may be what compels Wordsworth to assert that the incident could be blunted, the fears managed.

So, in the encounter with the veteran soldier, earlier in the *Prelude* (IV, 353–469), we have a projection of the profound sense of man as alien or intruder, though in this case a temporary or *ad hoc* resolution is found. And the resolution presents, in miniature, what Wordsworth was trying to conceive as a possibility. At the end of the episode, the veteran fades into the context of nature, just as (in a very different way) the dead maiden in "A slumber did my spirit seal" is made one with nature's "diurnal course," caught up

17

in a solemn and inevitable absorption into "rocks, and stones, and trees." In this particular instance, the veteran finally proves, like the leech gatherer, Michael, and other characters who represent Wordsworth's hope for human nature, to have a "demeanour calm," to come close to being "solemn and sublime." In other words, he possesses all the qualities usually located in nature and none that Wordsworth usually associates with man. Hence at the end of the incident the poet finds himself able to continue on his way "with quiet heart."

But the background of the encounter, however it may have been resolved, and the poet's first impressions, are extraordinarily revealing. Wordsworth, to begin with, is returning home, late at night, from a visit with friends. The contrast that this solitary walk presents with the earlier part of the evening is sharp. Certainly there is no conscious intention to refer back to the particular visit or evening-party, but there is still the brooding reflection that we are "parted," as he says, "from our better selves" by

> the hurrying world, and droop,
> Sick of its business, of its pleasures tired. (IV, 355–356)

This thought leads immediately to a passage in direct praise of "Solitude" — "How gracious, how benign" — and even of a "mere image of her sway" such as

> a public road,
> When, for the night deserted, it assumes
> A character of quiet more profound
> Than pathless wastes. (IV, 367–370)

But Wordsworth also remarks that an image of "Solitude" becomes "Most potent when impressed upon the mind/ With an appropriate human centre," a "hermit,/ Deep in the bosom of the wilderness," or a "Votary . . . Kneeling

18

at prayers" alone in some "vast cathedral." He goes on to suggest that the lonely veteran standing in the road was also a "human centre" embodying the "soul" of "Solitude." These lines represent Wordsworth's own effort to account for the deep impression made by the encounter.[6] What is striking about them is that the explanation does not seem to accord with the experience, as though Wordsworth himself could not recognize or admit what was involved. At least, when first seen the veteran is felt to be anything but "gracious" or "benign."

Before the encounter, the quiet and calm of the scene is emphasized. Except for the sound of a brook, there is complete silence:

> No living thing appeared in earth or air,
> And, save the flowing water's peaceful voice,
> Sound there was none.   (IV, 385–387)

Then suddenly there is the meeting with another person. At once the tranquil peace of the scene, and of Wordsworth's corresponding mood, is shattered. Instead of blending into the natural scene, the man intrudes upon it. He appears as an "uncouth shape," assertively "stiff, lank, and upright" (we may remember that the corpse emerges from the bosom of the lake "bolt upright"). Moreover, this innocent and solitary human being is seen as "ghastly in the moonlight." Even later on, after the meeting, his is a "ghostly figure." Also, when Wordsworth, still unperceived, first notices him,

6. In fact, lines 354–365 discussing the power of solitude when "impressed upon the mind" by a "human centre" were added subsequent to the 1805 version of the *Prelude*. As De Selincourt remarks, p. 525n., they were added, "doubtless, to explain the strange effect produced upon him by his meeting with the soldier. But . . . the rather elaborate style . . . contrasts awkwardly with the bare, telling simplicity of the narration that follows."

> From his lips . . .
> Issued low muttered sounds, as if of pain
> Or some uneasy thought.   (IV, 404–406)

The intrusion, in other words, is more than physical. It involves the presence of human pain and guilt in the natural world. Moreover, the guilt imputed may be something more than what Wordsworth usually associated with human nature. The first reaction may have been to see the man as guilty because he intrudes. Nor do later developments completely belie these impressions. He is, as Wordsworth learns, a veteran soldier, a reminder of the violent emotions unleashed in war. By association, he arouses a disturbing train of images in the poet's mind, yet, at the same time, being solitary and surrounded by the "vast cathedral" of nature, he gradually permits these images and associations to be managed. In fact, as it turns out, he has certain traits of character which offer a kind of catharsis; for when Wordsworth, learning that he is a veteran, is led to broach the subject of

> war, battle, and pestilence,
> Sprinkling this talk with questions, better spared,
> On what he might himself have seen or felt, (IV, 437–439)

the veteran answers calmly, with

> a strange half-absence, as of one
> Knowing too well the importance of his theme,
> But feeling it no longer.   (IV, 443–445)

It is partly this lack of feeling in the veteran which calms and subdues the agitations he had roused. Indeed, this "half-absence" suggests exactly what Wordsworth sought when faced with situations of emotional stress. But however the catharsis or resolution may have been achieved, the poet's immediate reaction may remind us of Robinson Crusoe's sudden fear when, after so many years of solitude, he suddenly discovered a human footprint in the sand.

— 4 —

We seem to have at the start, therefore, a conception of human nature quite different from what we associate with romantic primitivism. This is perhaps one of the values of reconsidering Wordsworth's poetic symbolism. It helps to get us away from any notion that he is an English, landscape-loving version of Rousseau. At least it qualifies any such notion in a fairly drastic way. The result is a gain not only in the interests of historical accuracy, and the judicial interpretation of Wordsworth himself, but also in seeing his relevance for the understanding of later poetry. It is hard to feel deeply involved when issues are bracketed in a simple, Rousseauistic way. Our own primitivism is a good deal more refined and elusive. Wordsworth has left a large body of theoretical statements, not only in his prose but in his verse, which make a veritable treasure-house for illustrating (or at least for documenting) the history of romantic primitivism. His avowed purpose, indeed, as he says in the Preface to the *Lyrical Ballads,* is to show man in his "natural" state; and that natural state, he also says, is one in which man is living in close communion with nature. Certainly Wordsworth concentrates on simple folk, who are supposedly formed or attuned to their surroundings. This can be taken for granted as an intention or hope in Wordsworth that is strong enough to be called a genuine preoccupation. Yet it can be joined with other feelings just as strong; and the result can be a chemical admixture, as it were, that has unique properties of its own.

The principal liability of the term "primitivism" when

it is applied to Wordsworth may be in suggesting a confidence that the state being idealized is historically natural, a condition from which man has fallen away. With it goes the optimistic suggestion that all we have to do is get back on a former track. Now Wordsworth says things, in an explicit, almost prosaic way, particularly in his earlier writings, that do fit in with this. Yet if we go beneath the surface, and also prevent certain obiter dicta from dominating our imaginations, we find something more complicated, more disturbing to him, and more significant for later poetry. The separation of man and nature that I have been sketching is not conceived as a new thing, caused by recent mistakes. It is darkly but still deeply felt as something intrinsic in human consciousness itself. Wordsworth's blasts against city life, against industrial growth, and the like do not arise from any very deep assurance that what came before was a true *beau ideal*. They are reactions to threats that are pressing at the moment.

Characteristically, Wordsworth never equates the human mind proceeding by itself with the permanent qualities of nature that suggest order and serenity. Instead, the symbolic equation of the confusion and conflict of human impulses is the city. The city is wholly man-made; and in the city human nature is effectively walled within its own confines. It is not so much an example of man having gone off on the wrong track as it is a symbol of the track human nature inevitably makes for itself. To some extent the city even suggests the almost aboriginal chaos of human passion and potentiality, left to itself, undirected and unformed by nature's influence. In a curious manner (curious because it is far from conventional romantic primitivism) Wordsworth almost exactly reversed neoclassic thought on this point.

The urban neoclassicist, of course, tends to assume that human nature retains its natural, primitive savagery unless it has been trained or molded by human civilization. The town with its conventions is man's garden, helping to protect him from his own instinctive barbarism. But to Wordsworth the "enormous City's turbulent world" reveals both the original state — the burden, push, and blind riot — and also the inevitable disease that human passion will create for itself when unprotected and unredeemed by nature. Hence his tone of "awed surprise," as Cleanth Brooks says,[7] when in "Composed upon Westminster Bridge" he is suddenly able to view the city as beautiful — "Earth has not anything to show more fair." The point, of course, is that at this moment before the city has awakened it seems "calm," "still," and susceptible to the benign influence of nature ("Open unto the fields"), and the surprise is so strongly marked in the sonnet precisely because this view of the city runs counter to Wordsworth's expectation. Almost invariably he dwells on the "folly, vice" and other "deformities of crowded life" where the "human heart is sick."[8] The most concentrated "epitome/ Of what the mighty City is herself" is found in the "blank confusion" of St. Bartholomew Fair, with its noisy babble, its "rivalship" of contending interests, its "grimacing, writhing, screaming," its human impulses "all jumbled up together." The city, in short, is viewed as "anarchy," and is to that extent "barbarian." The total result is that it can be "an unmanageable sight," just as the human mind can be so precariously unmanageable when cut off from the "Wisdom and Spirit of the universe."[9]

7. *The Well Wrought Urn* (New York, 1947), p. 5.
8. *Prelude,* VII, 578; VIII, 332; XIII, 204.
9. *Prelude,* VII, 676–732, *passim;* I, 401.

— 5 —

When Wordsworth discusses human psychology in a theoretical way, he is naturally more concerned with the means by which man can establish contact than with illustrating or rationalizing his separation. Here again, man's isolation does not appear as a point Wordsworth cared to labor abstractly or deliberately. It is something that he takes for granted; and the sense of it, in Wordsworth's treatment of the human mind, dominates his imagination most when he is concerned with more than theoretical discourse. The city, as a prototype of human nature walled within itself, is matched by another recurring symbol which is more directly associated with the individual mind. This is the image of the cavern or abyss, and the principal implication of the symbol is an inevitable, and fearful, isolation from any external medium through which the mind can be healthfully governed. There is also the suggestion of fertility and creation. For this cavern is a lair alive with impulses and imaginative stirrings. Creative achievement, indeed, is always associated with the "depths" or "recesses" of the soul: "Oh! mystery of man, from what a depth/ Proceed thy honours"; imagination "rose from the mind's abyss"; "from deep/ Recesses in man's heart," from "the hiding-places of man's power." [10]

But the effect of the image is to emphasize the solitude even of imaginative creation. So with the poet in particular:

> Possessions have I that are solely mine,
> Something within which yet is shared by none,
> Not even the nearest to me and most dear,[11]

10. *Prelude,* XII, 272–273; VI, 594; I, 231–232; XII, 279.
11. *The Recluse,* lines 686–688, in *The Poetical Works,* ed. Ernest de Selincourt and Helen Darbishire (London and New York, 1940–1949), V.

and Wordsworth goes on to say that his attempt is to "impart" these inward possessions. In other words, in creative activity the poet dwells on what isolates him from other men. Indeed, one can go further and say that it is the slightly variant or novel way of seeing which largely justifies the poet's effort. It is his contribution to human sensibility, to human knowledge, and, perhaps, in an extreme or purely ideal statement of romantic thought, it is an enrichment of the cosmos itself. Hence in a key passage Wordsworth speaks of the mind as "my haunt, and the main region of my song." Of course, Wordsworth is never so thoroughgoing as Blake, who at times conceives that every man creates and inhabits his own private universe. But he did assume that each man's vision is too unique and personal to be completely communicated. Hence the stress on the inadequacy of words. Even when most successfully used, they are in effect a compromise. When men possessing "the vision and the faculty divine" are "grasping with their greatest strength," words are often "but under-agents in their souls." "In the main," the visionary power lies in the "soul's deep valley" where it is "far hidden from the reach of words," far, in fact, "from any reach of outward fellowship." [12]

But the larger fear suggested by the cavern is not isolation from one's fellows. Rather it is of being pocketed or closed off from the external universe. "*Caverns* there were within my mind which sun/ Could never penetrate." Separated from what is outside, the mind can become "the blind and awful lair" of "madness," the "blank abyss" where man can be "lost within himself/ In trepidation." [13] By man "lost within himself" Wordsworth does not refer to subjectivism

12. *Prelude,* XIII, 273–274; "Yarrow Revisited," line 39; *Prelude,* III, 183–184; XIV, 217.
13. *Prelude,* III, 243–244; V, 151–152; VI, 469–470.

as the term is usually used. Instead, he refers to a nightmare state approaching "madness" in which the mind has nothing external on which it can fix and reflect itself. "Debarred from Nature's living images," and "compelled to be a life unto herself," the mind becomes "self-haunting." [14] To the extent that human feelings are violent the fear may be intensified. In this connection we are justified in noting the numerous testimonies from Wordsworth and those who knew him to the extraordinary turbulence and strength of his own feelings. De Quincey, for example, referred to the "preternatural animal sensibility diffused through *all*" Wordsworth's "animal passions." [15] Wordsworth himself speaks, in the *Prelude,* of his "unmanageable thoughts," of scenes that "Would leave behind a dance of images,/ That . . . break in upon his sleep for weeks" (VIII, 114–115). Similar evidence is provided by Wordsworth's reaction to the French Revolution:

> my nights were miserable;
> Through months, through years, long after the last beat
> Of those atrocities, the hour of sleep
> To me came rarely charged with natural gifts,
> Such ghastly visions had I of despair
> And tyranny, and implements of death. (X, 398–403)

When the mind can be haunted by such "ghastly visions," the need to climb out of it is desperately felt. One can understand the "trepidation" of man "lost within himself," isolated and "debarred from Nature's living images," and entombed within those "*Caverns* . . . which sun/ Could never penetrate."

14. *Prelude,* VI, 302–303; XIV, 284.
15. Quoted by Raymond D. Havens, *The Mind of a Poet* (Baltimore, Md., 1951), p. 367.

One of the most illuminating habits of romantic poetry is its tendency to dramatize the searching mind of man, and especially the poet himself as the quintessence of the searching mind, through the symbolic figure of the Wanderer, Outcast, or Solitary. In Byron, the poet as a type is presented as a man with capacities beyond those of most other men. Thus the poet associates himself with the sublimer elements of nature, with mountains, oceans, cataracts, and the like, because only in these can he find some mirror of his own titanic emotions. Furthermore, he is often pictured as an outcast. He has committed a crime that is in itself the expression of his more capacious nature; for most men would not have dared to conceive a like transgression. The outcast is wracked by guilt; and it is suggested that he bears without complaint an inward agony that lesser men could not support. The word "suggested" is used; for, when Byron himself becomes closely merged with the outcast, he must remind us of the woes he endures so that we may appreciate his uncomplaining fortitude. Coleridge's Ancient Mariner is, in some respects, a version of this Byronic figure, cut off from other men by the depth of his experience and by his own sense of guilt.

Wordsworth, of course, used the same image, or domesticated versions of it, to suggest similar attitudes. There are the various tours in London, the Alps, and France described in the *Prelude* and in many shorter poems as well. Perhaps nothing better suggests the appeal of the symbol than that the patriarchal and home-loving Wordsworth, "having," as Coleridge said, "even the minutest thing, almost his very Eating and Drinking done for him by his Sister, or Wife," [16]

16. *Collected Letters of Samuel Taylor Coleridge*, ed. E. L. Griggs (London, 1956), I, 291.

and later surrounded by many children, should claim that to some extent he cannot share the concerns of those who

> take in charge
> Their wives, their children, and their virgin loves,
> Or whatsoever else the heart holds dear.
>
> *(Prelude,* V, 152–154)

But the wanderer is not simply uninvolved in the common life of men; he has intense concerns of his own, is on a quest. In Shelley's *Alastor* or Keats's *Endymion* the quest suggests the pursuit of preoccupations peculiar to the poet as a special type. These preoccupations derive from unique endowments which allow him to enter realms of experience from which most men are barred. At the same time, they tend to isolate the poet still further. Wordsworth employs the symbol in a similar way. Though it was a very late addition, written when Wordsworth had otherwise ceased to be a wanderer, the powerful image in the *Prelude* of the statue of Newton is an example:

> Newton with his prism and silent face,
> The marble index of a mind for ever
> Voyaging through strange seas of Thought, alone.
>
> (III, 61–63)

Both because of his superior capacities, and because he is on a quest, the wanderer is often viewed with a mixture of fear and awe. These associations lie behind the emotions felt by Wordsworth when he says

> Yes, something of the grandeur which invests
> The mariner who sails the roaring sea
> Through storm and darkness, early in my mind
> Surrounded, too, the wanderers of the earth;
>
> .   .   .   .   .
>
> Awed have I been by strolling Bedlamites;
> From many other uncouth vagrants (passed
> In fear) have walked with quicker step. (XIII, 152–159)

The reference to strolling Bedlamites is perhaps particularly significant. To the "domestic" man the quest may seem not merely incomprehensible but a result of "madness." Perhaps it really is something bordering on insanity; Wordsworth does not always appear sure. And the uncertainty suggests that the poet, in so far as he identifies himself with the wanderer, is on the defensive. As a result, his assertions may become more extreme. What seems insanity may actually be reason — "in the blind and awful lair/ Of such a madness, reason did lie couched." And if the wanderer is mad, it is because he has been

> crazed
> By love and feeling, and internal thought
> Protracted among endless solitudes, —

"crazed," that is, by the ardors such a quest involves — and Wordsworth sometimes feels that he could willingly "share" the "maniac's fond anxiety, and go/ Upon like errand." [17]

But in Wordsworth the wanderer, as a symbolic character, is more usually presented without any particular reference to the poet as a special type. Examples can be found in "The Old Cumberland Beggar," "Guilt and Sorrow," *Peter Bell*, "Resolution and Independence" with its old leech gatherer — pacing "About the weary moors continually/ Wandering about alone and silently" (lines 130–131) — or in the first book of the *Excursion* which is itself called "The Wanderer." The symbol is so general and so habitually used that it may suggest an attitude to man as a species — that we are in some ways all wanderers, homeless and nostalgic within the natural universe. Of course, Wordsworth wanted to show a harmony between man and nature, and one could argue that the "Wanderer" in the *Excursion* or the Cumberland

17. *Prelude,* V, 145–160, *passim.*

beggar are instances of it, and that they are especially at home in nature precisely because they are footloose. In other words, if one thinks of the "trivial" bustle which fills so much of social life, one would argue that it is only by becoming a "wanderer" that man can hope to fulfill his own deeper needs. This is the positive content of the symbolism for Wordsworth. Negative implications are equally present but largely unacknowledged. They are necessarily involved in the notion of a quest, which at least implies that one has not yet attained final satisfaction.

Still more characteristically, the figure of the wanderer, in contrast with Shelley's avid journeyers in their rapid boats, often appears in Wordsworth as an onlooker, stationed, at least momentarily, in a position before which a large natural scene unfolds itself. Usually he looks from some ridge or promontory over a large body of water. Perhaps the finest of these many images is that of the

> lone shepherd on a promontory
> Who lacking occupation looks far forth
> Into the boundless sea.   (*Prelude*, III, 513–515)

In the typical occurrence of this image, the wanderer is uninvolved in the life he overlooks. His stance typifies his estrangement or alienation. It contrasts with the attitude of the reconciled man who is often symbolized as the child being embraced. Secondly, as long as the onlooker retains his position on the shore, the terrace walk, the boat, and the like he is safe. His position reflects a need to keep things at a distance. But most of all his stance suggests a desire to escape from the caverns of the mind in the contemplation of the external universe. The hope is that man "lost within himself" can look "with bodily eyes" from the "blank abyss" of his own mind; that he can "be consoled" by forgetting his restless and passionate confusion in the contemplation of nature; that he can turn to

> yon shining cliffs,
> The untransmuted shapes of many worlds,
> Cerulean ether's pure inhabitants,
> These forests unapproachable by death,
> That shall endure as long as man endures,
> To think, to hope, to worship, and to feel,
> To struggle, to be lost within himself
> In trepidation, from the blank abyss
> To look with bodily eyes and be consoled.
>
> *(Prelude,* VI, 463–471)

❦ II ❦

WORDSWORTH
The Linking of Man and Nature

Nothing is more widespread in contemporary criticism than our sense that the total work of an important writer embodies what Virginia Woolf once called a "private harmony." Here, of course, we differ from Renaissance and eighteenth-century critics, who frequently assumed that Homer, or some other poet, holds a mirror up to "nature" in all its fluid variety and scope. We are much more likely to think that any man has only a limited set of ideas or attitudes which are clarified and harmonized through a lifetime of effort, and hence to speak of the "universe" of some particular writer, or even of the "universe" of some major work. The word implies that the poetry consists of definite materials selected from a vaster potentiality, from what William James called the "blooming welter" of life, and ordered into a pattern. Hence one begins to define a writer's arrangement or vision of life when one considers not only what it includes, but also what has been left out. Wordsworth, Shelley, and Keats might all be described as "nature" poets. That is, they are "nature" poets if we mean that they closely observed natural phenomena, and that they expressed themselves largely through imagery and symbols drawn from nature. Yet despite their close observation, each of these poets focused primarily on particular aspects of nature to the exclusion of others, though what they focused on differed in each case.

Wordsworth was "haunted," as Whitehead said, "by the enormous permanences of nature." More or less ignoring the swift change and transformation that obsessed Shelley, he tended to notice "rocks/ Immutable, and everflowing streams." To a "mind intoxicate" with "the busy dance/ Of things that pass away," nature presents "a temperate show/ Of objects that endure." Even the images by which another poet might especially have depicted flux are often used by Wordsworth to express its opposite. In Shelley, for example, rivers and streams become metaphors of constant, sinuously rippled alteration; but in Wordsworth's poetry streams flow "in lasting current" and suggest the permanent qualities of nature — "Still glides the stream, and shall for ever glide." Here, of course, the double meaning of "still" puts exactly the qualities Wordsworth found in nature. Again Shelley might see a waterfall as an emblem of the turbulence and shifting variety of concrete life. Wordsworth, however, stands at a distance, and views even waterfalls as "stationary blasts." [1] Where Wordsworth does describe change and process in the natural world, it is slowed down until it scarcely intrudes upon the sense of permanence. Both Wordsworth and Shelley possessed, at times, a cosmic sweep; their imaginations extended to take in geological and astronomical mutations. But in Shelley these large scale transformations are speeded up until they become symbolic of the rapid flux he saw everywhere. In Wordsworth these planetary processes are retarded, and he dwells more on the unchanging continuity than on the dissolution of planets and stars.

1. *Prelude*, VIII, 170–171; XIII, 29–32; VI, 675; *The River Duddon*, "After-Thought," line 5; *Prelude*, VI, 626.

Often in Wordsworth's poetry the permanence of nature is felt most strongly by contrast with the brevity of human life. If, for the sake of condensing a potentially tedious exposition, we confine ourselves to the stream imagery already mentioned, we find that the "flowing stream" habitually gives rise to a "thought . . . Of Life continuous, Being unimpaired;/ That hath been, is, and . . . shall endure." This "thought" at once generates its antithesis, "the blind walk of mortal accident" where

> man grows old, and dwindles, and decays;
> And countless generations of mankind
> Depart, and leave no vestige where they trod.[2]

Usually this contrast is put more concretely, as in "The Fountain," where old Matthew, resting by a spring, reflects that it will "murmur on a thousand years,/ And flow as now it flows." At once he "cannot choose but think" of his own mortality. But the remorseless encroachments of time are not felt only in terms of individual life. In a situation frequent in Wordsworth's poetry, the stream flows by an architectural relic representing an enormous, vanished past. The men who built it are gone, and often the structure itself is falling into ruin under the "unimaginable touch of Time," but the stream is unchanged. Flowing forever with "unaltered face," it forms the stable background to the human shows passing on its banks.[3]

— 2 —

Wordsworth's treatment of man's impermanence thus seems to involve a good deal more than the matter of per-

---

2. *Excursion*, IV, 754–762.
3. *Ecclesiastical Sonnets*, "Mutability," line 14; "Yarrow Revisited," lines 105, 35.

sonal mortality. In fact, we begin to suspect that individual death itself becomes almost a symbol of something more troublesome. For one thing, as we have seen, the notion of impermanence — as contrasted with the unchanging presence of nature — extends beyond the mere individual to include whatever is characteristically associated with human nature or produced by it. There is, in Wordsworth, a comparative absence of the mixed pain and hope with which romantic and contemporary poets have tended to regard creative achievements. They have tended, that is, to see in the edifices of human thought, usually symbolized in architectural structures or some form of sculpture — Keats's Grecian urn, Yeats's bird of "hammered gold" or "moonlit dome" — a form of immortality which stands in sharp, often ironic contrast to flesh and blood. This is seldom the case in Wordsworth. Instead he insists that even the "consecrated works of Bard and Sage," what seem to be "adamantine holds of truth," will vanish. The creations of the "sovereign Intellect" may seem to "aspire to unconquerable life";

> And yet we feel — we cannot choose but feel —
> That they must perish.[4]

Only the "living Presence" of nature can be regarded as permanent and undying. Hence when Wordsworth insists on the mortality of man and his works, it should, perhaps, be construed as only a final instance of the chasm separating man from nature. Death itself is not an obsession with Wordsworth, nor does his quest primarily involve an attempt to find some reconciliation to the fact of death (as does that of Shelley, Keats, Yeats, or, for that matter, the Shakespeare of the sonnets). The great lines in the closing sonnet of *The River Duddon* — "We Men, who in our

4. *Prelude*, V, 15–42, *passim*.

35

morn of youth defied/ The elements, must vanish; — be it so!" — are not bravado. They are a real acceptance, even though the acceptance is not placid or joyous. But what is not accepted, and is a constant "trouble" to his "dreams," is man's isolation from nature while he lives. The quest for permanence, in so far as Wordsworth is concerned, should be regarded rather as a quest for a certain kind of stability and reassurance while we are alive. For it was the clamorous bustle of desire, and all that it creates, that Wordsworth especially hoped to escape. The primary need, in other words, is that man should "forget his feeling" in so far as it is turbulent and "unmanageable," should "mitigate the fever of his heart"; and the hope is that he can do this by dwelling upon whatever, not "touched by welterings of passion," seems to contain and infuse "Transcendent peace/ And silence." [5]

In the *Prelude* Wordsworth describes a dream which seems to suggest two ways in which man may hope to "manage" his feeling and escape from the stormy cavern of his own mind. He had been reading in a rocky cave and, laying aside the book, began to muse

> On poetry and geometric truth,
> And their high privilege of lasting life,
> From all internal injury exempt.   (V, 65–67)

Falling asleep, he dreamt that he was alone in a "wilderness." It was "black and void" (we remember that the mind can be a "dark pit" or "blank abyss"); and, as he looked about, "distress and fear/ Came creeping" over him (V, 72–74). At this point the usual wanderer figure appeared, this time in the guise of an Arab.[6] In his dream Wordsworth

---

5. *Prelude*, VI, 154; *Excursion*, I, 300; *Prelude*, VI, 138–140.
6. Cf. W. H. Auden's remarks on this passage, *The Enchafèd Flood* (New York, 1950), pp. 3–6.

felt that the Arab wanderer was a "guide . . . who with unerring skill" would "lead" him "through the desert." "Underneath one arm" the Arab carried a stone, and "in the opposite hand a shell." The stone, he told Wordsworth, represents "Euclid's Elements" — geometry or, more generally, abstract thought. The shell "is something of more worth," and it turns out to be a symbol of poetry or imagination in general (V, 72–89). Abstract thought and imagination, then, are both avenues by which man can ease or escape the burden of his feelings. The latter is "of more worth," but the tendency to view abstract speculation as an escape from the turbulence of personal feeling is still strong in Wordsworth, reminding us of Yeats in the Byzantium poems or of Johnson who, according to Mrs. Thrale, would turn to mathematics when he thought his fancy disordered.

When we speak of Wordsworth's attraction to abstract thought, and to geometry as a symbol of it, we do not picture him hurrying to purchase a copy of Euclid. We are dealing with a symbolic gesture which, of course, can become symbolic because it has some correspondence with literal human experience. At the same time, in view of Wordsworth's frequent attacks on mathematical logic and scientific abstraction elsewhere in his poetry, and his own aversion to studying mathematics at college, one may be surprised that he can discover any appeal in it, even as a symbol. The fact that he does so indicates how strongly he felt the need for a refuge, and it also suggests what he hoped to escape. The appeal of mathematics seems to be twofold. In the first place, through it one enters "an independent world" — a world "of permanent and universal sway" remote from "the disturbances of space and time." In the second place, geometry and abstract science are "created out of pure intelligence." By "pure" Wordsworth seems to mean not "touched

37

by welterings of passion." Thus he speaks of Archimedes as a "pure abstracted soul," [7] and the French Revolution was a time when there were many "speculative schemes"

> That promised to abstract the hopes of Man
> Out of his feelings, to be fixed thenceforth
> For ever in a purer element.   (XI, 225–227)

The hope, then, is that by the study of geometry man can center himself in a pure, unchanging, and independent world where he will escape from his own passions. Thus Wordsworth instances a person who was shipwrecked "upon a desert coast" (*Prelude*, VI, 144 ff.). He happened to have with him "A treatise of Geometry," and often he would "part from company and take this book . . . To spots remote." There he would draw "diagrams" upon the sand,

>   and thus
> Did oft beguile his sorrow, and almost
> Forget his feeling.   (VI, 152–154)

Generalizing upon this incident, Wordsworth remarks that although his own outward circumstances are very different, his needs are the same:

> So was it then with me, and so will be
> With Poets ever. Mighty is the charm
> Of those abstractions to a mind beset
> With images, and haunted by herself.   (VI, 157–160)

But the effort to compose or suppress feeling through turning to abstraction is seldom finally successful. In the more or less autobiographical history related in the *Excursion,* Wordsworth tells how before the Boy's "eighteenth year . . . Accumulated feelings pressed his heart." He was "subdued" by the "turbulence . . . of his own mind" (I, 280–284). In this situation, he turned to the intellect, and "from the

7. *Prelude*, VI, 166, 131; XI, 330; VI, 167, 138; XI, 435.

stillness of abstracted thought/ He asked repose" (I, 291–293):

> But vainly thus,
> And vainly by all other means, he strove
> To mitigate the fever of his heart. (I, 298–300)

Wordsworth, then, had little confidence in the "stone" of geometrical science as a resolution of the human dilemma. For abstract science works merely to suppress feeling. In fact, the "charm severe" of geometry — "the purer elements of truth involved/ In lines and numbers" — is

> Especially perceived where nature droops
> And feeling is suppressed. (I, 253–256)

Hence any consolation geometry may offer is precariously liable to disintegrate. "That genuine knowledge, fraught with peace" (*Prelude*, XI, 354), can only grow from whatever composes and so changes the character of human passion at the same time that it draws it forth.

The gestures toward abstract speculation are important mainly in illustrating how strong the need for stability is. Of course, Wordsworth urges that a union with nature is what frees the mind from the stir and thrust of its own dark emotions. But his poetry records a vast number of personal instances when the tranquillity seems to have been achieved in a different way. In these instances, one can see a number of psychological processes at work, all of which have as their result a tamping down and minimizing of immediate emotional concern. Feeling, in other words, is not shunted aside in these responses. On the contrary, it is actively present, but pitched in a diminished and manageable way. This, of course, suggests how these responses fulfilled a genuine need. If allowed to roam at large, the native passions of an anxious or restless heart will prey on the economy of personal life.

39

At the same time, they cannot be successfully caged, but must be gentled and domesticated while they are released. For Wordsworth, such a domestication could take place when the call to feeling is placed at a distance in space or time, weakened, so to speak, by the length of its journey. Or it could occur when what draws and focuses emotion is overwhelmed and almost lost in surrounding vastness. In either case, the result is that pressing human concerns are reduced in importance, and the heart is eased of their pull. In pursuing this subject, we shall have to consider the significance to Wordsworth of memory, history, the immensity of nature as contrasted with the human life it envelops, and a few other things. We shall be dealing, in other words, with reactions — both those which immediately involve nature and those which do not — which seem to have been sources of tranquillity and composure, but which Wordsworth did not usually recognize as such; for he almost invariably attributed the "calm existence that is mine when I/ Am worthy of myself" (*Prelude*, I, 349–350), to the union of the mind with nature.

— 3 —

The great enemy of human tranquillity, for Wordsworth, is

> passion over-near ourselves,
> Reality too close and too intense. (*Prelude*, XI, 57–58)

The desired attitude would be what he felt in the early days of the French Revolution:

> I looked upon these things
> As from a distance; heard, and saw, and felt,
> Was touched, but with no intimate concern.
> (*Prelude*, VI, 767–769)

As we have noticed, the various wanderers that people so much of Wordsworth's poetry seem placed in an attitude in which the totality of what they observe is seen as a single vista, in which, being reduced in scale, it becomes manageable. Even the city, the specific haunt of human stress and passion, can be contemplated with tranquil serenity from the vantage point of Westminster Bridge, particularly since, with its "smokeless air" it has not yet awakened and become a city. So, in the *Prelude,* as one leaves the city, its smoke, "by distance ruralized," is seen merely as a "curling cloud" (I, 88–89), as a part of the "face" of nature, instead of an indication of the presence of man. Wordsworth recollects such glimpses so frequently in his poetry because they were deeply satisfying to him. Viewed at a distance and amid the tranquillity of nature, man, with his desires and fears, can scarcely arouse strong feeling in the onlooker. Instead, he can be contemplated with a steady and detached calm. Furthermore, from a distance humanity, particularly rustic humanity, is seen together with clouds, hills, and trees virtually as part of a natural scene. No more a stranger, the human being seems reconciled and "fitted" to the surrounding universe.

But it is not only in a long spatial perspective that things can be viewed in this way. Through retrospection, events can also be contemplated "as from a distance" in time, and in the process even the most distressing occasions lose much of their power to obtrude and unsettle the mind's composure. Memory, then, provides another means through which human feeling, without being entirely shunned or suppressed, can be quieted and digested without any loss of personal tranquillity. By holding things at a distance, recollection enables the poet, like Emily returning to Rylstone, to receive

the memory of old loves,
Undisturbed and undistrest.   (lines 1754–1755)

In this connection it is important to note that the bulk of Wordsworth's poetry is retrospective. Indeed, his well-known formulation of the source of poetry — "emotion recollected in tranquillity" — exactly defines the desired state of mind and the role of memory in helping to achieve it. He wants the emotion, but he does not want it to be immediate and pressing. He goes on to say that in the "mood" in which "successful composition generally begins," the "emotion is contemplated till . . . the tranquillity gradually disappears, and an emotion, kindred to that which was before the subject of contemplation, is gradually produced." But he at once adds that the "emotion, of whatever kind, and in whatever degree . . . is qualified . . . so that in describing any passions whatsoever, which are voluntarily described, the mind will, upon the whole, be in a state of enjoyment." In other words, emotions "of whatever kind," even the more "painful" ones, are not to be allowed to intrude so far as to spoil the mind's "overbalance of pleasure." [8] Wordsworth is remarkably vague in explaining why or how the emotion is "qualified" so that the mind can retain its "state of enjoyment." The reader can only suppose that it is because the emotion is "contemplated" rather than immediately felt. The poet may vividly recollect the original powerful feelings, but he does so from such a distance that the recollected emotion cannot be oppressive and disturbing, but can only rouse and excite the mind to a pleasurable activity. The desired state, even if in recalling powerful feelings the "tranquillity gradually disappears," still remains, perhaps, to be "touched, but with no intimate concern."

8. Preface to the *Lyrical Ballads*, p. 940.

42

In addition to an unusually firm and active memory, Wordsworth possessed a powerful historical imagination, capable of vividly reconstructing the past and bringing it to his eye. In fact, his sense of history was so strong that sometimes, he says, it literally overwhelmed and obliterated his consciousness of the present. For example, once in his childhood as he "ranged at will" on "Sarum's Plain," "Time with his retinue of ages fled/ Backwards," and, becoming almost unaware of his present surroundings, he saw "Our dim ancestral Past in vision clear." He goes on, in the *Prelude* (XIII, 315–322) to describe the vision in detail — the "multitudes of men," the "single Briton clothed in wolfskin vest," and the like. Similarly, on his first entry into London, while sitting on the top of a coach, he saw

> vulgar men about me, trivial forms
> Of houses, pavements, streets, of men and things, —
> Mean shapes on every side.

But when he passed the "threshold" of the city "A weight of ages did at once descend/ Upon" his "heart," and the vivid sense of the enormous, vanished past momentarily usurped and virtually wiped out his consciousness of the "trivial" present (VIII, 544–552).

But we have been citing unusually intense and visionary experiences. Wordsworth's sense of history seems usually not to have blotted out the present but rather to have minimized its urgent stress and intrusion. Through the historical imagination, he was sometimes able to see the present, with all its restless concerns and demands, against so wide a background that it was reduced in importance and lost some of its power to agitate and alarm. When he was in France, "the experience of past ages" which he "carried about" with him prevented him from being "pressed upon" by "objects over near." In other words, Wordsworth was not at first

43

passionately committed to the revolutionary cause, or, as he
put it, "dipped/ Into the turmoil." Similarly, at Cambridge
he saw the present life of the college through a veil of history,
and therefore became more reconciled to it:

> here the vulgar light
> Of present, actual, superficial life,
> Gleaming through colouring of other times,
> Old usages and local privilege,
> Was welcome, softened, if not solemnised.

Even the "din" and confusion of London was "softened"
and made less oppressive by his vivid

> sense
> Of what in the Great City had been done
> And suffered, and was doing, suffering, still;

for his immediate consciousness of the "vulgar" and "trivial"
life of the city was swallowed up in his imaginative "sense"
of the "abyss of ages past." At such moments the city became
less a present reality than a token or symbol of human
destiny. As such, it could "support the test of thought," and
Wordsworth's "young imagination" could sometimes find
in it "no uncongenial element." [9]

— 4 —

In particular, the unsettling tug of immediate human
concerns seems often to have been lessened, for Wordsworth,
by his perception of an immense natural world surrounding
and engulfing these concerns. Seen against the large, tranquil
and impending forms of nature, human life itself becomes
reduced in importance and human passions are felt to be
less urgent and compulsive. Indeed, one sometimes has an
impression in reading Wordsworth — an impression so con-

9. *Prelude*, IX, 331–337; VIII, 505–509; 625–627; XII, 63; VIII, 628, 639–
640.

trary to his overt intentions and obiter dicta and so significant for later poetry — that man is a brief appearance on the surface, a kind of fungus momentarily clinging to the bleak, immutable rocks. For Wordsworth, the immediate result of this kind of contrast was, of course, that it tended to encourage a composed state of mind. We have already mentioned the incident in the *Prelude* (V, 435–455), where Wordsworth saw the body of a drowned man raised from a lake, but it is particularly relevant at this point. The episode occurred in Wordsworth's childhood. He crossed at twilight a peninsula on "Esthwaite's Lake," and saw on the "opposite shore/ A heap of garments." He watched them for a while, but no one came to claim them.

> Meanwhile the calm lake
> Grew dark with all the shadows on its breast,
> And, now and then, a fish up-leaping snapped
> The breathless stillness. (lines 439–442)

Next day, suspecting that someone had drowned, men sounded with poles for the body.

> At last, the dead man, mid that beauteous scene
> Of trees and hills and water, bolt upright
> Rose, with his ghastly face, a spectre shape
> Of terror. (lines 448–451)

Wordsworth, however, was not frightened, for, as he explains, he "had seen/ Such sights before" in "faery land." In this characteristic incident, the drowned man, a "shape/ Of terror," guiltily transgressing on the breathless stillness, is an image of humanity. Set against the enormous backdrop of lake and hills, he can make little impression. Even at the moment when he breaks the surface, Wordsworth notices the surrounding "beauteous scene." The fear inspired by the drowned man and the guilt he symbolizes have been swallowed in the immensity of nature. A similar episode is

45

Wordsworth's account of the death of a woodman in the forest (*Prelude,* VIII, 437–450). The man is "withering by slow degrees," dying in other words, but his death takes place

> 'mid gentle airs,
> Birds, running streams, and hills so beautiful
> On golden evenings, while the charcoal pile
> Breathed up its smoke.   (lines 446–449)

The charcoal pile breathing up its smoke may be an implicit metaphor of the man breathing up his soul. As such, it would help to define the tone of the verse, which, in any case, converts the death to something as natural and painless as the sunset which envelops it. Here again human suffering has been submerged in the tranquillity of nature, and the poet's feelings are not called upon. This type of response might seem of dubious moral worth; but it at least helped Wordsworth to reach and maintain the serene calm he sought.

One can even go further and suggest that the contrast of human life with the immensity of nature not only allowed Wordsworth to view human concerns with a detached composure, but that it also permitted, and at times even stimulated, feelings of tender benevolence directed to human life as a whole — feelings which he earnestly desired to cultivate, and which stand in marked contrast to the uneasy and frightened distress often provoked in him by the contemplation of specifically human life. One example is the description of a sunrise in the *Prelude*:

> Magnificent
> The morning rose, in memorable pomp,
> Glorious as e'er I had beheld — in front,
> The sea lay laughing at a distance; near,
> The solid mountains shone, bright as the clouds,
> Grain-tinctured, drenched in empyrean light;

46

And in the meadows and the lower grounds
Was all the sweetness of a common dawn —
Dews, vapours, and the melody of birds,
And labourers going forth to till the fields. (IV, 323–332)

Wordsworth goes on to describe how deeply he was moved by the spectacle. Like many of Wordsworth's most successful passages, this experience, so powerfully felt and so majestically conveyed, seems charged with some half-understood meaning working below the surface description. Wordsworth himself recognizes as much when, at the conclusion of the vision, he says "On I walked/ In thankful blessedness, which yet survives" (IV, 337–338). As in many such passages, the symbolic suggestion is obscure, and one can scarcely be explicit about it. But the significance of these lines rests in the contrast between the "common dawn" with its rustic chores, and what towers above it. The "solid mountains . . . drenched in empyrean light" are images or sudden revelations of natural glory and spiritual force resident in the cosmos. They are seen simultaneously with the common dawn, and the momentary vision is multidimensional and religious, discovering the numinous latent behind the concrete. At the same time the dawn draws its felt "sweetness" from the fact that it is "common," familiar, in contrast to the austere, unfamiliar glory of the mountain peaks. The laborers share in this "sweetness." In fact they are merely part of the landscape, and in such a setting can only be viewed with a tranquil eye of love.

A similar vision, less imaginatively intense, is that of the country people gathered for a fair upon the side of Mount Helvellyn. Dwarfed by the mountain which broods above them, they seem small, innocent, and helpless, and release a gush of sentiment. The *Prelude* describes Wordsworth's reaction quite explicitly:

47

>   Immense
> Is the recess, the circumambient world
> Magnificent, by which they are embraced;
> They move about upon the soft green turf:
> How little they, they and their doings, seem,
> And all that they can further or obstruct!
> Through utter weakness pitiably dear,
> As tender infants are.   (VIII, 55–62)

The comparison to infants should be noticed; for to Wordsworth the embraced infant almost always symbolizes man at home in the universe. It is, however, the contrast between the human beings and the immense natural surroundings which permits him to view the rustics as "pitiably dear."

Finally, it should be noticed that Wordsworth seems often to have been aided in "managing" his feelings by a kind of schizoid retreat, by a partial tendency to deny the reality of a present situation. That is, when immediately confronted with a circumstance which might be expected to arouse a distressing concern and to prey upon tranquillity, Wordsworth frequently reacts by viewing the circumstance almost as make-believe or dream. For example, he deals with the dying woodman partly by weaving an imaginary tale about him. He fancies "pangs of disappointed love,/ And all the sad etcetera of the wrong" as the cause of his death (VIII, 441–442). Hence he can react to the death as though the woodman were a character in a story. In the same way, Wordsworth remarks that when the body of the drowned man rose from the lake, "no soul-debasing fear . . . Possessed me." He himself proceeds to account for this by saying that his

>   inner eye had seen
> Such sights before, among the shining streams
> Of faery land, the forest of romance.   (V, 453–455)

48

He responded to the sight of the drowned man by almost denying its actual existence, seeing it instead as an episode in a romance; and the spirit of romance "hallowed the sad spectacle/ With decoration of ideal grace." Wordsworth also attributed this type of reaction to his friend, Beaupuy, who represents something of an ideal, and is praised for maintaining his serenity throughout the bloodletting of the French Revolution:

> He through the events
> Of that great change wandered in perfect faith,
> As through a book, an old romance, or tale
> Of Fairy, or some dream of actions wrought
> Behind the summer clouds.   (*Prelude*, IX, 298–302)

In this connection we may also note Wordsworth's discussion of meter in the Preface to the *Lyrical Ballads*, a discussion, one may think, which throws at least as much light on Wordsworth's own general attitudes as it does on the effect of metrical arrangement in poetry. He remarks, of course, that the "end of Poetry is to produce excitement in co-existence with an overbalance of pleasure." "Excitement" is desired, that is, as long as it does not become "unmanageable" and intrusive. But it may get out of hand: "excitement is an unusual and irregular state of the mind" and "may be carried beyond its proper bounds." The use of meter, therefore, is in "tempering and restraining the passion" so that it is not allowed to interfere with a composed and "pleasurable" state of mind. Wordsworth's discussion, as he himself recognizes, is quite unsystematic. In general, however, he seems to advance two main explanations of the means or processes by which meter can restrain feeling. In the first place, by association the presence of meter wakens in the mind a remembrance of all the other feelings with which metrical language has been "connected." In Wordsworth's terms, "the mind has been accustomed" to meter "in various moods and in a less excited state." Hence, meter arouses "an intertexture of ordinary feeling, and of feeling not strictly and necessarily connected with the passion" immediately present in the poem. This large background of "ordinary" and even irrelevant feelings tends to minimize and dissipate the excitement aroused by a particular metrical arrangement or poem. The principle involved probably differs only slightly from the tempering of excitement derived from a sense of history; for in both cases the immediate occasion is held against a backdrop of past associations and loses much of its power to provoke strong feeling. Even more characteristic is what seems to be Wordsworth's alternative explanation of the efficacy of meter in restraining passion. The attraction of meter, as he speaks of it, is that it tends "to divest language . . . of its reality, and thus to throw a sort of half-consciousness of unsubstantial existence over the whole composition." [10]

— 5 —

The habits of mind we have been considering — a denial that can at times seem almost schizoid, the retreat to memory, the sense of history and of the tranquil sweep of nature — are only some of the modes of response which helped Wordsworth to achieve the serenity he so earnestly sought. Wordsworth himself, of course, felt that whatever abiding composure the mind attained was the result of its being linked, intertwined, or united with external nature. The ideal is an imaginative union so intimate and complete that the mind, instead of being imprisoned and engulfed in its distinctive human qualities, can virtually absorb the tone and characteristics of nature. Probably this linking is the

10. Preface to the *Lyrical Ballads*, p. 940.

principal theme of his poetry, not only in the *Prelude* and the *Excursion* — though there it is most obviously foremost — but also in shorter lyrics which frequently take up some limited aspect of the larger concern and become fully meaningful only in the light of Wordsworth's general preoccupations. It is significant that in a passage which concludes the first book of the *Recluse* — a poem conceived on an overwhelming scale as the grand repository of his opinions and his major achievement — Wordsworth, in a mood of Miltonic self-dedication, announces his "high argument" to be how the mind of man can be "wedded" to the "goodly universe":

> — I, long before the blissful hour arrives,
> Would chant, in lonely peace, the spousal verse
> Of this great consummation.[11]

There can be no doubt that Wordsworth occasionally felt what seemed to be moments of oneness with external nature, and that he believed his mind to have been composed and to some extent permanently formed by such experiences. With a desperate, baffled honesty he repeatedly tries, throughout his poetry, to present these experiences as they had actually occurred; and he also tries to understand and explain the psychological processes involved — processes that established the union and permitted the composure. Wordsworth himself particularly stressed the role of either empathy or sympathetic identification in these moments of "linking."

From Hazlitt to the present day critics have tended to deny that Wordsworth possessed much sympathetic receptivity to the life around him. If it existed at all, it was certainly selective in accordance with his own intense preoccupations, directed only to some things, and specifically

11. Published as the "Prospectus" of the *Excursion*, lines 56–71.

to nonhuman identities. In any personal instance recreated in the poetry, there is always a question whether we are dealing with the psychology of sympathetic participation, or rather with an outright imposition of his own feelings upon nature in a way too subjective to be thought of as sympathetic. The forms of nature, and particularly those which Wordsworth focused upon, are so passive, so obviously open to interpretation and manipulation, so lacking in specific identity or character, that it is a question whether they can permit much sympathetic response. But then, if we fall back upon a psychology of simple projection, we must at once add that a particular natural scene was not so blank and featureless that it allowed any or all feelings to be projected. It acted rather as a filter, permitting and intensifying some kinds of emotional response and inhibiting others. What is certain, however, is that Wordsworth tended to construe his responses as either sympathetic or empathic. As one quick example, we might cite his remark that "my favorite grove,/ Tossing in sunshine its dark boughs aloft . . . Wakes in me agitations like its own." (*Prelude*, VII, 44–47). The point is that the psychology of sympathy has a central place in his theoretical discourse. It is usually conceived in terms of its salutary effect in drawing man toward the forms of nature. What is more important is that it provided a way of accounting for the formative control which nature is felt to exert as it stamps its own tone and spirit upon the mind.

It is perhaps significant that when Wordsworth is meditating a particular moment or instance in his own life, complexities and cross-lights come to the fore to tangle and confuse his account of the psychology involved. It is mainly when he resorts to theoretical and general discourse, or when he constructs a narrative dealing with persons other than himself, that an empathic psychology is advanced in a clear-cut and single-minded way. For example, in "Ruth," where Wordsworth tells the story, which he so often repeats in various forms, of a maiden deserted by her lover, the wayward behavior of the lover is partially explained by the influence of his early natural surrounding (lines 121–136). He had been reared in Georgia, amid a climate and flora Wordsworth conceived as tropical. "The wind, the tempest," and the "tumult of a tropic sky" may have been "dangerous food," encouraging or reinforcing the originally "impetuous blood" of the youth. Similarly, the "fair trees and gorgeous flowers" may have "wrought" upon him by feeding "voluptuous thought." In short,

> Whatever in those climes he found
> Irregular in sight or sound
> Did to his mind impart
> A kindred impulse.   (lines 127–130)

In accord with the impetuous and irregular character bred or at least intensified by his early environment, he deserted his bride. This example is unusual in that nature's influence is not altogether beneficent. Of course, Wordsworth's habitual view was quite the reverse, and he stresses the moral elevation and discipline derived from intercourse with nature. Obviously nature's formative control operates most powerfully when the mind is pervious and openly receptive. From this consideration derives, in part, the ethical justification of the "wise passiveness" Wordsworth urges. Only when the mind is undistracted by the pull of human concerns can it receive the stamp and tone of nature.

— 6 —

This theoretical resort to an empathic psychology is of endless consequence for Wordsworth's poetry. For one thing, it joined and supported his effort to see nature as actively beneficent. He speaks, that is, of the human capacity for empathy as something upon which nature deliberately plays after bestowing it in the first place. Transcendentalizing it in this way (but not, I think, very successfully) Wordsworth seems to feel freer to conceive nature, at times, as actually reaching out to man, and almost consciously molding him provided he is sufficiently receptive. Hence there are such statements as

> Nature oftentimes, when she would frame
> A favor'd Being, from his earliest dawn
> Of infancy doth open up the clouds
> As at the touch of lightning, seeking him
> With gentlest visitation.[12]

It is possible to feel that there is something desperate in Wordsworth's temptation to build so much upon this receptive empathy, and to construe it in such a way as to suggest that a maternal and almost conscious nature is reaching out and acting upon us through it. His attempts to do so seem more important as a symptom of how strongly he desired to think in these terms than as a key for interpreting his own achievement as a poet. Somehow the conception of nature as mother or nurse is most effective in Wordsworth where the maternal ministrations are only implied. The enormous capaciousness of nature is so vividly present in Wordsworth's poetry, its spotless and pure character is so largely impersonal, though not abstract, that attempts to personify it seem a little insincere. The insincerity is not a result of lack of earnestness. In fact, the earnestness is only too obvious. It is simply that the hope of conceiving nature in so directly animate and quasi-human a way runs counter to the weightier convictions of Wordsworth himself. The

12. *The Prelude*, ed. De Selincourt, version of 1805–06, I, 363–367.

wide, impassive forms of nature, however benign, and at the same time the nightmare cavernous isolation, the pocketed fret and self-laceration of man, are already too intrinsic in Wordsworth's own thinking and poetry to permit gestures in which nature becomes domesticated into tender and conscious anthropomorphism. Any interpretation, therefore, that concentrates on his obiter dicta about imaginative sympathy, or ties it up with current transcendental notions, may be documenting the history of ideas so far as one of Wordsworth's intentions is concerned. But it is not touching what is deepest in him.

But if we do not harness our thinking to Wordsworth's own theory, and turn instead to those passages where he attempts to recreate what was felt as a moment of "linking" or union, we find, more often than not, that he seems to be directly projecting or objectifying his own feelings in the appearances of nature. In this process, the external world becomes a kind of sounding board or echo, repeating or mirroring to the mind its own emotions. In the *Prelude* (XII, 235–266) Wordsworth relates how, in his childhood, he once wandered to a place "where in former times/ A murderer had been hung in iron chains." Some "monumental letters" commemorated the deed. Wordsworth noticed them in a casual glance and

> fled,
> Faltering and faint, and ignorant of the road:
> Then, reascending the bare common, saw
> A naked pool that lay beneath the hills,
> The beacon on the summit, and, more near,
> A girl, who bore a pitcher on her head. (lines 246–251)

Wordsworth goes on, saying

> It was, in truth
> An ordinary sight; but I should need

55

> Colours and words that are unknown to man,
> To paint the visionary dreariness   (lines 253–256)

which invested this scene. In later life he roamed the same area "in the blessèd hours/ Of early love." At this time

> Upon the naked pool and dreary crags,
> And on the melancholy beacon, fell
> A spirit of pleasure and youth's golden gleam.
>
> (lines 264–266)

On each of these occasions the scene is exactly the same. Wordsworth even notices the same items in the landscape. Moreover, it was an "ordinary sight," presumably incapable of arousing unusual feeling. But the mood breathed from external nature to the human mind is altogether different. What has happened, of course, is that on each occasion Wordsworth has objectified his own feelings in the landscape. Similarly, in "Guilt and Sorrow" Wordsworth describes a traveler — a former sailor as it turns out — moving across Sarum Plain. The sailor has committed a murder, and as he walks along he sees the body of a criminal hanging in chains from a gibbet. The spectacle aroused all his feelings of guilt, and it seemed to him that the stones of the plain, "as if to cover him from day,/ Rolled at his back" (lines 82–88).

This habitual reaction also helps to explain the moral guidance and correction Wordsworth felt he derived from nature. I have already referred to the famous episode in the *Prelude* where Wordsworth tells of his childhood theft of a boat. "It was," he says, "an act of stealth/ And troubled pleasure," and he felt guilty, though the guilt seems to arise less from the theft itself than from the agitated feelings which accompany it, making the youthful oarsman an intruder in the calm and silent landscape. As he rowed out on the lake,

from behind that craggy steep till then
The horizon's bound, a huge peak, black and huge,
As if with voluntary power instinct
Upreared its head. I struck and struck again,
And growing still in stature the grim shape
Towered up between me and the stars, and still,
For so it seemed, with purpose of its own
And measured motion like a living thing,
Strode after me.   (I, 377–385)

And though he returned the boat, the memory of what he
had seen worked for many days "with a dim and undeter-
mined sense" within him. The experience is not interpreted,
of course, as the subjective reaction of a guilty mind. Rather
it is construed as an instance of the moral chastening and
brooding dominance of nature. The context is significant.
Shortly before we have the equally notable scene in which he
steals a bird from someone else's snare:

and when the deed was done
I heard among the solitary hills
Low breathings coming after me, and sounds
Of undistinguishable motion, steps
Almost as silent as the turf they trod.   (I. 321–325)

Then, between this episode and the boat-stealing incident,
comes a great passage stressing that "terrors, pains, and early
miseries" have had a "needful part" in "making up" his
"calm existence." And after the boat-stealing episode occurs
a paean beginning "Wisdom and Spirit of the universe,"
the theme of which is the purifying of human feelings as
they come into contact with the "enduring things" of nature,
intertwine with them, and are tempered "by such discipline."
Disturbing memories of guilt, in other words, serve as the
principal personal stimulus in the most majestic single passage in the *Prelude* on the formative effect of nature. And,

57

for the poet himself, they are given a catharsis when they are swept up and enveloped by a larger context which reduces them to size and manageability.

We have here, in short, a vivid personal example of the way the mind reacts with external nature. Through the process of projection, nature could serve as the language or symbolic representation of feeling, and thus fulfill one of the needs more ordinarily served by pictorial art or by music. To the extent that this takes place, the mind at once begins to acquire a certain tranquillity from its relation to nature. For expression of any sort — even a grunt or exclamation — immediately helps to define feeling, to set it at a distance, so to speak, where one can then begin to contemplate and deal with it. To the extent that the expression is more complete, it more successfully types, labels, and orders feeling and so renders it less confusing and masterful. One can, however, go further in an account of the way in which emotion becomes calmed and composed when it is objectified in nature. For as feeling is expressed or reflected in an external medium, it inevitably takes on some of the qualities of that medium. Human emotions translated into the forms of nature acquire some of its own character. And if the forms of nature selected and focused upon are those which especially appear calm, unchanging, and ordered, the mind may achieve some degree of "Composure, and ennobling Harmony" (*Prelude*, VII, 771).

These processes in the imagination, then, may help to explain the calm Wordsworth derived from nature, and his feeling of union with it. But there were moments of intenser imaginative experience (of the sort to which we are tempted to apply the vague word, mystic)[13] when Words-

13. Havens, *The Mind of a Poet*, pp. 155–178, especially interprets these moments as "mystic," and he relates them to "those brief periods of ecstasy,

worth had a profounder sense of oneness with the external universe. These experiences must now be discussed; for by his recollection of them Wordsworth, in so far as he was able, maintained his sense of reconciliation, his conviction that man was not an alien resident of an indifferent cosmos. But if the experiences now to be discussed were more intense than most of those previously cited, they nevertheless involved the same kinds of psychological response. Usually these profounder feelings of oneness with nature seems to have arisen in moments of relative personal tranquillity when Wordsworth was looking out to a vast and quiet landscape. No gap sundered the mind from what it contemplated. Instead the life of the mind was wholly projected upon external nature. Often, the mind seemed to expand to the horizon:

> in these moments such a holy calm
> Would overspread my soul, that bodily eyes
> Were utterly forgotten, and what I saw
> Appeared like something in myself, a dream,
> A prospect in the mind.   (II, 348–352)

Here the "holy calm" is both encouraged and objectified by the landscape before him. The feelings are so completely embodied in what he sees that the imagery of nature is also

---

insight, and oblivion" described in the "literature of mysticism" (p. 160). One would not quarrel with the argument as Havens presents it. But unless the term is used precisely, it can involve the critic in difficulties. In particular, the term "mystic" may suggest that these experiences were essentially different in kind from those in which there was a less intense imaginative arousal. It is worth emphasizing, therefore, that, as Havens remarks, Wordsworth himself "never thought of" his experience as mystical (p. 167), and that "there was . . . no deep gulf between Wordsworth's mystical experiences and other memorable incidents in his life" (p. 171). Instead, as Havens admits, the "passages" which can be described as mystical "are likewise instances of the transforming power of the imagination" (p. 169). In other words, they do not differ in kind but only in degree from the usual processes of Wordsworthian "vision."

the imagery or expression of his own mood. When he was a child, Wordsworth said, these moments were not infrequent: "I was often unable to think of external things as having external existence, and I communed with all that I saw as something not apart from, but inherent in, my own immaterial nature." [14]

In these experiences Wordsworth often felt something more than an entire union with the outward universe. He was also conscious of a cherishing and love reciprocated from the cosmos to the human mind, and the feeling transformed mundane life, making it an Eden or "Paradise." What usually happened in these occasions, however, is that Wordsworth's own emotions of outgoing wonder and exalting praise were objectified in the visible scene, and seemed directed from the forms of nature to him. One such experience is described in the autobiographical section of the *Excursion*. "The Boy," stationed on "the naked top/ Of some bold headland" at dawn

> beheld the sun
> Rise up, and bathe the world in light! He looked —
> Ocean and earth, the solid frame of earth
> And ocean's liquid mass, in gladness lay
> Beneath him.

The gladness is, of course, the onlooker's emotion projected into the scene.

> Far and wide the clouds were touched,
> And in their silent faces could be read
> Unutterable love,

and this "love" also reflected the boy's emotion.

14. Note dictated to Isabella Fenwick on "Intimations of Immortality," *The Poetical Works,* ed. De Selincourt and Darbishire, IV, 463.

In such access of mind, in such high hour
Of visitation from the living God,
Thought was not; in enjoyment it expired.

. . . . .

His mind was a thanksgiving to the power
That made him; it was blessedness and love!   (I, 198–218)

Thus a theory resting on the psychology of projection may account not only for Wordsworth's belief that all of nature, even including lakes, stones, winds, clouds, and other inorganic forms was alive and sentient. It can also be used to explain his early faith that nature involved the presence of the divine. Although this is an unsympathetic view, naturally denying Wordsworth's claims for special illumination and for the powers of the imagination, it is reinforced by his own later development in which he seems to have come to rather similar conclusions, though he never made them so explicit.

In any case, the word "love," as Wordsworth uses it, describes the feeling accompanying these moments of reconciliation. In the first place, it implies a childlike wonder. and a praise for all external life; and when he was a child, Wordsworth said, he learned "To look on Nature . . . with a superstitious eye of love" (*Excursion*, I, 241–243). Similarly, the rustics feel

an overflowing love,
Not for the Creature only, but for all
That is around them, love for every thing
Which in this happy Region they behold.
                    (*Recluse*, lines 286–289)

Wordsworth has in mind here something very similar to one of the root intuitions of Coleridge in the "Ancient Mariner" or of Shelley in *Prometheus Unbound*. Self-concern, a sense

61

LIBRARY ST. MARY'S COLLEGE

of personal injury or guilt, for example, imprisons the individual, cuts him off from nature, and leads only to frustration and defeat. A more innocent heart and a more extensive vision turn to all existence with an eye of wonder and blessing:

> he who feels contempt
> For any living thing, hath faculties
> Which he has never used.[15]

Moreover, the love felt at such moments becomes a religious emotion, lifting the soul on "wings of praise . . . to the Almighty's Throne." As he "pored, watched, expected, listened, spread" his "thoughts" through what he calls a "wider creeping" he was aware of

> Incumbencies more awful, visitings
> Of the Upholder of the tranquil soul,
> That tolerates the indignities of Time,
> And, from the center of Eternity
> All finite motions overruling, lives
> In glory immutable.

But we remember that "God . . . is our home"; that "our being's heart and home" is within His "infinitude." Hence in these moments when the human soul seems linked to nature it seems also to touch and rest in its true home. They are brief preludes or anticipations of that final moment when "The Wanderer" will "advance . . . in peace of heart, in calm of mind/ And soul, to mingle with Eterniy." [16]

---

15. "Lines Left Upon a Seat in a Yew-Tree," lines 52–54.
16. *Prelude,* XIV, 186–187; III, 114–121; "Intimations of Immortality," line 66; *Prelude,* VI, 604–605; *The River Duddon,* XXXIII, 7, 12–14.

❧ III ❧

The Wordsworthian Withdrawal

One of the most obvious features of Wordsworth's poetry is the extent to which children appear as protagonists. For children, like beggars, itinerant pedlars, rustics, and other similar figures, represent "unaccommodated man," to use Lear's phrase, and permit Wordsworth, or so he would seem to think, to trace the "primary laws of our nature" without having to take account of secondary complications produced by social and urban life. But the child, as Wordsworth speaks of it, is not simply a purer distillation of the lonely rustic. Just as the sense of alienation from nature is often put in the symbolic figure of the wanderer, man in his moments of reconciliation becomes as a child maternally embraced and cherished by the cosmos. To use Wordsworth's own symbols in a rather crude way, the hope is that man can proceed from wanderer to child. In speaking of Wordsworth's child symbolism, one must inevitably point to the great ode on "Intimations of Immortality," which is, of course, central to almost any discussion of Wordsworth. But just as the themes of the ode reappear throughout Wordsworth's poetry, the metaphoric vehicle was far from being generated for that one occasion. Instead the ode simply brings it to the fore and spotlights it. We shall have occasion later on, particularly when speaking of the poetry of Keats, to argue that many of the major poems of the romantic movement involve, in method or structure, the scrutiny of a symbol, or nexus of symbols, intimately expressive of the poet's deepest preoccupations: the poet hopes to find a symbol through which he can fully represent the object of his quest, and which, at the same time, offers some assurance that the desired end can be attained. For example, the method of the "Ode on a Grecian Urn" or "Ode to a Nightingale" is to explore a central symbol until it finally discloses unwanted implications. The same thing happens in Wordsworth's ode, though the poem sticks less closely to its central symbol and finally goes beyond it to assertions which contradict what the symbol implies and violate the tone of the poem.

Perhaps one might begin by noting Wordsworth's emphasis on maternal love; for no form of human love is presented with a more fervent sympathy. One of the main reasons for the endorsement seems to be the effect on the child of the maternal care:

> blest the Babe,
> Nursed in his Mother's arms, who sinks to sleep,
> Rocked on his Mother's breast; who with his soul
> Drinks in the feelings of his Mother's eye!
>
> *(Prelude*, II, 234–237)

Here the child is surrounded — one might almost say engulfed — by his mother. "No outcast . . . bewildered and depressed," conscious only of a brooding love exercised on his behalf, the child seems utterly safe and so "sinks to sleep." In short, he rests in the lap of his mother as the human being, in his happiest moments, seems to dwell in the cosmos, watched over by a protecting and guiding love. Indeed, the symbol was so firmly established that it often becomes explicit — though not necessarily conscious — when Wordsworth pictures a natural scene. He refers to the "breast of Nature," to a boat "upon the breast/ Of a still water," to the "smooth breast" of the Derwent, and to "mountains over all, embracing all." [1] Many other phrases of a similar tenor might be cited. Perhaps the most clear-cut instance is the description, already quoted, of the rustic fair on the side of Mount Helvellyn (*Prelude,* VIII, 55 ff.). Viewed against the mountain men and women become reduced in size until they are seen almost as children. "Old Helvellyn" broods over the scene virtually as a mother or a nurse:

> Immense
> Is the recess, the circumambient world
> Magnificent, by which they are embraced. (lines 55–57)

Nature puts forth a loving care on their behalf; "for all things serve them" as a mother serves her child:

> Them the morning light
> Loves, as it glistens on the silent rocks;
> And them the silent rocks, which now from high
> Look down upon them. (lines 63–66)

In this passage, the numinous force present in nature is made actively benevolent in accordance with the mother-child symbolism. But at other times, it is conceived in a more impersonal way. When this takes place, Wordsworth's attitudes toward it tend to be expressed in imagery of the sea. The symbol, of course, appears at the close of the River Duddon sonnets, where the river flows "in radiant progress toward the Deep," and where the final passage into the sea is compared to the speaker's own death when he hopes "to mingle with Eternity." In the *Prelude* (XIV, 4 ff.), to take another example, Wordsworth describes the "full-orbed Moon" which "gazed" upon a canopy of "hoary mist." The mist itself rested upon the "main Atlantic," and through a rift in the mist, "A fixed, abysmal, gloomy, breathing-place,"

1. *Prelude,* X, 232; IV, 257–258; I, 283; VIII, 95.

the voice of the sea seemed to rise, and he heard "the roar of waters, torrents, streams/ Innumerable." In this passage the moon becomes

> The emblem of a mind
> That feeds upon infinity, that broods
> Over the dark abyss, intent to hear
> Its voices issuing forth to silent light. (XIV, 70–73)

Any number of similar instances could be cited. The point is that the symbol is relatively fixed in the total imaginative pattern of Wordsworth's poetry. Hence the child's reactions to the sea have a special significance. For the child is also "a mind/ That feeds upon infinity"; though "deaf and silent," the child, in the ode on "Intimations of Immortality," reads "the eternal deep." But the child feels a contact so continuing and intimate that it is quite unawed and at ease. In the sonnet beginning "It is a beauteous evening, calm and free," the speaker walks by the seashore with his child. The sea, described as "the mighty Being" is

>   awake,
> And doth with his eternal motion make
> A sound like thunder—everlastingly. (lines 6–8)

The child, however, seems "untouched by solemn thought." The reason is that the moment is not an unusual one for her; she lives habitually in touch with the large, rolling power figured in the sea:

> Thou liest in Abraham's bosom all the year;
> And worshipp'st at the Temple's inner shrine,
> God being with thee when we know it not. (lines 12–14)

The children in "Intimations of Immortality" who "sport upon the shore" of the sea possess the same familiar ease. The grown man, although he can occasionally glimpse the sea "in a season of calm weather," is in general forced to remain "inland far." But the children are always upon the shore; and, being accustomed to the sea, are able to play in its presence.

> Hence in a season of calm weather
> Though inland far we be,
> Our Souls have sight of that immortal sea
> Which brought us hither,
> Can in a moment travel thither,
> And see the Children sport upon the shore,
> And hear the mighty waters rolling evermore.
>
> (lines 165–171)

Thus the child as a symbol tells us much about what is felt when man is united to the external universe. At such moments, no longer a wanderer or outcast, he is safely at home and conscious of a brooding love directed toward him. The contact is intimate, complete, and passive in that it is not achieved by an act of will. On the contrary, it is either directly bestowed by nature or else it is the product of responses over which he has no control. Moreover, as it banishes all desire and fear it releases a joy which is innocent and almost playful. The joy is felt to be something latent in human nature, a joy normally blocked as restless and crowding anxieties seal the ego within itself, and which emerges as these anxieties are allayed. It should be emphasized that this childlike joy does not result from the attainment of any specific desire. Often the romantics associated it with a rather spontaneous creative activity. In any case, its content is mainly a deeper sense of one's own vitality, a fuller intensity of being alive, combined with a sense of the kindly beauty of the cosmos and all that has part in it. The enemy, in other words, is egotism — the egotism of desire as well as the egotism of fear — and the child represents its antithesis — an innocent, undemanding, and spontaneous re-

67

sponse to the world. But this response does not proceed as a sole and independent thing, welling from certain elect souls possessed of an abounding gusto. Rather it is permitted only by feelings of security and trust.

Of course, the child is a common symbol in romantic literature, perhaps in all literature, of a certain desired state of mind. One thinks especially of Blake and Shelley. But Wordsworth uses the symbol in an unconventional way, or perhaps we should say that he did not think of it as a symbol at all. Coleridge, of course, liked to insist that a good symbol partakes in the reality it renders intelligible, but in the case of the child, at least, Wordsworth seems to have gone much further, and to have conceived that the child *is* what it represents. In other words, he would view a present, living child as literally and actually embodying the desired state of mind. Now in writing poetry it makes a great deal of difference if you naturalize a key symbolic conception in this way. In the case of Wordsworth, it created very large — one might almost say central — critical difficulties. It committed him to all the implications which can be drawn from his naturalistic presentation of children. Needless to say, Wordsworth's children are not wholly naturalistic; there is still some selectivity in the presentation. But they certainly tend in the direction of a literal naturalism. The point is that whatever is felt to be true of living children will then have some bearing on what they symbolize. Furthermore, if we are speaking of children in a naturalistic way, certain things must be said or the presentation becomes false. Thus the symbol controls the poet in an unusually active and direct manner. If, on the other hand, the poet refuses to be controlled by his symbol, making, in a naturalistic context, statements which the reader feels to be false or even strained, he may bring about a loss of empathic involvement.

— 2 —

Wordsworth's minor poems offers several instances of this way of talking about children and of the difficulties it creates. In "We Are Seven," he adopts the pose of the matter-of-fact adult, and confronts a "simple Child." There is, perhaps, some intention to take the girl out of the everyday world and to imply that she incarnates a nature spirit. Thus we are told that she had a "rustic, woodland air," and was "wildly clad." Also the speaker rather eerily emphasizes that "Her eyes were fair, and very fair," almost as though there were something peculiar and striking about them. But this intention, if it exists, is associated with a naturalistic, highly particular description. The reader learns that she is "eight years old," and that she engages in all the domestic activities expected of "cottage" girls — "My stocking there I often knit,/ My kerchief there I hem." Thus the reader may conceive the "simple Child" as a woodland spirit, but he must also see her as a little girl, and because of this literalism the poem exposes itself to the objection of Coleridge that the child's notion of death is not probable or typical: she "would have been better instructed in most Christian families." [2] After meeting the child, the speaker asks

> 'Sisters and brothers, little maid,
> How many may you be?'
> 'How many? Seven in all,' she said,
> And wondering looked at me.   (line 13–16)

It develops, however, that two of the brothers and sisters are dead. On hearing the news, the adult, significantly employing a mathematical logic, remarks that "If two are in the church-yard laid,/ Then ye are only five." But the child

2. *Biographia Literaria*, ed. J. Shawcross (London, 1907), II, 113.

69

insists that "we are seven," and the argument drifts along and closes, each side maintaining its position with equal obstinacy and defiance:

> 'But they are dead; those two are dead!
> Their spirts are in heaven!'
> 'Twas throwing words away; for still
> The little Maid would have her will,
> And said, 'Nay, we are seven!'   (lines 65–69)

The upshot, of course, is that the child has a very different angle of vision, understanding either more or less of death than the adult. Thus, the original description of the "Child" as "simple" appears rather equivocal. From the point of view of the speaker, the girl is "simple" in that she is incapable of comprehending the fact of death. But from the point of view of the reader who comes to the poem with a wide experience of Wordsworth's poetry, the child may be right in her simplicity. If, however, we attempt to read it in this way, we may not find the poem successful. It is a question whether the reader will accept Wordsworth to the point of believing the child. He might be persuaded that a "woodland" spirit could tell him something about death. But it looks like willful obscurantism to claim that a "cottage" girl should be trusted in her observations. At the same time, it should be said that we have gone outside the poem for this interpretation. In the poem itself, there is little intimation that the child is necessarily right in her view. In fact, in the first stanza the speaker apologizes for the "simple Child," explaining that it can hardly be expected to "know of death." Thus the poem maintains a very neat balance, and refuses to align itself on one side or the other. Nevertheless, the dramatic situation seems a little grotesque. The speaker argues earnestly and at considerable length, laboring to convince the child as though some important issue were at stake. This earnestness is pedagogic in character, and for Wordsworth something serious is involved. The matter-of-fact speaker represents the adult world actively seeking to destroy the just confidence of the child in its own intuitions.

This, however, does not alter our impression; for such considerations, though lying behind the poem, are not intrinsic in it. Of course, it would be possible to argue that the great earnestness pumped into an apparently trivial episode forces the reader to go behind the scene. But this, I think, would be over ingenious and false to our response. We do feel something grotesque in the poem, and the grotesqueness arises from a disparity between the tone of the poem and the situation it dramatizes. To put this more concretely, it comes from the picture of an adult engaged in eager argument with an eight-year-old cottage girl whose notions he opposes at length. Thus the poem leaves itself open to the criticism implied by Max Beerbohm in his cartoon, "William Wordsworth, in the Lake District, at Cross-purposes," in which the lanky poet, standing in the rain, buttonholes and questions a wide-eyed, flabbergasted child. An even more characteristic poem is "Anecdote for Fathers." Here a father asks his little boy whether he would rather be on the "smooth shore" of Kilve "by the green sea,/ Or here at Liswyn farm?" The boy prefers Kilve but cannot say why. When pressed for a reason, he happens to catch sight of a weathercock, and replies "At Kilve there was no weather-cock;/ And that's the reason why." We may not find much significance in this answer, but the father is more than satisfied with it:

> O, dearest, dearest boy! My heart
> For better lore would seldom yearn,
> Could I but teach the hundredth part
> Of what from thee I learn.   (lines 57–60)

It is the very inconsequence of the boy's reply which is instructive. The child's unhesitating answer, grounded on irrational and inarticulate feelings, here stands as a rebuke to the mental processes of age, tethered and straitened as they are by the restless desire of rational explanation.[3]

Thus the child can be thought to possess a kind of knowledge or insight usually denied to the adult with his confined and fading imagination. As we have seen, Wordsworth believed that many men may possess the visionary capacity without being able to translate their experience into words. The child is but another instance of this. What is important is not that such intuition should be conscious or communicable, but rather the effect it has on the human being who possesses it. With this in mind, we can take a brief look at one of the main battlegrounds in the criticism of Wordsworth, the account of the child in stanzas seven and eight of the ode on "Intimations of Immortality." Our intention is not to masticate once again this much chewed bone, but merely to note what has given rise to the critical scuffle. For the difficulty does not proceed, as Coleridge seems to imply, from the "magnificent attributes" ("best Philosopher," "Mighty Prophet," etc.) bestowed on the child in stanza eight. The poem has attempted to prepare us to accept these "magnificent attributes." For the child is not, as Coleridge suggests, "a *philosopher*" in a sense that would be "equally

3. It should be noted, however, that Wordsworth himself construed this poem in a different way. For a long time, "Anecdote for Fathers" was subtitled "Showing how the art of lying may be taught," and in later life, writing to an unknown correspondent, Wordsworth explained that his "intention was to point out the injurious effects of putting inconsiderate questions to Children, and urging them to give answers upon matters either uninteresting to them, or upon which they had no decided opinion." See *The Letters of William and Dorothy Wordsworth, The Later Years,* ed. Ernest de Selincourt (London, 1939), I, 253. This explanation seems to be another instance of Wordsworth's anxiety to discover a rational and edifying motive for the emotions expressed in his poetry. Such anxieties usually arose after the poem had been written. Often, as has been noted, they caused him to tinker with the poem. In this case they merely resulted in an interpretive subtitle.

suitable to a *bee,* or a *dog,* or a *field of corn.*" It is not a
"philosopher" in that it has part in the pantheistic being
of nature. In fact, the metaphysics in Wordsworth's great
ode are anything but pantheistic. "Heaven" and "Earth" are
sharply dissociated from each other, touching only in the consciousness of the child. Of course, Coleridge denies that
Wordsworth believed "the Platonic pre-existence," and seems
to say that he employed the myth as a symbolic framework
to convey the "sense" of the poem. Wordsworth later (1843)
made a very similar claim, being alarmed that the myth had
given "pain to some good and pious persons." It was not his
intention to "inculcate . . . belief" in "a prior state of existence." Neither, on the other hand, is he ready to relinquish
belief: "let us bear in mind that, though the idea is not
advanced in revelation, there is nothing there to contradict
it, and the fall of Man presents an analogy in its favor." In
any case, the ode, he says, employs the myth mainly as an
expressive device: "I took hold of the notion of pre-existence
as having sufficient foundation in humanity for authorising
me to make for my purpose the best use of it I could as a
Poet." [4]

Now one seldom believes a myth in the same way that
one believes a mathematical proposition. At the same time,
in Wordsworth's ode the myth is more than a way of con-
veying or talking about something which is otherwise conceived and understood. The use of myth is to provide some
account of experience which remains inscrutable except in
mythical terms. It fulfills, that is, a psychological need, and
we accept it for the sake of the order and peace that it brings.
Thus if Wordsworth did not literally confide in the myth
of pre-existence, he needed, accepted, and used it, and he

4. *Biographia Literaria,* ed. Shawcross, II, 120–121; Fenwick note to "Intimations of Immortality," *The Poetical Works,* ed. De Selincourt and Darbishire, IV, 464.

used it not only in the ode but, as we shall see later, in many other poems as well. For the myth offered an over-all explanation, making a place both for the peculiar "glory" of the child's world and for the subsequent fading of this "glory." And more than that, it served to authenticate or make valid the vision of the child as opposed to that of the adult. Thus it provides the structure of the ode, and the reader must possess some sort of sympathetic commitment to the myth in order to respond to the poem. In that commitment, we understand that the child is in contact with "Heaven," eternity, or permanence. It is possessed by certain essential truths which are lost as we grow older, and which we then toil "all our lives to find." In this sense, perhaps, it is a "prophet." It knows the object or end of man's search. We should also remind ourselves again of Wordsworth's tendency to equate the imaginative intuition which the child embodies with "clearest insight" or knowledge. The imagination, as he frequently says, is but "Reason in her most exalted mood," in touch with truths essential to human life, and the child is a "philosopher" in that he embodies man's "best" philosophy or "highest Reason."

But having said all this, we must at once add that the poem throws obstacles in our way if we wish to sympathize with the "magnificent attributes" appropriated to the child. The difficulty does not lie so much in the attributes themselves as in the fact that they must be read in conjunction with the picture of the little child in stanza seven. For we see the child as a toddler on the nursery floor, a "six years' Darling . . . Fretted by sallies of his mother's kisses." Here, in other words, the ode raises the same critical problem that we found in "We Are Seven," except that in the ode it appears in a more radical and striking way. In "We Are Seven," to repeat, the child is at once a nature spirit and a cottage

74

girl. That she is described in detail as a cottage girl makes it harder for the reader to assent to what she says of death, blocks a sympathetic involvement, and renders the dramatic situation grotesque. In the same way the ode presents the child as both a "best Philosopher" and a "six years' Darling," and the extended image of the "six years' Darling" is both sentimental and realistic. Thus the poem invites precisely those associations which make it most difficult to think of the child as a "philosopher" or "Seer." The failure to note this vitiates the remarks of G. Wilson Knight, for example. He sees the child as symbolizing "life," and urges its fitness as a symbol by citing instances in Shakespeare, the Bible, and Christian belief where the child appears as a symbolic fig-ure.[5] But even if one admits the force of this kind of argu-ment by analogy (which there is no need to do), there is a question whether the poem can be said to use a symbol. Instead, it seems to say that certain things are true of children, and so, needing only to create a poetic faith, quite unneces-sarily raises issues of fact. In other words, the trouble in these stanzas does not lie in the thought expressed, as Coleridge seems to imply, so much as in the technique or method of the poem. Of course, Wordsworth himself tended to view children in this way. That is what causes the em-barrassment. He is too faithful to his own conceptions, or, at least, he shows them too openly, and the reader, unable to share or participate in such notions, disagrees and tempo-rarily withdraws.

We said before that the ode could be described as the exploration or trying out of a symbol or web of symbols through which man might be assured of the reconciliation he seeks. But the point is that almost no reassurance can finally be obtained. For if the child is Wordsworth's usual

5. *The Starlit Dome* (London, 1941), pp. 43–48.

way of suggesting what "we are toiling all our lives to find," the ode — in contrast to much of Wordsworth's poetry — faces up to the implication that the grown man cannot hope to find it. This can be inferred, in the first place, from the explanation of the child's visionary power by the myth of pre-existence. Wordsworth, as we pointed out, tended to express the joy and peace felt in union with nature or God by calling such moments an experience of "Heaven" or "Paradise." Hence the child can be said to dwell in "Paradise" ("Heaven lies about us in our infancy"). More often, however, the child is described as a previous inhabitant of "Heaven" who becomes an exile or alien on earth. For example, in the city of London Wordsworth noticed a young boy who would have been "The pride and pleasure of all lookers-on/ In whatsoever place"; but in the city especially he seemed "A sort of alien scattered from the clouds." Elsewhere he speaks of the child as having departed from his "native continent" in entering "earth and human life." [6] Perhaps the most prominent instance of this metaphor occurs in the ode on "Intimations of Immortality." Here the child "cometh from afar," from his true "home," to the "Earth," and the "Earth" becomes a "homely nurse" who "doth all she can" to make her "Foster-child . . . Forget" his heavenly home. In this passage the "Earth" seems kindly, has "no unworthy aim," but it is sometimes compared to something sinister. Both in the ode and elsewhere it is described as a "prison-house" where the child, its "inmate," endures a "state of meagre vassalage."

The notion is of potential power cramped and frustrated. This is especially characteristic of Wordsworth. He usually maintained that, by conceiving the external world through the imagination, the mind escapes being "enthralled" by

6. *Prelude*, VII, 347–350; V, 537–538.

"sensible impressions." [7] Instead, it colors or modifies sense impressions and seems partially to create what it observes. Hence he habitually described the processes of imaginative vision as the exercise of power, the exertion, as he says in the *Prelude,* of a "domination . . . upon the face of outward things" (XIV, 81–82). The child especially possesses this power and domination:

> Our childhood sits,
> Our simple childhood, sits upon a throne
> That hath more power than all the elements. (V, 507–509)

This type of association underlies the reference to the "imperial palace" in stanza six. What is "imperial" about the child is his imagination. But after he has come to mortal life, a "foundling prince reared by the peasants," [8] he cannot exercise his power and gradually forgets it. As the myth of pre-existence emerges in the ode it carries with it several inferences which should be noted. In the first place, the goal of man's quest is spatially located. It is to be found not on earth but in heaven. Of course, "Heaven lies about us in our infancy," but this substantiates the point. The child comes from afar clouded in a heavenly atmosphere which cannot maintain itself on earth. Though the child can move from one to the other, the two realms are essentially dissociated. They can even be said to conflict with each other, or, at least, consciousness of one obliterates that of the other, for just as mortal life effaces our remembrance of heaven, so "sense and outward things" vanish from the consciousness of the child in those brief moments when he seems mindful of his former home. God does not stand in nature, and hence man living his earthly life cannot hope to find what he seeks. Furthermore, the imagination through

7. *Prelude,* V, 518; XIV, 106.
8. Brooks, *The Well Wrought Urn,* p. 128.

which man draws into eternity is not, in this context, conceived as an inherent human endowment which the child especially asserts. It is not an active process of visionary insight. Those truths which "we are toiling all our lives to find" rest on the child as a memory. What he recalls can never again be directly known. Because the glory glimpsed in childhood is itself a memory in the child, it will fade in time. Thus even if, as Coleridge suggests, in the myth of pre-existence Wordsworth uses "symbols of time and space" to convey "modes of inmost being, to which . . . the attributes of time and space are inapplicable and alien," [9] it must also be said that the implications of the symbolism run counter to what Wordsworth would have hoped to demonstrate.

It may be, however, that we look too scrupulously at the myth of pre-existence. What justifies us — if we are justified — is that similar implications crystallize in the child imagery, and that they are faced, developed, and made the theme or subject of the ode. For the central fact is that the child will grow up, losing, in the process, the joyful sense of reconciliation with nature. Of course, Wordsworth's own memories of childhood helped to determine the symbolic significance of children in his poetry. In the same way his own experience seems to have somewhat paralleled the gradual loss of visionary power and felt oneness with nature — a loss which the child, as a symbol, inevitably implies; and one of the large themes of his poetry is the effort to find some compensation for this loss, or at least to adjust it. But even without reference to Wordsworth's autobiography, the child symbolism suggests that the desired state of mind cannot, in fact, be maintained. Moreover, in the ode, there is something even more

9. *Biographia Literaria*, ed. Shawcross, II, 120.

disturbing. The child wants to grow up. He even takes "earnest pains" to do so. It is this that the poet dwells on in stanzas seven and eight. In actively seeking and practising the normal business of human life the child is "at strife" with his own "blessedness." Hence when the poet addresses the child, asking "Why with such earnest pains dost thou provoke/ The years to bring the inevitable yoke," the question is not rhetorical. It suggests a deep-seated recognition of something radically wrong. Human nature, it would seem, is so innately corrupt that man not only cannot attain his true "blessedness," but does not even want it, and this is true even of the child who still recalls his former "home."

Thus, to embody the desired state of mind in children tends to make the whole thing seem purely ideal and perhaps wishful. In the first place, it forces the conclusion that the grown man cannot recapture or return to it. Furthermore, the fact is that Wordsworth was seldom able to find even in children an unquestionable example of what he wished to assert. To simplify a very complex matter, we can say that children are presented in one of two ways. Either, as in "Nutting," portions of the *Prelude,* and other poems, they are little prototypes of human nature, passionately greedy and desirous, only partially and uncertainly receptive to the formative control of nature. Or else, in many poems of which "We Are Seven" is an example, children seem to possess none of the human characteristics which especially alienate man from nature. Hence, the desired state of mind does not appear to be achieved by modifying or transforming the human qualities which bar it. Instead, the felt union with nature seems to rest on children as something inevitably associated with childhood. But Wordsworth's conception of the assertive individuality of the mind is fixed and pervasive,

79

and the child represents more what Wordsworth would wish than a state of mind possible to be attained by adult humanity.

In fact, there is something undeniably and even strongly regressive about Wordsworth's use of the child as a symbol. Of course there are numerous disclaimers — notably in "Tintern Abbey" and the ode on "Intimations of Immortality" — but the later lines in the ode about finding "strength in what remains behind," in "years that bring the philosophic mind," are not a real credo. In the first place, the last two stanzas violate both the tone and the logical scheme of the poem. The tone is so nostalgic or elegiac that it becomes almost impertinent to end by saying that the speaker has only "relinquished one delight." The logical pattern of the poem does indeed move from the fact of loss to a consolation. But the consolation, to be convincing, must stem from the basic premises of the poem. Hence the logically acceptable recompense is found in stanza nine in the fact that the truths which wake in childhood will "perish never," and the recollection of them will continue to "uphold us." The lofty ethical sympathies of the two concluding stanzas are not strictly relevant to what the poem has said previously. Furthermore, the language of the "Ode" is, on the whole, precisely evocative only so long as Wordsworth is talking about what has been lost. When, in the last two stanzas, the poem describes what has replaced this loss, the language, though resounding and noble, is less precise. Through the course of the poem the reader possesses a close sympathetic sense of the theme, but in the last two stanzas he loses touch with the poem, can hardly grasp the kind of experience which lies behind the language and to which it points. It is as though the poet himself could scarcely conceive or know exactly what he was talking about.

As he grew older a number of things — among them personal griefs and misfortunes (such as the death of his brother) plus the disappointments and losses inevitable in aging — seem to have gradually weakened Wordsworth's earlier hope that the "Spirit of the universe" exercised a loving care on the behalf of man. Of course, we are speaking very generally. Many critics have denied that Wordsworth's views of things underwent much change from his youth to his old age, and it is true that the majority of the late poems do not seem inconsistent with the earlier ones. For on the whole, the late poems can be described as effusions in praise of meekness, tranquillity, order, and repose in the human mind and in society, and, except for some wild intellectual oats in response to the French Revolution, these are qualities which Wordsworth always valued and espoused. But there is a distinction. The late poems simply have not the same weight of thought and feeling behind them; they do not scoop or sift to the same degree. Hence there is nothing remarkably consistent either. Wordsworth's greater poetry usually involves a semi-autobiographical probing in quest of possible sources of tranquillity. The theme, in other words, is how tranquillity can be achieved, and, in the later poems, this theme is no longer central. Perhaps there was a gradual failure or leaking of energy: Wordsworth reminds one of Jacob, wrestling with God in his early manhood and afterwards lapsing into the commonplace of day to day. Perhaps the difficulty is more to be explained by the fact that it takes a grain of sand to make a pearl. It may be that Wordsworth was too successful in his quest for composure and tranquillity, that having smoothed his bed, so to speak, he then went to sleep. In any case, if we want to inquire whether there was a metamorphosis in Wordsworth's attitudes, it would not be sensible to draw many inferences from the slight and often trivial performances which, unfortunately for the scholar, make up the bulk of Wordsworth's later verse. Instead, we should concentrate on poems written when Wordsworth was still actively seeking, still forming his attitudes, and still capable of mobilizing and bringing to bear his massive poetic resources in a sustained way. I have in mind poems written between approximately 1805 and 1815, and especially the "Elegiac Stanzas," "The Happy Warrior," *The White Doe of Rylstone,* the "Ode to Duty," and "Laodamia." In taking the poems up in this order, I am, of course, violating the sequence in which they were composed, and it is important to remember that the "Ode to Duty" was written before the death of Wordsworth's brother. It seems permissible, however, to ignore chronology; for the attempt is only to sketch in large outline, and the "Ode to Duty" and "Laodamia" benefit from a prior consideration of the other poems.

The fine "Elegiac Stanzas" touches on most of the major themes of this period. Here Wordsworth affirms that the intuition of serene benevolence at the heart of the mystery — the fancy "that the mighty Deep/ Was even the gentlest of all gentle Things" — is an experience of "Elysian quiet," a "chronicle of heaven" under a "sky of bliss." At one time he would have believed that this vision of a "steadfast peace that might not be betrayed" was also a glimpse into "the soul of truth";

> How perfect was the calm! it seemed no sleep;
> No mood which season takes away or brings.　(lines 9–10)

It seemed that the sea "could not cease to smile." Of course, this vision alienated him from common humanity. For one thing, in all men the imagination lies "In the recesses of

[their] nature, far/ From any reach of outward fellowship";
and to the extent that the poet is a visionary, he is fostering
what is unique in him. But Wordsworth now feels in addition
that it is possible to conceive nature as maternal only by
ignoring or even willfully refusing to see much of the common experience of men. In other words, his former notion
was founded on a limited or exclusive premise. A union with
a benevolent universe can seem to be a living reality only if
one withdraws from the arena of human life into "the fond
illusion" of the "heart," and Wordsworth renounces the
visionary experience:

> Farewell, farewell the heart that lives alone,
> Housed in a dream, at distance from the Kind!
> Such happiness, wherever it be known,
> Is to be pitied; for 'tis surely blind.   (lines 53–56)

Of course, this distrustful eye inevitably withers the visionary capacity:

> A power is gone, which nothing can restore;
> A deep distress hath humanized my Soul. (lines 35–36)

The soul becomes humanized both by losing the visionary
power and also by becoming aware of the "agonies, the strife/
Of human hearts," to borrow Keats's phrasing. It becomes
aware of "This sea in anger," "the deadly swell," and the
"pageantry of fear." The language of the poem might also
imply that the soul does something more than simply note
the significance of the darker side of human experience.
We might infer from the phrasing that to become humanized
would mean, among other things, to share or participate
more vitally in the feelings and concerns which preoccupy
most men.

This is not, in fact, the case. With the lost sense of a benevolent cosmos, the mind, instead of seeking to achieve the

joy, love, and security of the child in a maternal universe, must now fortify itself to face indifference. Hence there is a retreat into stoicism, and this transfer of allegiance probably provides the most vital theme of Wordsworth's later verse. This is not to deny that earlier poems occasionally showed similar attitudes. There is, for example, the rock-like and scarcely human old man in "Resolution and Independence" (1802) whose "firm . . . mind" seemed "apt admonishment" and example to the poet's unstable emotions. I am speaking of an over-all tendency, and in the later verse the stoicism shows itself in many explicit ways and more generally in the attraction to subject matter drawn from classical antiquity. For the necessary pattern and example to human nature is now found in "Roman dignity inviolate" through "all turns of fate." [10] As this quotation suggests, the need for stability and permanence is as pressing as ever, but nature has shown itself to be unreliable, and the desired steadfastness cannot be found through union with it. The human soul must itself be steadfast and unchanging, pitched above the "infirmities of mortal love," as Wordsworth calls them, impervious to hope, fear, or desire, and the suggestion seems sometimes to be present that the soul exists almost in open hostility to nature. Thus earlier poems often speak of human beings in terms of nature metaphors, as flowers or other vegetable life, and man becomes an organic part of a living whole. In these later poems, however, the good man is not a vegetable but a "warrior," a "man in arms," and a "happy Warrior" only when, resisting alike the temptations of ambition and "tender happiness," he "finds comfort in himself and in his cause." Thus in the "Elegiac Stanzas" the symbol of the soul is the "Castle" impenetrably "cased in the unfeeling armour of old time," which "braves . . . The lightning, the fierce

10. "The Pillar of Trajan," lines 49–50.

wind, and trampling waves." Alternative and related symbols occur in other lesser poems — for example, the image of the "votive Column" or "obelisk" standing in its isolated, massive integrity amid the "wrecks of Time," uninjured by the human passions which have "never ceased to eddy round its base," and, to take one more example, in natural rock formations such as the "Cave of Staffa" which endures unhurt the "assault of Time" and the "whole Atlantic weight/ Of tide and tempest." [11]

Perhaps the implications of such images are drawn most explicitly — at least in an abstract way — in *The White Doe of Rylstone*. Of course, there is much more in this rather complex narrative than mere overt sermonizing, but the little inserted sermons bear directly on what we have been saying. In an especially significant speech, Emily's brother, in a spirit of prophecy, sees the coming destruction of all that Emily loves. In this situation he counsels her to

> depend
> Upon no help of outward friend;
> Espouse thy doom at once, and cleave
> To fortitude without reprieve.   (lines 542–545)

She should, that is, anticipate and cushion her loss by abandoning hope and seeking, through fortitude, an "undisturbed humanity." For "prayers," "wishes," "Hope" itself, are a futile and needless trouble. She can "depend/ Upon no help of outward friend" because — glossing the line — "outward" circumstances, being subject to time and accident, do not offer the absolute reliability man seeks. Only the soul can be stable and unchanging, and then only when, as the poem makes plain later on, it is "impenetrable" to "mortal love." For *The White Doe of Rylstone* is a Wordsworthian Saint's

11. "The Pillar of Trajan," lines 1–35, *passim; Itinerary Poems of 1833*, XXXI, 13; XXIX, 9–10.

Legend. It depicts "victories in the world of spirit," and it is "intended" that Emily should "be honoured and loved" by the reader.[12] There is every intention to bestow the highest praise when near the end we are told that Emily "stood apart from human cares," or that

> Her soul doth in itself stand fast,
> Sustained by memory of the past
> And strength of Reason; held above
> The infirmities of mortal love;
> Undaunted, lofty, calm, and stable,
> And awfully impenetrable.   (lines 1623–1628)

Indeed, Wordsworth was apparently so sure of his doctrine that he was willing to impute moral, intellectual, and imaginative blindness if a reader were unresponsive to his poem: "Let [Charles] Lamb be ashamed of himself in not taking some pleasure in the contemplation of this picture . . . Lamb has not a reasoning mind, therefore cannot have a comprehensive mind, and, least of all, has he an imaginative one." [13]

— 4 —

What we find, then, is a withdrawal not simply from the "trivial" and crowding passions of urban life, but from all feeling whatsoever. But the withdrawal takes place not simply because Wordsworth has been taught to distrust impulse and desire. If it were only that, it might seem rational, even, to some readers, exemplary. But it often seems that something else is involved, something much more deep-seated and pathetic. Wordsworth seems finally to have felt that for the sake of peace he would sacrifice all. To care was too

---

12. *The Letters of William and Dorothy Wordsworth: The Middle Years,* ed. Ernest de Selincourt (London, 1937), I, 198, 197.
13. *Ibid.,* p. 198.

much trouble. We can remind ourselves here that Wordsworth seems to have possessed an innate tendency to violent
emotional responses. At the same time, there was a conscience active, scrupulous, assertive, unsleeping, and inquisi-
torial, ready to question and check any spontaneous gesture.
In all this there may be reason to suspect a conflict resulting
in continued uneasiness. What can scarcely be questioned,
in any case, is that Wordsworth carried within him a great
deal of what today we might call floating anxiety. But prolonged anxiety becomes fatiguing, and, when every gesture
or motion may release it, it becomes easier not to move, not
to care, not to feel. Hence the need to withdraw. He was,
as he says in the "Ode to Duty," weary of "chance desires."

Thus it may not be altogether facetious to point out that
the need for a withdrawn and protected stability is so strong
that Wordsworth, "thankful . . . For the rich bounties of
constraint," [14] sometimes says he would like to be a prisoner.
One might cite here "Nuns fret not at their convent's nar-
row room," where the poet says that " 'twas pastime to be
bound/ Within the Sonnet's scanty plot of ground," that
"Souls . . . Who have felt the weight of too much liberty"
may "find brief solace there." But though the thought is
altogether characteristic, such rather playful utterances are
not what we have in mind. Instead we are thinking of
Wordsworth's earnest, stoic affirmation of the "sacred laws"
which, as he says, in "Dion," are "eternal bars" man should
not overleap. Of course, as expressed in "Dion" and elsewhere this conception has the weight and profundity of a
long, philosophic tradition. What is peculiarly characteristic
of Wordsworth is not his sense and need of the fixed bars of
moral law, but instead the personal motivations which give
rise to this need. Here our text is the beautiful, movingly

14. "The Pass of Kirkstone," lines 57–58.

honest "Ode to Duty." Like many of Wordsworth's better poems, the "Ode to Duty" is a highly individual, particular, semi-autobiographical expression. Wordsworth takes pains to say exactly what he means, and what he means is not what the reader might have expected. Of course, Duty in the poem represents the Stoic conception of law, of absolute principles of right and wrong inwoven in the cosmos. Thus it is both a "light to guide" and a "rod/ To check the erring." But man does not always require a conscious awareness of these principles. There are those who, by following the spontaneous impulses of the heart, do the "work" of Duty and "know it not." Such men are happy; they can, with occasional guidance from Duty, hold a "blissful course"; their love and joy is largely unerring in its motion toward the right. The speaker — "to myself a guide" — has been equally free and spontaneous, and, blindly reposing his trust, has perhaps erred. But the ethic of spontaneity, the trust in the natural impulse of the heart, has not shown itself radically treacherous. There is no suggestion that it has led the speaker very far or dangerously astray. There has been no crisis, no catastrophe, no "disturbance" of the "soul" or "strong compunction" to convert the speaker to Duty. Rather it is because he is tired of "unchartered freedom," feels the "weight of chance-desires," simply does not want to be perplexed or disturbed by them, that he supplicates for an external control. Thus the attraction to Duty is not so much for the sake of moral guidance as such. Rather Duty is invoked mainly because it calms "the weary strife of frail humanity," and the speaker prays to live a prisoner or "Bondman" to the "Stern Lawgiver" not because it is necessary to the good life, but because in the chains of law one finds "a repose that ever is the same."

"Laodamia" carries the point of view even further. In this

beautiful narrative, Laodamia herself is an example of "rebellious passion," unable or unwilling to accept her fate, the death of her husband, and seeking, as she sees the shade of Protesilaus, to revive "the joys/ Of sense." But the law, embodied in the "just Gods whom no weak pity moved," is inexorable, Protesilaus must again depart, and because Laodamia will not submit, she dies and is "doomed to wear out her appointed time,/ Apart from happy Ghosts." Protesilaus, however, having sacrificed his life for the success of the Grecian cause, is an example of duty, and as a result he achieves a quiet and unchanging happiness. It is perhaps significant, even though Wordsworth is here constrained by the myth he retells, that this happiness is won after death. At least, the opportunity to express himself in these terms may partially account for the attraction to this particular myth. For the Elysium to which Protesilaus goes is above all safe: "No fears to beat away," no "strife," the "future sure," it is a place of "blissful quiet." As Yeats's Crazy Jane remarks, "All find safety in the tomb," and in Wordsworth the need for security seems to have become so strong that he was occasionally willing to seek it in the grave. All of the romantic poets declared themselves, at times, to be "half in love with easeful death," but they were spurred by different motives. Shelley and sometimes Keats (who is a more complicated case), like Shakespeare in the sixty-sixth sonnet, had moments of fatigue with what is nasty and ungrateful in earthly life. Shelley, moreover, saw mortal experience as a kind of veil and obfuscation of the eternal. But Wordsworth's attraction to death does not rest on these familiar attitudes. Here, as elsewhere, he was more original. He was driven by intense anxieties and fears, and he sought rest and safety. Hence there are such ghastly expressions as that "At the Grave of Burns" where the speaker, reflecting that Burns's son, a "stripling," had just died, finds in the thought "some sad delight." For those who have early found the "quiet bed" of the grave "are blest." And what the speaker most emphasizes, as justifying his feeling, is that the dead young man "is safe." One could also cite a poem "effused," as Wordsworth said, at the grave of George and Sarah Green, a couple who had died in an accident. This poem, he remarks, "is the mere pouring out of my own feelings," and in it he describes the grave as "a covert tempest-proof," a "shelter" where they are "safe" from "all agony of mind," from "fear, and from all need of hope." [15]

Thus the retreat into stoicism may have been compulsive as well as ethical, the result of unmanageable fears, of a need for security, as well as of a fuller experience of life. For as he grew older, Wordsworth does indeed seem to have known a gradual weakening of the visionary imagination, but he did not therefore — despite numerous abstract assertions — begin a more empathic or wider participation in the common cares of mankind. Instead he mainly developed a distrust both of vision and impulse, a felt need to discipline emotion, and perhaps a wish to cut losses by suppressing all feeling. Instead of bridging a distance from other men — to hark back to the "Elegiac Stanzas" — the stoic retrenchment may have ended in another sort of dehumanizing of the soul, less fruitful of successful poetry. For on the whole, Wordsworth's most successful subject was his own emotions autobiographically presented. In repressing feeling, he failed to add to his capital, and when his fund of childhood recollection was exhausted, he had no comparable theme to rouse and release his poetic power. The peace Wordsworth finally achieved may remind us of the grim remark on the Pax

15. Quoted from *Letters: The Middle Years*, I, 194–196. This is the first version of the poem, and it "varies considerably," as De Selincourt remarks, from that in the Oxford edition.

Romana which Tacitus attributes to the Briton, Calgacus: *Ubi solitudinem faciunt, pacem appellant.*

— 5 —

In a sense, then, Wordsworth, in the "Elegiac Stanzas" — where he speaks of the "fond illusion of my heart" — and elsewhere, is a perceptive critic of his own poetry, recognizing what has been the major critical charge against him from Hazlitt, Keats, and Coleridge to our own time. The issue, of course, has been that his "view of things" or "criticism of life," to use Arnold's phrases, was extremely subjective: that in the intensity of his personal preoccupations he made an unusually limited and selective use of experience; that with his confidence in the imagination he endowed his own impressions or intuitions with an absolute credence and authority; and finally, of course, that his interpretations of human experience were often too personal to be sympathetically received or readily shared by most readers.

It is, however, doubtful that the charge of subjectivism would have had much significant content or meaning to Wordsworth. Certainly his conception of the poetic imagination appears to justify, at least in a theoretic way, his own practice as a poet. There are, of course, several facets to Wordsworth's theory of the imagination, and at different times some are emphasized more than others. But at least some common qualities seem to persist in all his thinking about it. To begin with, he rarely conceived the imagination as a solely visionary capacity. It is not, as it seems to be in Blake, an organ of insight that automatically jumps beyond the concrete world into a purely ideal realm. Neither is it a merely inventive power, capable of spinning something out of nothing. At the same time, the imagination is not, for that reason, simply the amalgamated union of empirical consciousness, as it seems to be in many English and Scottish critics of the late eighteenth and early nineteenth centuries. Instead, Wordsworth seems to have believed, as he says in *Peter Bell*, (lines 144–145) that "in life's daily prospect" the mind may both "find" or receive from the senses and "create" whatever makes up the content of human consciousness and that the creative activity can take place without primary reference to the data supplied by the senses. We can go further, and note that as the imagination works more powerfully, it becomes increasingly independent of the senses. There is also the notion that if one concentrates deliberately on sense perception, "pampering" oneself "with meagre novelties/ Of colour and proportion," one lays "the inner faculties asleep." [16]

But if the imagination can and should go beyond sense experience, it is not, and should not be, isolated from what the senses can bring. Although it transcends man's empirical consciousness, it also works through it, and its visions are always, to some extent, "reared upon the base of outward things." In fact, Wordsworth's usual symbol of the "very spirit" in which "higher minds" possessing the "glorious faculty" of imagination "deal/ With the whole compass of the universe" is the shedding of light. The symbol is made explicit in the last book of the *Prelude* when Wordsworth powerfully describes the vision from Mount Snowden of the moon coloring and transforming a mist which lay about the mountain and stretched out over the Atlantic. But the symbol is equally present and obvious elsewhere in his poetry — in the ode on "Intimations of Immortality," in the fine passage on the creative imagination, in the *Prelude,* where he speaks of the "auxiliar light" which came from his mind and "on the setting sun/ Bestowed new splendour"

16. *Prelude,* XII, 116–117, 147.

(II, 368–370), and in numerous places where he speaks about poetic creation in terms of light imagery, as in the "Elegiac Stanzas":

> The light that never was, on sea or land,
> The consecration, and the Poets dream. (lines 15–16)

Indeed, in the Preface to the *Lyrical Ballads* Wordsworth says that it was his purpose to present "incidents and situations from common life," and "at the same time, to throw over them a certain colouring of imagination." This way of symbolizing the process of imagination suggests, of course, that the mind transforms at least the appearance of external things, partially creating what it perceives. At the same time, the act of imagination is clearly a proceeding towards what is outside, and cannot be regarded as entirely independent and isolated.

The word imagination, as Wordsworth states in the "Essay Supplementary" to the Preface of 1815, is used by him only because "Poverty of language" forces him to do so. Actually it is, as he says in the *Prelude,* but "another name" for "Reason in her most exalted mood" (XIV, lines 190–192). Any attempt to pin down the implications of the term, then, must obviously rest upon his theory of the mind as a whole. Throughout the more significant references to the potentiality either for destructiveness or growth in the human mind, there is always the implication that the mind (and therefore the imagination) is, first of all, assertive, individual, unique in many of its instinctual demands and appetites, and to some extent isolated. Yet there is also the implication that its creative independence can lead to growth and become valuable if it is able to merge or involve itself in certain healthful aspects of nature. There is the suggestion or hope, more often than not, that the ability to do this is somehow latent in the imagination at the start. To go back to Wordsworth's habitual image of the cavern, the creative activity of the mind is, by definition, always an activity of that particular mind and not of another. It is working within its own pocket, so to speak, of the universe. But granted the conception of the mind as cavern, there is still the intention or hope to climb out of it.

— 6 —

Man's approach to nature is thus inevitably lonely and personal; he must walk to it on his own feet, and carry with him the pedlar's pack of his own emotions, character, and experience. The conception of man as a wanderer or alien — of Newton as a mariner "Voyaging through strange seas of Thought, alone" — is again relevant. Truth, in the most complete meaning of the word for Wordsworth, represents this union, or rather this journey towards union. Truth, in other words, is not conceived as a purely objective thing — something on which all men will agree once they are turned toward it and are shaken awake. Instead Wordsworth seems to gravitate constantly toward a conception of truth as a process of coming together, as a union of the perceiving eye (an eye possessing unique, individual attributes) with the perceived object. The external object is not denied to exist by itself (and here we have the stubbornly empirical strain); but only the perceived object is known; and the adjective "perceived" at once suggests the qualification that the process of truth is an act of perception where what is brought to the perception makes its own contribution. Such a point of view is eminently pliable, as a kind of theoretic appendix, to Wordsworth's thesis of the search and need for union with nature. In so far as he is concerned with the salutary, direct impact of nature upon the mind of man,

94

this gives a psychological support or at least illustration: in the state of union, the perceived object, with its reassuring qualities, is acting upon the perceiving mind. If such an infused sanity, health, or reassurance is construed as objective by us, the psychology takes on that tincture, linking itself with traditional, classical conceptions of mind; and it is not difficult to discover eloquent lines or phrases in Wordsworth that would embellish this interpretation. We should also note that, in Wordsworth's thinking as a whole, one predominant element or theme is at all times the accessibility of nature to man and the need of man to exploit that accessibility. But having said this, we should remember the Janus-like quality of the psychology. This is indeed its virtue — that it looks in two ways at once. And if, in the interpretation of Wordsworth's own mind and poetry (as distinct from obiter dicta, or even persistent ideals that do not control his own activity as a poet), we find that certain distinctive or personal qualities are compulsive and dominant, it is justifiable to note that his theory of mind is equally pliable in this way. Ultimately, it is more pliable as far as actual practice is concerned.

Indeed, we may feel that his theoretical psychology is important mainly because it justifies, rationalizes, or at least sets no bar to his practice as a poet. There is nothing particularly uncharitable in stating this. The point is only that Wordsworth's theory of mind can give a defense of the subjective qualities of human nature. If this is acknowledged, then the theory of mind ceases to be a matter of pressing concern. We rarely go to poets to find information or solace in the theoretical architecture of their abstract thinking. This applies, certainly, to anything we are to get out of Wordsworth.

But it is at least appropriate that Wordsworth should

have felt the need for a theoretical justification and reassurance. There was strong reason for misgivings. For no major poet in literature, who has insisted so strongly upon the need for clearing and stabilizing the mind through a direct communication with nature, has at the same time, in his own feelings and interests, moved so compulsively into a selective use of experience. Selectivity is, of course, inevitable in poetry. Classical art presupposes it, often with the same ideal of stability. On the other hand, what at once cuts Wordsworth off from most classical and neo-classical selectivity (in fact what cuts Wordsworth off from most varieties of stylized or selective art) is the direct, emotional naturalism with which he is willing to commit himself to concreteness. Yet at the same time he is very selective in his empiricism. We have stressed that Wordsworth, in seeking what is permanent within the process of nature, concentrated on those aspects of concrete nature which seemed most enduring, and drew some of his controlling symbols from them. The withdrawal to the hills or mountains, to the brooding cliffs and the calm lakes, to the overhanging presences of the large, concrete forms of nature is what we have in mind. We have noted also, not that he retreats from those rapid, chemical changes of nature with which Shelley, for example, is obsessed, but that he hardly notices them. When they do intrude themselves upon him, there is the instinctive tendency, as we have said, to try to minimize and "manage" them. The pushing of them away in order to gain perspective, the habitual desire to stand apart and wrap them, so to speak, into a single, manageable unit, provides a strong example. The attempts to minimize the present by vividly resurrecting the past are another example; for it can naturally lead to a selecting of objects that permit this most easily. The appeal of quiet ruins, and of their counterpart, the aged and worn human figures we find in Wordsworth, is that they have less of an assertive present to get in the way. They invite retrospective feelings that can be easily handled, and permit a "recollection in tranquillity" that is already half-prepared for the mind. The desire to get things into perspective in this way has a certain kinship with the desire, in "Personal Talk," to sit by the fireside in solitude ("To sit without emotion"), removed from the meaningless chat and rivalry (as Wordsworth viewed it) of human contact. The tendency of Wordsworth, in his later years, to give up the claims of vision, and to retract or blunt his demands into a conventional stoicism is the next step in this reduction in personal involvement. Stoicism, it has been said, would have us cut off our hands lest we feel toward a thing and our feet lest we are led to walk to it. It implies a retraction of desire, a premature settling for a stalemate in which struggle or desire do not enter as troublesome complications. The withdrawal of Wordsworth from the arena of concrete experience has a significance that is not only historical. It also highlights the dilemma of the modern writer — the writer who shares a response in which the tug toward concreteness, however strong, is at once matched, modified (and all too often neutralized) by his uneasy and eviscerating realization that the human mind is, in Meredith's phrase, "hot for certainties in this our life," and that the "certainties" for which it seeks transcend the quasi-permanence of mountains, blank sky, and the giant brooding cliffs that haunt the imagination of Wordsworth.

The relevance of Wordsworth to our own time is not only that the course he followed may offer a general parallel or prototype to contemporary writers. He is also an example of a course that human nature as a whole is tempted to follow. In the face of any kind of anxiety, at least two types of reaction may become dominant and even compulsive. In the first place, the sense of anxiety leads to a struggle to reduce it. This struggle is inevitably lonely and personal. It brings about an intense preoccupation and self-involvement, a turning of the eye inward, and a concomitant lack of interest in the problems and concerns faced by other people. Certainly, a strong sympathetic engagement in the lives of fellow men and women is not one of the notable features of contemporary poetry. Instead, the modern poet often tends, like Wordsworth, to be an onlooker, viewing events in individual lives from a distance, and commenting upon them. Secondly, anxiety brings with it an inevitable temptation to retrench. There has been little desire, during the past half century, to follow the precise course or adopt the special terms of the Wordsworthian withdrawal. But the manner of retreating is still compulsive. The manner that we have in mind involves a selectivity that is made in the name of security; and the security is one which, in turn, involves a sort of minimizing of the present. The tendency of poetry, particularly in the twenties, to present discrete and minute fragments of experience, deliberately avoiding too much reference to the wider context of all experience, would be simply an extreme example of the inclination, written so large in Wordsworth, to get on top of the present and make it manageable, while retreating from what cannot be immediately managed or dealt with. The historical imagination, as it operates not for the enlightenment of the present, but for the melting and subsuming of it into a broader, less distressing context, can serve similar needs and here we may think especially of Yeats. The tendency, with its innumerable ramifications in various types of formalism, to resurrect with greater subtlety and refinement the doctrine of art for art's sake is another instance. In short, the sense that human experience and feeling, life itself, is unmanageable creates a need to master it in some way. We may organize and pigeon-hole according to systematic dogma, whether traditional and ready-to-hand or privately concocted; but if we do not achieve or espouse a system of belief, the unremitting complexities of living may result in a pervasive anxiety, fatigue, and desire to withdraw. The writer's eye turns from the full horizon of life toward what can be immediately mastered and managed. All this provides a larger nucleus from which to consider the problems and compulsions that have beset the poetry of the past half century; and of this Wordsworth is a prototype, almost a caricature.

Finally, we have noted that the main critical attack on Wordsworth, from his own time to the present day, has focused on his subjectivism. Here, too, he represents the dilemma of the modern poet; for it is almost inevitable that the modern poet will seem to be subjective. One of the things which we expect in the total work of any major poet is an inwoven vision of things. In the absence of any generally accepted interpretation of life, the poet must create his own, and he must create it on the basis of his own experience, which is necessarily limited. To other men, drawing upon a different fund of experience, his way of looking at things will inevitably seem restricted and subjective. The recourse to various poetic modes, such as irony, which permit opposite points of view to be included, may sometimes palliate but cannot resolve the problem. Furthermore, the dilemma is especially acute in a sophisticated age in which there is not only no generally accepted point of view, but instead many conflicting ones, all demanding the attention of educated men. At such a time, the poet, in order to maintain confidence in the validity of his own vision of things — a confidence without which it would be far more difficult to write poetry — must assert the authority of his own personal experience. Because he is on the defensive, his voice may tend to become strident, and his assertions unnecessarily extreme. In fact, he may in some cases feel compelled to protect himself from the intrusion of alien visions by deliberately refusing to listen. Thus Wordsworth mirrors, in a very striking way, one of the central problems of the contemporary poet. We could almost say that his confidence in the imagination enabled him to write. Certainly it underlay his impressive poetic success. At the same time, this confidence encouraged the muffling subjectivism that is his principal limitation.

✠ IV ✠

SHELLEY
Man's Eternal Home

Much of Shelley's work can be separated into a poetry for mass public consumption and a relatively difficult, personal, and private art, and in this, as in some other ways, his verse can be taken as prophetic of the future course of poetry in the nineteenth and twentieth centuries. The *Masque of Anarchy* was intended for the public that reads newspapers, and *The Cenci* for that which goes to plays: both were deliberately aimed at a large audience, and in them the poet is, in some sense, writing down. On the other hand, such poems as *Epipsychidion* and "The Witch of Atlas" were written for himself, his friends, and sympathizers, a sect of Shelleyans which had, in his own day, a very limited membership. Undoubtedly any poet would like to reach a wide audience, and most English poetry has been written in the confidence that such an audience would be found sooner or later. But poets have also composed for a clique or cult, and with little regard for a larger public. What is relatively novel in Shelley, and has become more urgent in our own day, is the sense of a dilemma, the desire for a large audience and the fear that one cannot expect it when one writes as one would wish. As Yeats put it, "There are two ways before literature — upward into ever-growing subtlety . . . or downward, taking the soul with us until all is simplified and solidified again. That is the choice of choices — the way of the bird until common eyes have lost us, or to the market carts."[1] There is certainly reason to doubt that the consciousness of this dilemma has been a healthy thing for modern poetry. For one thing, the tug in opposite directions makes for uncertainty in performance. But at the same time, the dilemma seems to be inescapable. For the knowledge that one is writing a difficult, relatively private poetry creates an antithetical ideal. As though suspended on the end of a pendulum, the further we go in one direction, the more we feel the pull of the other. Yet, as has been said, most of the genuine difficulty which we find in modern poetry stems not from self-indulgence but from a strenuous, partly successful effort to resolve problems which poets had seldom confronted before. Granted the milieu, the intentions, the points of view, the compelling needs, in all of which the romantics were partial prototypes of contemporary poetry, the difficulty becomes inevitable.

It is, of course, doubtful that Shelley recognized this problem in quite such a clear-cut way. With a recurrent, unsuppressible optimism, he continued to hope that even his more elaborate and difficult poems might find a wide public, and in that spirit he wrote, for example, to Ollier, expressing a mingled fear and confidence for the success of *Adonais*.[2] Hence, as Newman White (following Mary Shelley) points out, he was deeply distressed by the hostility of the reviews and the indifference of the public to most of his work, and this disappointment finally caused him not, per-

---

1. W. B. Yeats, "Discoveries," in *Essays* (London, 1924), p. 330.

2. To Ollier, Nov. 11, 1821, in *The Complete Works*, ed. Roger Ingpen and Walter E. Peck (London and New York, 1926), X, 335. Cf. To Hunt, Jan. 25, 1822, p. 351: "My faculties are shaken to atoms, and torpid. I can write nothing; and if Adonais had no success, and excited no interest what incentive can I have to write?"

haps, to write less, but to become somewhat self-pleasing and careless in his art. As Mary Shelley put it, he might have obtained "a greater mastery over his own powers . . . if public applause crowned his endeavours," and "the want of it took away a portion of the ardour that ought to have sustained him while writing." Hence if Shelley was only partially conscious of the problem, Mary was fully aware of it, and, she tells us, she "earnestly entreated" him to compose "in a style that commanded popular favour." But this Shelley could seldom bring himself to do, and as a result he wrote "without the hope of being appreciated." [3] In saying this, however, Mary is probably putting the matter too strongly. On the whole, Shelley's own remarks indicate a deep uneasiness and anxiety rather than despair, although in the "Advertisement" to *Epipsychidion* he admits that the poem "must ever remain incomprehensible" to many readers.

But in the case of Shelley it is possible to stress a further premise which especially tended to alienate him from many of his readers. It is not simply a matter of his unpopular doctrines, though often, of course, they presented something of an obstacle; it is again a question of style or poetic mode. For if there is a tradition in modern poetry which links Wordsworth and the Eliot of the *Four Quartets,* and which may be described as a meditative, quasi-autobiographical, relatively "loose" type of verse, there is also a rather nebulous counter tradition which includes many poets in certain moods and especially pertains to Blake, Shelley, and Yeats. Adopting the term the romantics themselves used, we can call it a poetry of "vision." It is rather difficult to describe this poetic mode in a precise way. Examples include most of Blake's poetry, for instance the lyric which begins "O rose

3. Note on "The Witch of Atlas," p. 383; note on *The Cenci,* p. 334; note on "The Witch of Atlas," p. 383.

thou art sick," Coleridge's "Kubla Khan," Shelley's "Witch of Atlas" and "Triumph of Life," Keats's dream of Moneta in *The Fall of Hyperion,* Browning's "Childe Roland to the Dark Tower Came," and Yeats's "Byzantium." The list may seem rather miscellaneous, but some common characteristics can be noted, though not all characteristics, of course, will hold true for each poem. In the first place, these poems are the reverse of naturalistic. The scenes and events depicted in them never occurred in the common ways of life, and in seeing them the poet did not look with what Blake called "the mortal and perishing eye." Putting this another way, we can say that these poems involve the intense contemplation of symbols, but the symbols themselves are not located in the natural world. Instead, they are "out of nature," to use Yeats's phrase, contemplated in a realm of fantasy or imagination. In the second place, the symbols are presented as though they were fraught with significance, but the significance is not spelled out in the poem. The poet offers few clues in the form of overt explanation and comment to guide the reader in his interpretation. Thus the meaning and force of the poem lies in the articulation of symbols with each other, and the poem may be susceptible of many interpretations. It is a statement, but, unlike an allegory, the statement is not limited and translatable. Thirdly, the symbols may be brought into relations with each other for which the natural world offers no warrant. When Shelley says that the Witch of Atlas would travel in her boat *under* the surface of a river the statement is meaningful in terms of what the river represents; but in order to grasp it the reader must relinquish usual expectations and be gathered into the logic of the symbols.

In short, the poetry of vision, when it is not overtly presented as a dream, at least proceeds on the analogy of dream experience. Poets could write in this way because of a metaphysic and a psychology which encouraged them to trust the visionary imagination. In describing or, in Blake's term, "copying" the dream or vision, the poet has penetrated to a meaning or truth beyond the reach of reason and inscrutable to it. But as the poetry of Keats particularly indicates, the confidence in vision has seldom been unqualified and wholehearted. The poet usually makes concessions. To the extent, however, that this confidence exists, there is an obvious danger that the poet will seem merely subjective, fantastic, and obscure, especially to that inevitable majority of his readers who do not share his premises. This certainly applies to the poetry of Shelley, and in his case there is a further disadvantage. Mrs. Blake once remarked to Seymour Kirkup, "I have very little of Mr. Blake's company, he is always in Paradise," [4] and Mary Shelley made very similar complaints of her husband, though she put them in a more conventional way. For the imagination of Shelley tended to dwell among cloudy symbols of good and evil, superhuman figures such as Laon and Cythna, Prometheus, Jupiter, Asia, and the Witch of Atlas. Though they are drawn from a less eccentric body of lore, these protagonists share many of the liabilities of Blake's Los, Enitharmon, Vala, and his other mythological creations. As Johnson remarked of Milton's *Paradise Lost,* the "inconvenience" is that "neither human actions nor human manners" are portrayed. "The reader finds no transaction in which he can be engaged, beholds no condition in which he can by any effort of imagination place himself; he has, therefore, little

4. Sir Thomas Reid, *Life, Letters, and Friendships of Richard Monckton Milnes* (1890), II, 222.

natural curiosity or sympathy. . . . The want of human interest is always felt." [5] In a sense, then, Mary Shelley was not unwise when she urged Shelley to adopt "subjects that would more suit the popular taste," [6] but she may have been unsympathetic; for she was, in part, asking him to forego his faith in the imagination as he understood it.

Shelley's manner of using symbols is worth particular attention, not only because it gives his poetry much of its distinctive character, but also because it implies or proceeds from deep-seated metaphysical premises. The point is that in developing symbols, Shelley, as compared with Wordsworth, tends to denaturalize images taken from the concrete world. For example, in the work of both poets children have almost the same symbolic significance. But in using the child as a symbol, Wordsworth, as we noted, would present him in full naturalistic detail. Shelley goes to the opposite extreme, and his symbolic children are almost never a duplication of nature. In fact, he often describes the child as having wings. In theory, there might be considerable advantages in Shelley's way of abstracting symbols from nature. A successful symbol, one might think, would be one which has enough clarity of outline and limitation of detail to be immediately felt. Furthermore, as was noted in Wordsworth, a detailed representation of all the circumstances connected with any event in nature inevitably permits or even encourages associations not pertinent to the symbolic meaning. But to use symbols in a non-representational way may imply that the particular event in nature is not by itself of primary importance. For Wordsworth, the actual phenomena of nature seem to have possessed some special significance in and of themselves. They are "consubstantial" (to borrow

5. "Milton," *Lives of the Poets*, ed. Hill (1905), I, 181–183.
6. Note on "The Witch of Atlas," p. 383.

Coleridge's word) with ultimate truth or reality. They are, as Wordsworth put it, "imbedded in a quickening soul," and whatever can be "beheld" is charged "with inward meaning." Hence any mode of poetry which takes us away from the full concreteness of things, removes us, at the same time, from truth, and Wordsworth sometimes seems to think, if we may generalize from his occasional practice, that he has done something significant if only he has faithfully reproduced an actual occurrence or circumstance. But Shelley's manner of employing symbols at once implies that the concrete has little correspondence with the "deep truth." It suggests that man can find no substantial equivalent in nature through which he can know the realm of ultimate truth, and that he can only conceive it through the exertions of thought or spirit building in partial independence of what is seen in the natural world. In other words, this approach to poetic symbolism exploits concrete nature as raw material from which elements can be drawn by the artist in the process of inventing symbols. But the symbols themselves are felt to be only approximations. They inevitably fail to convey fully the "deep truth" which, as Demogorgon says, "is imageless." [7]

— 2 —

The critical reputation of Shelley has sagged in the present century. Sometimes, indeed, his verse has been singled out and subjected to analytic persecution. This being the case, those critics who do respond to Shelley's poetry become restless, and feel challenged to show that Shelley's poetry does conform, at least in some ways, to the currently fashionable criteria of poetic accomplishment. It may not be possible to discover much wit, irony, drama, or concern with abrasive,

7. *Prometheus Unbound*, II, iv, 116.

particular fact in his verse, but one can still attempt to show, by means of detailed and ingenious explication, that many of his poems display complex metaphoric interrelation and organic completeness. These efforts often highlight aspects of Shelley's sensibility little noticed before, but they are best when conducted as a limited war, an effort to hold a defense perimeter from which, at some later time, Shelley's reputation may advance. For ideals of poetic integrity were not militant in Shelley's imagination; in comparison with most English poets, he tended to write in a loose, relatively spontaneous way, and his longer poems, such as *Epipsychidion,* often have a rather episodic character. On the other hand, sympathetic critics also try to remind us that there are many ways of reading poetry, that the standards prevalent in our own time are not absolute or final, and there has been a concern to define the mode of Shelley's poetry and so to state principles of evaluation which justify his verse, or at least make a place for it. It is scarcely possible to quarrel with this approach, but again it cannot be pushed to an extreme which denies the claims of anti-Shelleyans. The X-ray of our contemporary criticism may penetrate only to some things; but it is nevertheless very penetrating, and what it is equipped to disclose, it does not find in Shelley. Indeed, this lack of bony firmness and structure may explain the interest in quoting Aldous Huxley's reference to Shelley as a cross between an angel and a white slug. Now if the current orthodoxy has any merit, it will not neglect a major poet. From the middle of the nineteenth century to the present day, there have been few attempts to deny the merit of Wordsworth or Keats, though the grounds of estimation have been constantly changing. This may suggest one distinction between major and minor poetry. A major poetry fulfills diverse critical expectations, and so survives from one age to the next. A minor poetry is not necessarily inferior in all respects, but it is more limited in its resources. If we apply this distinction, it seems clear that Shelley cannot be numbered among what he called "the splendours of the firmament of time." He could do many things supremely well, but the poetic values of the early and mid-twentieth century are, on the whole, precisely those which Shelley does not exhibit. And if there is no reason to feel that our standards are complete and unquestionable, there is also no reason to believe they are wholly beside the point.

Quite aside from whatever satisfactions may or may not be found in Shelley's verse, it poses certain problems which are fundamental to poetry as an art. If he is not a major poet, it is for reasons that tell us much about his more successful contemporaries, and, indeed, about most of the widely recognized English poets. For in some rather basic respects, Shelley seems to stand outside the main tradition of English poetic style. Most poets, that is, would seem to have shared at least two assumptions. In the first place, there is the belief that the concrete is in some sense real, important, and worth dwelling upon, and, secondly, there is the related faith that words themselves are important and, if used precisely, can be trusted to lay bare significant kinds of truth. In the absence of these premises, it would seem, one could scarcely labor at poetry or any other verbal art. The striking thing about Shelley, then, is that at bottom he did not share these notions, or, at least, he shared them less than any other English poet worth mentioning. Despite the frequent delicacy and splendor of his imaginative constructions, he possessed a temperament which can be described as in some ways anti-poetic. There are some lines in Yeats's poem,

"Vacillation," that bear directly on this point. In a brief
dialogue between *"The Soul"* and *"The Heart,"* the Soul
says:

> Seek out reality, leave things that seem.
> *The Heart.* What, be a singer born and lack a theme?
> *The Soul.* Isaiah's coal, what more can man desire?
> *The Heart.* Struck dumb in the simplicity of fire!

Shelley, perhaps, came as close as any poet can to the
danger Yeats so well describes as being "struck dumb in the
simplicity of fire." In the face of the vast bulk of writing he
accomplished in a short life, one can hardly say that he was
struck dumb in any literal sense. But in his urgent preoccupation with ultimate reality he left things that seem far
behind, and, in attempting to express the ineffable, he
often becomes inarticulate. Hence much in his poetry that
has aroused critical complaint — the vagueness, the insub-
stantiality, the abstraction, the lack of dramatic sense —
should be viewed not as special, perhaps unfortunate stylistic
mannerisms, but as the revelation of a particular sensibility.
They can be seen as inevitable results of his way of looking,
or not looking, at the world. Keats wrote in a letter to
Shelley that *"an artist* must serve Mammon," and if we extend the meaning of "Mammon" beyond what Keats had
in mind, taking "Mammon" as the patron or representative
of this world, the remark still remains pointed and apt.

— 3 —

We can start with the matter of vagueness. It has been
much discussed in connection with Shelley's poetry, and
the intention here is merely to distinguish some kinds or
causes of vagueness, and to relate them to other aspects of
Shelley's imagination. In general, the pervasive unsubstan-
tiality of Shelley's verse must be taken as expressing a com-

parative lack of interest in the concrete. This want of interest shows itself, for example, in a tendency to disengage emotion from whatever circumstances may have kindled it, thus focusing only on the passions aroused. Especially in the shorter lyrics, one finds a vagueness in specific reference, a relative absence, in other words, of an instinct or felt need for drama. The brief "Lament" which begins "O world! O life! O time!" vents feelings of hopeless loss and world-weariness, but these emotions float by themselves, disembodied and detached from any dramatic occasion. Also, in this and similar poems, the imagery, if it can be called imagery — "Fresh spring, and summer, and winter hoar" — tends to lack specification and individuality. This fact, however, may simply indicate a particular poetic intention. For in poetry an image which is concrete and precisely individuated usually qualifies what is being said. It has character, so to speak; it invites attention and will not fade virtually unnoticed into an over-all context. But the use of images in these lyrics is not so much to arouse or define emotion. They are employed rather to receive feelings already generated, and to allow them to flow unchanged. Of course, it is possible, by the application of particular critical standards, to argue that poems similar to "A Lament" are not successful precisely because of the characteristics we have described. Certainly such poetry leaves a great deal to the reader. And the difficulty is that unless the reader is unusually suggestible, or unless the mood expressed immediately fits his own, he may not respond.

But the grounds of critical objection are often quasi-moral rather than aesthetic. Both in Irving Babbitt and his followers and also in more analytic writing, there is a suspicion that feeling unattached to precise referents and so, it may seem, indulged for its own sake, is untrustworthy, morbid, or in some other way undesirable. This may or may not be just; but it is a premise which neither Shelley nor at least two generations of his readers would have shared. Throughout the nineteenth century, it was assumed that one of the uses of poetry, both for the poet and his readers, is simply to liberate emotion. Of course, as soon as it is urged in a single-minded way, this notion becomes naïve, but it remained as an ingredient in more sophisticated discussions. And the numerous, almost pathetic tributes to the power of romantic poetry to waken emotion and so to lend some needed release, vitality, and refreshment to the dry routine of daily life should teach us charity in our criticism. At least they help to explain the vogue of poems such as "A Lament." In approaching this poetry, the reader would be likely to bring with him a readiness to respond; he would, in fact, be actually seeking to have his emotions stirred. Thus the poem could work less by empathic response directed to the poet than as a stimulus to the reader. Because of its very vagueness, both in reference and imagery, it could become a vehicle for moments of self-expression in the reading public. It provides a frame for emotion; it is a trigger or signal, and whether the signal will be received depends in part on the expectations brought to the reading of poetry.

Of course, much romantic poetry moves toward the expression of strong, personal feeling, and, in calling attention to this aspect of Shelley, one seeks merely to mark a difference in degree. For not only shorter poems such as the "Ode to the West Wind," but also extended passages in such longer works as *Epipsychidon* and *Prometheus Unbound* are couched in a rhetoric of what one might almost call frenzy. Perhaps it is verse of this kind that has tempted critics to apply the epithet "shrill" to Shelley; for the passions involved are seldom qualified or complex. Instead, the ardor and intensity spring like some fast-growing weed from a single emotional root. Putting it another way, one can describe much of Shelley's verse as a poetry of exclamation or outcry. He writes as a man seized and overfilled for a while with one emotion which must be voiced, but can only be put in expressions fundamentally repetitive. This at once suggests one of the liabilities of this mode of poetry. It is virtually a law of taste that an exclamation must be short. When, for example, the reader comes to the last act of *Prometheus Unbound* and finds that, despite all the surface variegation, it is actually but an extended exclamation point, there is a strong possibility that tedium will be felt. This suspicion is further reinforced by the fact that even sympathetic critics, when discussing the last act, have been reduced to brevity and an exclamatory style.

But there is another liability which this mode of poetry would seem to have entailed. For in these moments of outburst there is often a vagueness in the use of imagery and metaphor which does not necessarily inhere in the image or metaphor by itself. It is a matter of the lack of individuality which results from being part of a crowd.[8] For example, in the opening section of *Epipsychidion* Emily is apostrophized in a chain of metaphors:

> Sweet Benediction in the eternal Curse!
> Veiled Glory of this lampless Universe!
> Thou Moon beyond the clouds! Thou living Form
> Among the Dead! Thou Star above the Storm!
> Thou Wonder, and thou Beauty, and thou Terror!
> Thou Harmony of Nature's art!   (lines 25–30)

Of course, such nouns as "Wonder," "Beauty," and "Terror"

---

8. Cf. the discussion of Shelley's imagery in Raymond D. Havens, "Shelley the Artist," *The Major English Romantic Poets,* ed. Clarence D. Thorpe et al. (Carbondale, Ill., 1957), pp. 175–177.

have their own obvious liabilities, and tend to muffle these lines in abstraction. It is, however, possible to claim that the individual metaphors — the "Moon beyond the clouds," the "Star," and the like — are, in their context, sufficiently suggestive. But huddled as they are along an impulsive stream of ecstatic feeling, they may shift and flicker so rapidly that they serve partially to diffuse the impact of what is being said. No particular image is fixed or planted in the mind, and as a result the passage as a whole may seem a dazzling blur. It should be admitted that these lines are an extreme example, but they are not atypical, and there are several possible speculations which might help to explain this way of writing. For one thing, these metaphors can be described as a further instance of what has already been noticed in the brief lyric "A Lament." Here again words are adapted not so much to modify or give precision, but to receive and carry ecstatic feelings which, it is hoped, have already been inflamed. In other words, Shelley here puts language to work in a rather unusual way, aspiring, as Walter Pater said all art aspires, to the condition of music, that is, to a relatively pure emotion sustained through time. But since words must be used, and since they tend individually to summon defined meanings and complex associations, they must be mixed and hurried in such a way that the reader will not pause to study their content. And there are several enticements in the verse to persuade the reader to move rapidly. The grammar is simple and exclamatory, consisting largely of brief parallel clauses; each metaphor has an immediate clarity when taken by itself, and, taken together, they are repetitive in content and tone; the reader may be already empathically caught up in the excited onrush of the speaker's emotions. Another possible cause of this way of writing might be that the poem here attempts to express the ineffable. No single image or metaphor could begin to hold what the speaker has in mind or the emotions felt with respect to it. Thus it is approached through many metaphors, and the hope seems to be that in the mixture of ingredients an explosion will take place, that the reader will somehow pass beyond the veil of words to an intuitive apprehension. Such a passage, then, may suggest a certain distrust of language. It is not through words precisely put together, but rather by an intuitive sympathy stimulated, of course, by what is said, but finally transcending it, that the poet can hope to communicate. Adapting a phrase of Wordsworth's which has already been cited, one can say of Shelley that when he was "grasping" with his "greatest strength," words were but "under agents" in his "soul."

— 4 —

In talking about some elements of Shelley's poetic style, the attempt was to begin a sketch or description of his particular way of arranging or ordering experience. It might seem that this approach involves the deliberate choice of a winding road; for Shelley left a number of prose fragments (not to mention letters) which, exploiting the language of systematic philosophy, define, or attempt to define, his beliefs. The difficulty, however, is that one is concerned not so much with beliefs themselves, as beliefs turned into poetry, and what a writer believes, or says he believes, and what he is able to funnel into poetic expression may be rather different things. Furthermore, abstract language, especially when handled by a poet, may tend to a rather crude generality. We have seen that what Wordsworth actually tends to notice in nature, what comprises his usual stock of images, modifies and enriches our notion of his fundamental attitudes themselves. So with Shelley. A reading of his poetry quickly indicates how obsessed he was by flux and transformation in the natural world. He habitually observes gleamings and dartings — for example, the swift transformation of colors in an insect wing. More especially he notices how contingent circumstances modify the appearance of things. Perhaps this imagery is most characteristic when it presents things acquiring or changing color as various kinds of light play on them. Of course, Wordsworth also tended to see and record such phenomena, and in his poetry the light thrown upon an object and altering its appearance often becomes a metaphor of the imagination at work. In Shelley's verse, however, such descriptions carry rather different implications. For one thing, there is usually the emphasis that the coloring received is shifting and evanescent. Moreover, the light is often projected upon such things as mists or clouds which have no permanent or innate color of their own. For example, Shelley describes "a vaporous spray/ Which the sun clothes in hues of Iris light." Here the "vaporous spray" is felt to lack distinctive individuality, and the aspect it assumes is a clothing that can be put off or changed. But this applies to more solid and tangible objects as well. Shelley speaks of a church "whose pinnacles/ Point from one shrine like pyramids of fire" as the sunset is "clothing in hues of heaven" its "dim and distant spire." [9] In *Prometheus Unbound* the Third Voice (from the Air) puts the idea very baldly:

> I had clothed, since Earth uprose
> Its wastes in colours not their own.   (I, 82–83)

The remark has a scientific basis of sorts, but it also implies Shelley's habitual way of thinking about material concretions. In fact, imagery of this sort occurs frequently enough to

9. "Orpheus," lines 79–80; "A Summer Evening Churchyard," lines 13–16.

acquire an important symbolic function, suggesting that matter can have little or no character of its own, and that it derives whatever identity it has from the influences that play upon it.

A corollary can be found in the constant motion that Shelley notices in the natural world; he seldom presents anything that suggests repose or permanence. Even those objects that another poet might have used as metaphors of rest and stillness are observed to be darting or dancing. One thinks of Keats's sonnet which employs a "Bright Star" as a symbol precisely because it appears to be "stedfast." In Shelley's poetry even the stars "whirl and flee,/ Like a swarm of golden bees." A star "scatters drops of golden light" until "it is borne away, away/ By the swift Heavens that cannot stay"; the earth, instead of following its slow planetary orbit, "dances about the sun." Similarly, if he pictures a mountain, he may see not the Wordsworthian stillness, but a "sun-awakened avalanche." [10] In fact, images of repose and solidity in Shelley's poetry seem to exist mainly to dramatize the force that shakes them. When the Furies are unleashed in *Prometheus Unbound* Ione remarks, "I hear the thunder of new wings," and Panthea replies, "These solid mountains quiver with the sound/ Even as the tremulous air" (I, 521–523). Perhaps a passage in "The Witch of Atlas" put Shelley's conviction of universal impermanence most powerfully. The animate spirits of nature hope to live forever in the presence of the witch:

> 'This may not be,' the wizard maid replied;
> 'The fountains where the Naiades bedew
> Their shining hair, at length are drained and dried;
> The solid oaks forget their strength, and strew

10. "The Cloud," lines 53–54; *Prometheus Unbound*, II, ii, 18–20; "The Cloud," line 8; *Prometheus Unbound*, II, iii, 37.

Their latest leaf upon the mountains wide;
The boundless ocean like a drop of dew
Will be consumed — the stubborn centre must
Be scattered, like a cloud of summer dust.' (lines 225–232)

Although tinged with nostalgia, these lines, with their driving, assertive rhythm, are an unequivocal statement, summing up the inevitable decomposition of all material things from the fountains to the "stubborn center" of the earth itself.

What is true of physical nature applies even more to human life, whether for the individual or entire nations. The generations of mankind are "rapid, blind/ And fleeting," and Shelley's imagination, as "Ozymandias" suggests, tended to dwell on the decay of empires. Babylon is now dust; "Rome has fallen, ye see it lying/ Heaped in undistinguished ruin." [11] With this sweeping vision of change and dissolution, Shelley naturally conceives time as an unresting, inevitable force hurrying all things to a death. His habitual symbol — a universal, almost a trite one — of time, or of life in time, is the stream on which even "Worlds on worlds are . . . borne away" as if they were "bubbles on a river." [12] But the stream imagery suggests not merely "the flood of time." It is also employed in a rather more subtle way, as Carl Grabo points out, to suggest the unceasing flow of human consciousness.[13] These ramifications of the image

11. "The Witch of Atlas," lines 615–616; *Prometheus Unbound*, I, 191; "Fragment: Rome and Nature," lines 1–2.
12. "Hellas," lines 197–200.
13. *The Magic Plant* (Chapel Hill, N. C., 1936), pp. 146–147. One ramification of this symbolism is that by means of it Shelley "continually meditates," to quote Yeats, on the "mysterious source" of the stream of human existence. Sometimes, as in "Mont Blanc," the source is a mountain. More frequently, however, streams in Shelley's poetry arise in caverns, often as a fountain. The point is discussed in detail by W. B. Yeats in his discussion of "The Philosophy of Shelley's Poetry," *Essays*, pp. 96–98. Although Shelley

are, however, entirely consistent. For the theme of much of Shelley's poetry, as of Eliot's *Four Quartets,* is the relation of time and eternity. At sudden and unpredictable moments human consciousness may move out of time into what both Shelley and Eliot would call "reality." But for the most part human consciousness is inextricably bound to the "turning world." Held in what Eliot calls "the enchainment of past and future," it moves with or through time, and thus the sad implications of the stream imagery become applicable to the mind itself. One of the implications of the stream is that "its waves are unreturning." [14] As Cythna says in *The Revolt of Islam,*

> Alas, our thoughts flow on with stream, whose waters
> Return not to their fountain — Earth and Heaven,
> The Ocean and the Sun, the Clouds their daughters,
> Winter, and Spring, and Morn, and Noon, and Even,
> All that we are or know, is darkly driven
> Towards one gulf.   (lines 3775–3780)

The gulf, of course, is death, or, at least, a loss of personal existence in "the utmost Ocean/ Of universal life" (lines 2594–2595). All are driven to it because all are caught in the stream, and its push is irresistible.

Alternatively, when concrete life is not viewed as a tossing bark borne rapidly away on an irresistible stream, Shelley sees it trapped in meaningless cyclical repetitions. The cyclic pattern is observed, for example, in the seasonal "change and motion" of the "revolving year," [15] as in the "Ode to the West Wind," or "The Sensitive Plant," and in the

---

usually associates water imagery with the world of time and generation, he also at times used the sea, "the utmost Ocean/ Of universal life" (*The Revolt of Islam,* lines 2594–2595), as a symbol of the One. Cf. on this point *The Magic Plant,* p. 281.

14. "Lines: 'That time is dead for ever,'" line 9.

15. *Adonais,* lines 165, 155.

endless transformation of water to vapor and rain. The latter sometimes becomes a metaphor of human life; for men are

> Clouds
> Driven by the wind in warring multitudes,
> Which rain into the bosom of the earth,
> And rise again, and in our death and birth,
> And through our restless life, take as from heaven
> Hues which are not our own.[16]

But the cyclic pattern applies not only to the individual. It may characterize any change taking place in the world of time, and hence, like Yeats, Shelley sometimes conceived history as moving in cycles. "Some think" Ahasuerus "has survived/ Cycles of generation and of ruin" (*Hellas,* lines 153–154) and that his

> spirit is present in the Past, and sees
> The birth of this old world through all its cycles
> Of desolation and of loveliness.   (*Hellas,* lines 745–747)

The future golden age Shelley fondly envisaged in *Hellas* will be the completion of a cycle, the repetition of the "great age" of the past:

> The world's great age begins anew,
>   The golden years return,
>   .   .   .   .   .
> A brighter Hellas rears its mountains
>   From waves serener far
>   .   .   .   .   .
> A loftier Argo cleaves the main,
>   Fraught with a later prize;
> Another Orpheus sings again,
>   And loves, and weeps, and dies.
> A new Ulysses leaves once more
> Calypso for his native shore.   (lines 1060–1077)

16. "Fragments Connected with *Epipsychidion,*" lines 126–131.

But, of course, the golden age reborn must again be suc-
ceeded by an age of "hate and death." Thus the cyclic
pattern affords no comfort, and the final wish expressed in
this great lyric is the moving, triple iteration of the word
"cease."

> Oh, cease! must hate and death return?
> Cease! must men kill and die?
> Cease! drain not to its dregs the urn
>   Of bitter prophecy.
> The world is weary of the past,
> Oh, might it die or rest at last!   (lines 1096–1101)

It is an injunction, first of all, to the poet to cease speaking,
to end his poem at the vision of utopian happiness. More
than that, it expresses an urge to cease the process of thought,
to withdraw from the cyclic vision of history; for if it is
pursued, the prophecy must inevitably become bitter. Finally,
it expresses a wish that history should itself cease with the
new "great age," but, if the cyclic pattern makes this wish
sentimental and impossible, then the prayer must be that
the "world" may "die."

— 5 —

Perhaps Shelley's most effective presentation of this attitude to life in time occurs in the first 175 lines of the unfinished "Triumph of Life." One characteristic of Shelley's
poetry is that rather than unravelling the implications of a
dominant comparison, it weaves together multiple strands of
metaphor which are, in effect, variations on a single theme.
So here the poem makes use of a number of images, all of
them recurrent in Shelley, and the images are linked together by associations which were themselves relatively fixed
and stable. The poem begins with a brief and graceful introduction which leads into a "strange trance" during which a

vision is "rolled upon the brain" of the poet. As he sat beside a public way, he saw "a great stream/ Of people . . . hurrying to and fro." The stream image here might not have much significance by itself, but it is picked up later when the crowd is described as a "mighty torrent," and becomes, as it usually does with Shelley, a metaphor of a force which irresistibly compels the individual. All of the people were hastening onward without apparent volition of their own, each "borne amid the crowd, as through the sky/ One of the million leaves" is hurried by the autumn wind. The reference to leaves blown through the sky recalls the "Ode to the West Wind" where leaves are also compared to people, "Pestilence-stricken multitudes," driven by the wind. But in the "Ode" the violence of the wind is but the prelude to the coming of a storm, and the storm also follows in "The Triumph of Life." For as the poem continues, the visionary has an impression of confused and pointless motions of the leaf-people, and then of a cold glare which "obscured . . . The sun," and is the "herald" of the coming storm. Just as in the "Ode" the west wind is compared to a chariot, the chariot of life speeds on "the silent storm/ Of its own rushing splendour." The "Shape" of Life sits within, and "o'er what seemed the head" can be observed "a dun and faint aetherial gloom/ Tempering the light," and this "cloudlike . . . gloom" is, of course, an image of the dark clouds of the storm. Also, the movement of the chariot is accompanied by "thick lightnings" (lines 29–96). The point is, then, that in the multiplication of metaphors, Life is figured in the onrush of a chariot, and the chariot is itself compared to a storm. Moreover, as in the "Ode" and elsewhere in Shelley, the storm itself is associated with overwhelming violence and daemonic intoxication.

In the poetry of Shelley, as of Keats, major poems are often organized around a metaphor or symbol relatively fixed in the poet's imagination, and the poem itself simply ex-plores or works out whatever the symbol may imply. Thus the "Ode to the West Wind" builds with storm and seasonal metaphors which occur elsewhere in a more incidental way; "The Cloud" elaborates one of the images most common in Shelley; "The Sensitive Plant" unites and carries into detail such recurrent symbols as the seasons of the year, the garden, the poet or the Platonic lover as a flower, and, of course, the transcendent ideal figured as a beautiful woman; and this last metaphor is fully developed in *Epipsychidion*. In the same way, the vision of Life riding in a chariot can be described as a determined pursuit of a habitual image; for the chariot of Life is both the last chronologically and the most extensively described of numerous chariots in Shelley's poetry, and in "The Triumph of Life" the full implications of the image are revealed. In *Prometheus Unbound*, to cite one example, Demogorgon comes in the "earthquake of his chariot" (III, i, 50) to overthrow Jupiter, and the chariot here becomes a metaphor of the irresistible onrush of time and fate. For the chariot in which Demogorgon arrives is not actually his own but rather the car of the particular Hour or moment of time during which this de-nouement takes place, and each of the inevitable hours is personified as a "wild-eyed charioteer" riding in a car like the chariot of Life, drawn "by rainbow-wingèd steeds" (II, iv, 130–132). Again in *Hellas* Shelley described Destiny as "The world's eyeless charioteer," and her car is drawn by "earthquake-footed steeds" (lines 711–714). The reference to the earthquake in both these instances suggests that same overwhelming and destructive violence in the chariot's for-ward motion which, in the "Triumph of Life," is implied in the comparison of the chariot to a storm, and, to mention one more parallel, the charioteer Destiny in *Hellas* is eyeless just as the "Janus-visaged Shadow" on the chariot-beam of Life's car has his eyes banded (lines 93–99), thus suggesting the lack of direction or point in Life's forward motion.

The hurtling onrush of Life drives all living things along with it. In the "Triumph of Life," the conception, as Shelley says, is specifically of a Roman triumphal procession when prisoners taken in battle were marched through Rome yoked to the chariot of the victorious conqueror. Though it here receives a rather special reference, Shelley frequently employed the metaphor of life in time as a shackling or "enchainment," to use Eliot's word, of the human spirit. In the "Ode to the West Wind," a "heavy weight of hours has chained and bowed" the youthful poet. Man must "wear/ These heavy chains of life," [17] and Urania, mourning for Adonais, says

> I would give
> All that I am to be as thou now art!
> But I am chained to Time, and cannot thence depart!
> (lines 232–234)

Mahmud knows that Ahasuerus will appear "When the omnipotent hour to which are yoked/ He, I, and all things shall compel." [18] And even after the transforming of the earth in *Prometheus Unbound,* Shelley writes that "chance, and death, and mutability" are still "The clogs" of the human spirit "which else might oversoar/ The loftiest star of unascended heaven" (III, iv, 201–203). Accordingly, in "The Triumph of Life" the throng about the chariot is

---

17. "Fragments Connected with *Epipsychidion*," lines 123–124.
18. *Hellas,* lines 189–190.

"a captive multitude . . . driven" wherever it rolled. The "captives fettered" consist of all those whom Life has subdued, and Shelley seems to construe submission as meaning any kind of commitment to life, any desire or endeavor directed to something in human life. Thus Plato walks in the triumph, his heart having been "Conquered . . . by love"; but Socrates knew neither joy nor woe, and hence is not in the pageant (lines 119–120; 457; 121; 258; 255).

But in addition to the Roman triumph, another image from classical antiquity lies behind the conception of "The Triumph of Life." Those clustered around the chariot are not all sullen captives; there are also "agonizing pleasure," "fierce song and maniac dance/ Raging around," "a ribald crowd," people "fierce and obscene," and a "wild dance" that "maddens in the van." "Those who lead it . . . Outspeed the chariot . . . Throw back their heads and loose their streaming hair," and dance round Life until they fall senseless and the chariot passes on (lines 110–160). In *Prometheus Unbound* Shelley had spoken of the "maddening wine of life" (II, iii, 7), and here in the "maniac dance" he surely has in mind the Dionysian revellers. Life is the god Dionysus, intoxicating and maddening his attendants. This madness, of course, cannot be confused with the madness of inspiration. Neither is it akin to the emotions of the maniac in the cryptic "Julian and Maddalo," but when in that poem the maniac cries "What power delights to torture us" (line 320), the question carries us forward to *Prometheus Unbound* and finally to "The Triumph of Life," where the final cry of the poet — "Then, what is life? I cried" — may be a very similar question. The "Triumph of Life," of course, is unfinished, but as it stands the question is rhetorical; for it has already been answered in the first vision of the chariot of Life. The poem sums up, with little need for qualification, what Shelley came finally to see in human existence.

— 6 —

With this attitude, Shelley, no less than Wordsworth, sought some principle of permanence in the cosmos. As with other romantic and modern poets, the quest for permanence, and for the reassurance it brings, should be regarded as a natural human protest against the constant, meaningless, uncontrollable flux and change sensed in his own emotions and in the world around him. He hoped to find something more than "Whatever is begotten, born, and dies," to borrow Yeats's phrase, some stability unmodified by accidents of neighborhood and out of time. Shelley and Wordsworth, though they share the quest for permanence, come to opposite resolutions of the dilemma; and Shelley, like Wordsworth, represents an attitude which many poets since the beginning of the nineteenth century have been tempted to adopt. The attitude involved might be called a flight to abstraction, although the phrasing may seem unsympathetic. Wordsworth at least in the poetry written before 1805, tended to locate the desired permanence in the concrete or natural world, seeing permanence as part of the living oneness of the cosmos. Shelley, however, is closer to Blake, for he bifurcated or split the universe into the concrete, with its unending flux, and a world of thought or spirit behind or beside the concrete, but only fleetingly in it.[19] In con-

19. We are speaking here of a tendency writ large in Shelley's poetry, and the statement necessarily involves an oversimplification of detail. At times, Shelley attempts to resolve this dualism, either by declaring that the cosmos is all matter, or alternatively that it is all mind. These notions, however, do not play a major rôle in his poetry, and to me they seem imposed *ab extra* from a desire for philosophic respectability. The dualism, however, is

trast to the material cosmos, this transcendent reality is immortal and unchanging. It was symbolized in many ways; but for our immediate purposes the most important points are that it is the ultimate locus of truth or reality, and that, except for momentary visitations, it is sharply dissociated from concrete nature.

"Mont Blanc," for example, was written early in Shelley's career, but in these fundamental respects it is entirely characteristic. However doubtful one may be about details of interpretation, the outline of the poem seems clear enough. It begins with an image of the stream suggesting the "universe of things" as it "flows through the mind." The mind itself, as so often in Shelley and in romantic poetry in general — and here, as elsewhere, the poem especially shows the influence of Wordsworth — has "secret chasms" from which waters are "welling" (line 122). These are "the source of human thought" which brings its "tribute . . . Of waters" to the flowing "universe of things," lending splendor to it (lines 1–5). After this preliminary section, the poem describes the ravine with the stream running through it. The symbolism is vague, but in contrast to the mountain towering above it, the ravine seems to suggest concrete life. Thus it is described as a "many-coloured, many-voicèd vale." Above it "sail/ Fast cloud-shadows and sunbeams," suggesting the shifting light and shade Shelley habitually observed in nature. Similarly, the poem here refers to the "chainless winds," "rainbows," "unresting sound" and "ceaseless motion" that characterize the life of the vale (lines 13–33). At the same time, as the poem makes clear, the "dark, deep Ravine" is also an emblem of the

---

grounded in emotions since it embodies what was perhaps deepest in Shelley, the protest against things as they are and the longing for a better world.

> human mind, which passively
> Now renders and receives fast influencings,
> Holding an unremitting interchange
> With the clear universe of things around.   (lines 37–40)

It should be noted, in passing, that the symbolism of the poem marks no clear distinction between the human mind and the phenomenal world.

The stream of Arve, which in the first section was a figure of the "everlasting universe of things" flowing through the mind, seems now to have changed in metaphoric significance. One critic, citing the statement that "Power in likeness of the Arve comes down" (line 16) from the mountain, points out that the Arve has now become "the symbol . . . of 'Power' pervading the passive Ravine." The Power is identical with the Power which later in the poem Shelley symbolizes in the image of the mountain. Thus the mountain and the stream begin to suggest the immanent and transcendent aspects of the same Power.[20] The Arve is said to descend "Bursting through these dark mountains like the flame/ Of lightning through the tempest" (lines 18–19); and, as we shall see later, both the comparison to flame and the insistence on the suddenness of its visitation are entirely characteristic of Shelley. Equally characteristic is the statement that the "caverns" of the mind echo to the "Arve's commotion," and that no other sound can tame or blot out the human consciousness of transcendence (lines 30–31).

But beyond the Ravine, and the content of human consciousness which it symbolizes, there is a "remoter world," known perhaps in sleep, perhaps in death when the "veil of life" is lifted. Of this Mont Blanc is the symbol. "Still snowy, and serene" it pierces "the infinite sky" (lines 49–61).

20. James A. Notopoulos, *The Platonism of Shelley* (Durham, N. C., 1949), pp. 206–209.

With its ice, rock, and "frozen floods" (lines 63–64), it "seems eternal," and one should also note in passing that this remoter world is associated with death. In the fourth section, having established the landscape as symbolic, the poem generalizes upon it. All "living things that dwell" on earth and all "the works and ways of man" are "born and die." They "revolve, subside, and swell" in constant change. But the ultimate reality and force of the cosmos does not reside in these concretions. Instead, Power, symbolized as the mountain, "dwells apart in its tranquillity,/ Remote, serene, and inaccessible" (lines 85–97).

— 7 —

"Mont Blanc" is, however, an early poem, and though it is entirely characteristic in postulating a remoter world, the particular symbolism employed did not tend to recur. For however appropriate for some purposes, the mountain, stream, and vale also impose certain implications contrary to what were, or came to be, Shelley's own convictions. To represent ultimate Power in the mountain and the stream means that it is always present to human consciousness, and though he might have wished to believe this, Shelley was seldom able to do so. Moreover, the symbolism does not naturally or gracefully suggest what gives Shelley's art much of its intensity and direction, the aspiration — more eager than in any of the other romantics with the possible exception of Blake — to escape from the organic, shifting, phenomenal world, and to rise into the transcendent permanence. With this pattern of rejection and aspiration, it was perhaps inevitable that through most of his life Shelley should formulate and express his beliefs in Platonic terms. For whatever else it may include, Platonism, as matters so diverse as the death of Socrates or the concept of Platonic love would indicate, involves a rejection of the concrete as it is in favor of a fixed ideal. Hence for most of his mature life, Shelley seems to have conceived the desired permanence in Platonic or quasi-Platonic terms; and, like all Platonists, he habitually symbolized transcendent reality in images of light.

Critics have frequently noticed and explored this light symbolism, and there is no need to discuss it in detail here, though it may be helpful to outline some of the main ways it appears in Shelley's poetry. The sun, in particular, suggests the reality to which man aspires. In *Prometheus Unbound*, Asia is metaphorically equated with the sun. At the time of her first "uprise," a radiance like "the sun's fire filling the living world/ Burst" from her (III, v, 22, 27–28). When Prometheus recalls his curse and the earth is transformed, Asia is again "unveiled" and her "smiles . . . Make the cold air fire" (II, v, 20, 50–51) and this, of course, dovetails with the passage in *Adonais* where the One, equated with "Heaven's light," is described as the "Light whose smile kindles the Universe" (lines 460–461, 478). Hence in aspiring to escape from the flux of mortality, man seeks a "diviner clime," a "sunnier strand." In Plato's myth of the cave, the philosopher is one who has escaped from the cave and is able to look at the sun. Hence, the men of "godlike mind" who sometimes appear in the world may be compared to eagles, for, in accordance with the bestiary tradition, eagles can fly in the full intensity of the sun. Thus Francis Bacon was an "eagle spirit," and in "The Triumph of Life" the "sacred few," those who Life could not lead in the triumph, merely "touched the world" and then "fled back like eagles to their native noon" (lines 128–131).

With this web of implications in mind, one can turn to the lines in *Adonais* which are probably the most famous single passage in Shelley,

> The One remains, the many change and pass;
> Heaven's light forever shines, Earth's shadows fly;
> Life, like a dome of many-coloured glass,
> Stains the white radiance of Eternity,
> Until Death tramples it to fragments.   (lines 460–464)

The radiance of Eternity is the light emanating from the sun. Drawing upon scientific lore, Shelley conceives it as white until it strikes the dome of the earthly atmosphere, when, of course, it takes on color.[21] But the word "stains" is ambiguous. It means that "Life" gives color to the white radiance, but it also implies that "Life" casts a certain undesirable stain, "the world's slow stain" from whose "contagion" Adonais is now "secure" (lines 356–357). In other words, the color obscures the "white radiance of Eternity" which man seeks, just as the dome by its architectural implications suggests that bodily life itself imprisons man, blocking his heavenward flight. Hence it is desirable that death should trample the dome into fragments, and the metaphor is immediately followed by a direct injunction to "Die,/ If thou wouldst be with that which thou dost seek" (lines 464–465). But again it is especially the water vapor in the atmosphere which stains, and thus such frequent images as the sun drawing up dew, or burning away mist, acquire important symbolic overtones. These overtones become explicit at the end of *Adonais* where the poet, seeming to find himself in the process of approaching the "abode where the Eternal are," speaks of the light of heaven which beams on him as "Consuming the last clouds of cold mortality" (lines 495; 485–486).

21. Earl R. Wasserman, "'Adonais': Progressive Revelation as a Poetic Mode," *ELH*, XXI (December, 1954), p. 306: "The 'dome,' of course, is a metaphor for the sky . . . Because this atmospheric dome diffracts the rays of the sun, it stains the radiance of eternity, which is outside the atmosphere, and thereby produces color, the quality of the world of mutability."

As an image of transcendent reality the sun suggests both
that it is beyond the concrete and that it exercises some
powerful influence within the realm of nature. Moreover,
because we associate the sun with fire, Shelley's symbolism
begins to fall into the kind of complex associative nexus or
pattern which, in the modes of romantic and modern poetry,
often provides a fertile ground for successful composition —
although Shelley's associations were seldom as stable as those
of Wordsworth or Keats. For another of Shelley's habitual
ways of suggesting the transcendent reality is through imagery of fire. Of course, this was also traditional in neo-Platonic thought, and it has been exhaustively studied in connection with Shelley. Briefly summarizing what Shelley implies through this symbolism, we can say that Platonic reality
is the "fire for which all thirst." It is veiled or obscured to
human eyes while man dwells on earth, but the "eclipsing
Curse/ Of birth" cannot quench it. Instead, it "must glow/
Through time and change, unquenchably the same." [22] Such
words as "quench" and "unquenchably" suggest the association which runs throughout *Adonais* of the realm of birth
and death with water. In this pattern of metaphor, the gen-
eration-water realm of earthly life is hostile to the fire-perma-
nence.[23] But the latter is the fire for which all thirst." The
paradox of thirsting for a fire is resolved, however, in the
neo-Platonic image of transcendent reality as a "burning
fountain" (line 339). The image, as Carlos Baker has suggested, resembles the "well/ Of crimson fire" in which the

22. *Adonais,* lines 485, 480–481, 340–341.
23. Wasserman, p. 282: "Throughout the poem there is a recurrent opposition of two nature symbols: light, or fire, the life symbol, and moisture,
the symbol of mortality." The article traces in considerable detail the use
of water and fire imagery in *Adonais.*

Witch of Atlas lies,[24] and in a metaphor it annihilates antinomies of mortality and spirit, generation and permanence. In keeping with neo-Platonic tradition, Shelley, like Wordsworth in his great ode, sometimes says that the spirit of man comes to human life from the burning fountain of ultimate being. Life itself is a "decaying flame" to which the individual brings a "portion of the Eternal," touching the world with "living flame." At death, "the pure spirit shall flow/ Back to the burning fountain whence it came." [25]

The fire symbolism also suggests that the transcendent reality is immaterial. Shelley's conception of it is, perhaps, further clarified by his association of fire not only with ultimate being, but also with human thought. The association has a persistent gravitational force in Shelley's poetry, and only a few representative instances can be cited. Human thought is a "dying flame" momentarily nourished by glimpses of the "Eternal." [26] In his "Defence of Poetry," Shelley argued that poetry, or at least genuine poetry, as contrasted to the "mosaic" type produced by painstaking care and revision, is the result of an "evanescent visitation." "It is, as it were, the interpenetration of a diviner nature through our own"; and the mind, having been momentarily kindled by the divine fire, "in creation is as a fading coal." [27]

24. "The Witch of Atlas," lines 278–279. Carlos Baker, *Shelley's Major Poetry* (Princeton, 1948), p. 210. Newman White, *Shelley* (New York, 1940), II, 370, has noted the recurrence of the same image in "The Triumph of Life," lines 345–347:

> the sun's image radiantly intense
> Burned on the waters of the well that glowed
> Like gold.

25. *Alastor,* line 247; *Adonais,* line 340; "The Triumph of Life," line 130; *Adonais,* lines 338–339.

26. "Hymn to Intellectual Beauty," lines 44–45.

27. *Works,* ed. Roger Ingpen and W. E. Peck (London and New York, 1926–1930), VII, 135–136.

133

The writers of the past have left "the stamp/ Of ever-burning thoughts on many a page"; thoughts which sustain the hopes of man amid a "dark ruin" are like "fires that flare/ In storm-encompassed isles." The "quenchless words" of Greece are "sparks of immortal truth." [28] But fire is a metaphor not simply of thought, but of whatever in man is not inevitably involved in the flux and decay of matter. For example, in *Prometheus Unbound* the furies which torment Prometheus cannot "obscure . . . The soul which burns within," and Jupiter elsewhere remarks that "The soul of man, like unextinguished fire,/ Yet burns toward heaven" (I, 484–485; III, i, 5–6). As one ramification of this metaphoric pattern, the minds of the wise are frequently spoken of as "lamps within the dome of this dim world" ("Ode to Liberty," lines 226–227):

> the love from Petrarch's urn,
> Yet amid yon hills doth burn,
> A quenchless lamp by which the heart
> Sees things unearthly.[29]

This complex network of equations which associates fire with human "thought," "mind," or "soul" has important consequences for Shelley's poetry. The common denominator of the fire symbolism tends to make soul an equivalent of thought. Hence human thought is what corresponds in man to the "Eternal." As the typically Shelleyan symbol of a hermit dwelling in a tower suggests, it is to some extent possible to turn from concrete experience and withdraw into "thought." But if thought can be imaginatively identified with the "fire for which all thirst," then the absorption in thought is an earthly analogue of the desired escape from

28. *The Revolt of Islam*, lines 1478–1479, 3154–3156; *Hellas*, line 97.
29. "Lines Written among the Euganean Hills," lines 200–203.

concrete life to a transcendent reality. But this point will be developed later.

To the fire and sun symbolism should be added the star as an image of transcendent reality. Like the sun, the star is beyond the earth and yet shines upon it. Moreover, the star "burns," and, like fire, it is associated with human thought. Thus in the "night of time" stars represent the

> kings of thought
> Who waged contention with their time's decay,
> And of the past are all that cannot pass away.
>
> (*Adonais,* lines 430–432)

Milton's "clear Sprite" is a star that "Yet reigns o'er earth"; and in the realm of earthly existence, what Shelley calls "the firmament of time," the "kings of thought" are "splendours" which climb like "stars to their appointed height." Similarly, the "quenchless words" of ancient Greece are "Stars of all night," and the "holiest dreams of highest spirits/ Are stars beneath the dawn." [30] But as a symbol the star permits some implications to follow more naturally and hence more convincingly than the fire symbolism. We have seen that the fire of ultimate being cannot be quenched by the mist or moisture of earth. The fire-water symbolism perfectly dramatizes a split between earthly existence and transcendent reality, but the notion that the fire is quenchless is simply an assertion, weighted, it is true, by the ardor of Shelley's conviction, but not rooted in the natural experience of the reader. In other words, the assertion is not helped to win poetic faith and credence by any correspondence of the symbolic interrelation of the images with their actual interrelation in the natural world. This lack of correspondence is, of

---

30. *Adonais,* lines 35–36, 388–390; *Hellas,* lines 97–98, 111–112.

course, characteristic of Shelley, but does not always make for a successful use of metaphor. In the context of the star symbolism, the counterpart of the quenching of the fire would be the star ceasing to shine. Through the symbolism, Shelley can represent the star obscured by the clouds of earthly existence. But even though it may be temporarily lost to human eyes it still shines behind the "veil of Heaven." [31] Like the fire, it is quenchless, but the symbolic vehicle now acquires force and conviction from its truth to the order of nature. Furthermore, like the fire the star is an image of something desired. But here again, Shelley, by a dazzling use of metaphor, fixes its power of attraction in the realm of natural experience; for in a recurrent expression he speaks of "the desire of the moth for the star." [32] The metaphor is based on nature, for by the moth's tropism to light, the star would be automatically and irresistibly attractive to it. At the same time, of course, it dramatizes the inaccessibility of the star. It is worth noting that, like the "burning fountain," the star can be reached only at death. So, in *Epipsychidion* (line 223), the moth, in flitting toward the star, is seeking "A radiant death, a fiery sepulchre."

31. *Adonais,* line 493.
32. "To ———," line 13.

℣ V ℣

SHELLEY

Visitations of the Transcendent World

One of the legacies of the romantic period is the heightened concern in literature with types of psychological experience outside the usual limits of consciousness. The romantics recognized and talked about a wide variety of processes ranging from secondary perception to what they might call either outright hallucination or imaginative "vision." Indeed, from the perspective of our own time, we may feel that the great romantics struck a healthy balance in these matters. They did not deliberately pursue the strange and occult in human experience, either by a direct assault, like Rossetti or Yeats with their interest in the supernatural, or, like De Quincey or Rimbaud, by consciously distorting their own powers of perception. On the other hand, they did not explain away such things by appealing to a strict rationalism. In fact, most of the major romantics actually testified to brief moments when the mind seemed to achieve some vital contact with an unseen, transcendent power, and much of the romantic effort can be described as an honest meditation of the validity of such experience. Wordsworth, as we have seen, turned especially to the recollection of these moments as a source of reassurance and security. They were no less significant to Shelley; it was only at such times that living man could know the permanence that lies behind the concrete. What seems to take place, as Shelley speaks of it, is a sudden jump or transference of consciousness to another realm, or, alternatively, an invasion from the transcendent into human life, and much of his poetry attempts to describe such experience. We can start with one of his earlier poems, the "Hymn to Intellectual Beauty," in which Shelley summarizes by means both of abstract language and of autobiography much that he puts elsewhere in a more metaphoric way. Although there is no need to discuss the poem in detail, a number of general points can be made. In the first place, there is an "unseen Power," represented in the poem by a quasi-Platonic "Spirit of BEAUTY." [1] "Life's unquiet dream" receives whatever grace and truth it has from the play of this unseen Power upon it. The "awful shadow" of this Power visits the variegated world of "Doubt, chance, and mutability," and mortality is passive to its visitation. When it descends into human consciousness, it creates a state of mind which Shelley terms "ecstasy," but its visitation is incontant, and the "Spirit of BEAUTY" will inevitably "pass away and leave . . . This dim vast vale of tears, vacant and desolate." Once man has known this "awful LOVELINESS,"

1. Joseph Barrell, *Shelley and the Thought of His Time* (New Haven, 1947), pp. 126–127, makes clear the extent to which the "Hymn to Intellectual Beauty" differs in fundamental respects from Plato himself. Of course, Shelley's idealism was never strictly governed by any one philosophic system. Indeed, his idealism seems to have been more an emotional attitude than a system of ideas; and when we use the word "Platonic" in relation to Shelley, we are referring more to a habit of mind encouraged by a long philosophic tradition than to a body of specific doctrine. That is to say, we are using the word in the way most commentators on Shelley have employed it. For example, James A. Notopoulos in his lengthy book on *The Platonism of Shelley* takes up not only the "direct" influence of Plato on Shelley, but also what Shelley owed to the Platonic tradition in philosophy and literature and to the "natural" Platonism of his own mind. Notopoulos also discusses differences between Shelley and Plato in connection with the "Hymn to Intellectual Beauty" (p. 202).

however, he remains henceforth bound and dedicated in worship of it.

The experience recorded in the "Hymn to Intellectual Beauty" is an autobiographical prototype of a number of similar events depicted in Shelley's poetry through the use of symbols. As such, it helps to pin down and clarify the content of Shelley's symbolism; but the symbolism itself expresses the felt contact with transcendence — an experience that Shelley felt words could scarcely duplicate — with a more nuanced precision. One of Shelley's habitual ways of suggesting Intellectual Beauty, or what he frequently Platonized as Intellectual Beauty, is by a surpassingly beautiful woman or goddess. Asia, the Witch of Atlas, the "veilèd maid" known by the protagonist of *Alastor* in a dream (line 151), and the female "shape" seen by Rousseau in "The Triumph of Life" (line 352) are all more or less equivalent. They stand for the permanence to which man aspires; and hence are invariably associated with images of light, fire, stars, and sun. Moreover, in keeping with the Platonic implications, these figures are often veiled, and the veil suggests the inability of mortal eyes to see the full splendor of heavenly Beauty, either because it is, as Shelley says in "The Sensitive Plant," too bright for "our organs, which endure/ No light" (Pt. III, lines 136–137), or because the bodily shape in which it is clothed necessarily involves some obscuring of its full radiance. At moments man has some intimate experience of the transcendent reality symbolized by these supernatural women. In the context of this symbolism, the experience may be presented as a sexual union, or more usually as a dream or vision in which the ideal is seen by human eyes. Once known, the beauty of these figures acts henceforth like a magnet, drawing the soul after it. The plot of *Alastor*, if it is a plot, dramatizes this, but the theme is found in many other poems. For example, those who drank the "strange panacea" of the Witch of Atlas "lived thenceforward as if some control,/ Mightier than life, were in them" (lines 594–597). As the "Hymn to Intellectual Beauty" made clear, the sudden vision of the Platonic reality lifts the human psyche into ecstasy. "The souls" of those to whom Asia appears, in *Prometheus Unbound*, "Walk upon the winds with lightness" (II, v, 68–69); and the dream union with the veiled maid of *Alastor* is an experience of "irresistible joy" (line 185). Moreover, the intensity of this ecstatic realization obliterates all consciousness of anything else. For example, in "The Triumph of Life" Rousseau says that the presence of the fair "shape," "no less than the sweet tune/ To which" she moved, blotted out "the thoughts of him who gazed on" her (lines 382–384).

The reference to "the sweet tune" is itself significant; for the effect of music is a frequent metaphor in Shelley of the impact of the vision on the human soul. Music is compared to something divine for which the heart thirsts. It is like the "strange panacea in a crystal bowl" which the Witch of Atlas presented to human lips; for in hearing music we are like one who

> drinks from a charmèd cup
> Of foaming, and sparkling, and murmuring wine,
> Whom, a mighty Enchantress filling up,
> Invites to love with her kiss divine.[2]

Like the vision of Intellectual Beauty, music "overpowers," and reveals "some world far from ours." [3] Moreover, it suggests the irresistible attraction which the vision exerts. A common symbol in Shelley's poetry of the soul is a boat swept

2. "Music," lines 19–22.
3. "To Jane: The Keen Stars were Twinkling," lines 19–22.

forward on the current of a stream. Hence when the pull of music is compared to a "many-winding river" inevitably hurrying the boat-soul into an experience of rapture, it becomes, in the light of Shelley's habitual preoccupations, a metaphor of the attraction of Platonic reality:

> My spirit like a charmed bark doth swim
> Upon the liquid waves of thy sweet singing,
> Far far away into the regions dim
> Of rapture.[4]

Furthermore, Shelley often symbolized the ecstatic state of mind created by a knowledge of Intellectual Beauty as an island paradise to which the boat-soul voyages. In *Prometheus Unbound*, Asia, hearing the song of the spirits, says "My soul is an enchanted boat . . . Upon the silver waves of thy sweet singing." Driven by "the instinct of sweet music," she goes "through Elysian garden islets . . . to a diviner day." The music finally brings her to "A paradise of vaulted bowers . . . Peopled by shapes too bright to see" (II, v, 72–108, *passim*). In this instance, the voyage to paradise involves a return to a pre-birth existence in which the soul is united with the One. We may also note that at the close of *The Revolt of Islam,* a boat "borne by the musical air" carries Laon and Cythna to "Elysian Islands."

— 2 —

The skylark in Shelley's ode is probably one of his most successful representations of the ecstatic gladness arising in the flight to the transcendent realm. The ode is a particularly striking example of what was a common poetic procedure with Shelley and especially with Keats; for the symbol is not static through the course of the poem. Instead it goes through a series of transformations, shifting constantly in

4. "Fragment: To One Singing," lines 1-4.

significance as the poet himself wonders what to make of it. Of course, the poet's relation to his symbol changes in a corresponding way. At the beginning of the poem the lark has almost reached the culmination of its heavenward flight, thus contrasting with Keats's "Ode to a Nightingale." For in Keats's ode, the nightingale is first presented as an actual, living bird. It is only through the course of the poem that the nightingale gradually becomes an "immortal Bird" and enters realms where the poet cannot follow. The reverse process takes place in Shelley's ode; for in the opening lines the lark seems to have already escaped from earth and ascended into "Heaven." Hence it has lost its mortal form, has died, so to speak, in the body, just as man must die in order to approach "the abode where the Eternal are," and has become pure "Spirit." In fact, it seems inconceivable that it ever was mortal, and in a hyperbole the poet exclaims "Bird thou never wert." Hence at the beginning of the poem, the speaker views the lark from without, apostrophizing it with a rapt enthusiasm but still with a consciousness of separate identity. In other words, in Keats's ode the first impressions of the nightingale are as from within the life of the bird. Only by identification with the nightingale can the poet speak of the lightness of its wings or of the "full-throated ease" of its singing, and such phrases indicate that it is the empathic imagination of the poet, as well as his senses, that reaches toward the bird. In Shelley's ode, however, the poet, proceeding only from what he can see and hear of the lark, suggests at once that he stands removed from it.

Having said that the lark is already in "Heaven," the speaker at once qualifies the statement. If the lark has not quite reached Heaven, it is at least "near it," and is mounting "Higher still and higher/ From the earth." But the "radiance of Eternity," to quote *Adonais,* still shines beyond the lark, and as it is approached the lark seems gradually to lose its mortal nature, becoming translucent to the light of Heaven. Hence the lark is compared to a "cloud of fire," and the cloud, a fixed metaphor of "cold mortality," here acquires and even transmits the qualities of the heavenly realm. In other words, the lark still retains the merest gauze of mortality, and thus becomes an image of the poet working in an ideal way, inspired by a near contact with transcendence and mediating his heavenly vision to mankind "in profuse strains of unpremeditated art." But in the ode, Shelley's symbol allows him to go further; for if the lark is an image of mortality in its flight to transcendence, the point is that the image enables the poet to describe the heavenward ascent as finally successful and completed. It should be remembered that although transcendent reality is constantly present behind the concrete world, it is usually invisible to mortal sight. Hence the skylark becomes unseen as it enters the heavenly realm, and is compared to a "star of Heaven/ In the broad daylight," or to the "silver sphere" (either the moon or the morning star) which fades "In the white dawn clear/ Until we hardly see — we feel that it is there." In this passage, of course, Shelley is putting metaphors to work in an unusual way. What actually takes place is that the lark becomes invisible as night deepens in the sky, and in the realm of nature the only correspondence between the lark and the star is that they both fade from human vision, the one in evening shadow gathering around its flight, the other in the "white dawn clear." But there is a natural associative leap from evening to stars, and, because the star is a fixed image of the transcendent, the context here reinforces the association. Shelley's imagination then takes another jump, equally habitual, moving from skylark to star to the star fading at dawn — a recurrent image of the disappearance of transcendent reality. The passage may still seem to describe a weak and confused correspondence, but it is a very clear example of the extent to which Shelley's verse moves on a level of symbolic rather than naturalistic propriety. Another version of the star is, of course, the moon, and the skylark is more appropriately (in view of the time of day) and even more directly merged with the transcendent when it is compared to the moon shining behind a cloud and diffusing its radiance through it.

If the lark represents mortality ascending to Heaven and can thus be employed as a metaphor of the poet, there is also another premise which qualifies the conception. For the lark, as the poem later reveals, is like Keats's nightingale or Yeats's swan (in "Leda and the Swan"), either "Sprite or Bird," either pure spirit or animal nature, or both, but in either case it is not human. Thus although it can be used as a symbol of what man would wish, the very choice of symbol posits a certain envy and despair; for it also implies that man himself cannot "come near" the "joy" which the lark possesses. In the poem, human nature is directly represented in the speaker, and as the lark flies higher and higher, the speaker remains fixed in the concrete world. But even though the lark, becoming "unbodied" and "unseen," is virtually incorporated in Eternity, it can still be heard, and the song of the lark thus brings the speaker into a momentary contact with transcendence. As always, the poet's experience of transcendent reality blots out consciousness of anything else: "All the earth and air/ With thy voice is loud." All of this, however, is not said in any overt way. Instead, it emerges very obliquely and inferentially when we refer to Shelley's habitual associations and attitudes.

It was noted that when the beautiful women who represent "deep truth" appear to men they are almost always veiled.

Mortality cannot fully or directly know ultimate truth. Even in his moments of deepest insight, man can glimpse only the shadow of the unseen Power. Hence when the skylark has merged with transcendence, it becomes unknowable: "What thou art we know not." The only way man can express his partial intuition of the deep truth is by trying to find "What is most like thee" in the concrete world and using it as a symbol or emblem of ultimate reality. But the deep truth, as Demorgorgon says, is "imageless," and any symbol will be only a partial approximation at best. The quick flux of metaphor which now begins in the ode "To a Skylark" is, then, simply a particularly clear-cut instance of Shelley's usual procedure. As the poet tries to find an image, the "unbodied" skylark is successively compared to a "Poet hidden/ In the light of thought," a maiden in a tower, a glowworm, and a rose. But these metaphors are less and less apt. The effort to know the spiritualized skylark ends in failure, and the poet gives up the struggle to find an image:

> All that ever was
> Joyous, and clear, and fresh, thy music doth surpass.
>
> (lines 59–60)

But as we read the poem this quick succession of metaphors distracts attention from the lark itself. It also seems to have a similar effect on the speaker, dissipating the rapt emotions in which the song of the lark was felt to be an experience of Heaven and returning the speaker to a more ordinary state of consciousness. In this mood, the speaker can no longer maintain confidence in his symbol, or, to put it another way, he cannot now affirm that the lark is a "blithe Spirit" which has never been a bird. Instead, as he again addresses the lark, he expresses some uncertainty, describing it as "Sprite or Bird," and, as the poem concludes, the lark becomes more obviously a bird. The objects of its "happy strain" are "fields, or waves, or mountains," or love of its own kind. But the point is that as "Sprite or Bird" it can be contrasted with man. For the life of man involves "languor," "annoyance," "satiety," discontent, and "pain"; the bird knows only a "clear keen joyance." Furthermore, even if these ills were not characteristic of human life, men could not reach the outgoing gladness of the skylark:

> If we were things born
> Not to shed a tear,
> I know not how thy joy we ever should come near.
>
> (lines 93–95)

For the lark has a special insight, a depth of vision into mortality and death (and presumably what follows it) which goes beyond even what man can imagine or dream. As always, Shelley thinks of the ecstatic delight symbolized by the lark as the product or accompaniment of this more than human vision:

> Waking or asleep,
> Thou of death must deem
> Things more true and deep
> Than we mortals dream,
> Or how could thy notes flow in such a crystal stream?
>
> (lines 81–85)

— 3 —

But the ecstatic joy arising in the visionary contact with Intellectual Beauty is short-lived; for, as the "Hymn to Intellectual Beauty" states, the vision itself quickly fades from human eyes. In *Alastor*, the dream union with the veiled maid, dissolving in the very moment it was experienced, was immediately lost, and "night/ Involved and swallowed up the vision" (lines 151, 187–189). Similarly, the fair shape described by Rousseau in "The Triumph of Life" "waned in the coming light" (line 412). Of course, if the experience of Intellectual Beauty lifts the soul into ecstasy, the loss of such experience plunges man into a deep depression and despair. This, indeed, is the theme of "The Sensitive Plant," though it is only by reference to associations habitual with Shelley that the poem discloses its full significance.

Most obviously, "The Sensitive Plant" illustrates and draws upon Shelley's more general use of bowers, gardens, paradisal islands, and the like in his poetry. These are frequently described, lavishly not to say lovingly embellished, and the bowers are usually secluded so that the protagonist can withdraw or escape into them. In representing them, Shelley is, in part, simply imagining an ideal dwelling place, and as a result an outright wish-fulfillment may seem to be involved. But in *Alastor,* in act three of *Prometheus Unbound,* in "The Sensitive Plant," in *Epipsychidion,* and elsewhere, the bower or island is also the place where human consciousness — the Sensitive Plant in this case — is united with Intellectual Beauty. For example, the protagonist of *Alastor* dreams of a sexual union with the veiled maid while he sleeps in a natural bower. Often the bower is also a cave, as in *Prometheus Unbound,* which, like the Elysian island of *The Revolt of Islam* or *Epipsychidion,* suggests the withdrawal from the concrete world taking place in the union with transcendence. For example, the cave to which Prometheus and Asia will retire after the transformation of the earth is "All overgrown with trailing odorous plants,/ Which curtain out the day." The day, of course, may represent the realm of common experience. In the cave, Prometheus hopes to escape the flux and decay involved in human life. "We will sit and talk of time and change," he says, "As the world ebbs and flows, ourselves unchanged" (III, iii, 11–12, 23–24). In other words, the bower or cave may almost seem an image of the

147

transcendent world. At least, it may be associated with the transcendent, not only by means of star and fire symbolism, but also because it usually incorporates the notion of permanence directly suggested by structures of stone such as caverns and architecture. For example, the retreats described in *Prometheus Unbound* and *Epipsychidion* include a temple or tower, and one might also take note of such a casual phrase as that of Asia when she speaks of the "diviner day" to which her soul is led as a "paradise of vaulted bowers" (II, v, 104).

But the symbolism may also avoid the notion of withdrawal in that the unveiling of Intellectual Beauty can make a paradise or garden of the human world. Here, of course, one thinks especially of *Prometheus Unbound,* and the changed earth there described may be interpreted either as a literal renovation or as a metaphor of the "precious seeing" which, as Shakespeare said, love adds to the eye. In either case, the change can be attributed to the unveiling of Intellectual Beauty, and Shelley's expression may seem to resemble that of Wordsworth, who stresses that when men feel themselves at one with the natural world and with the numinous power resident in it, they possess

> an overflowing love,
> Not for the Creature only, but for all
> That is around them, love for everything
> Which in this happy Region they behold!
>
> (*Recluse,* lines 286–290)

At least, in Shelley's poetry the presence of the transcendent creates a similar kind of love. In "The Sensitive Plant" each flower

> was interpenetrated
> With the light and the odour its neighbour shed,
> Like young lovers;   (Pt. I, lines 66–68)

and the theme of interconnection runs through many of

148

Shelley's bowers. The foliage enclosing the cave to which Prometheus and Asia hope to retire is described as a "quick growth of the serpent vine,/ And the dark linked ivy tangling wild" (III, iii, 135–136). In other passages Shelley imagines bowers of "interlaced branches" or "odorous plants" entwined. This entwining and interlacing suggests the love felt in the bower, just as in the "Witch of Atlas" the witch makes a figure of Love by kneading "fire and snow/ Together"; for "all things together grow/ Through which the harmony of love can pass" (lines 321–324). Thus in the entwining foliage, the indiscriminate wreathing together of every element of the bower, Shelley may suggest even more directly than Wordsworth the love which all things in nature must share. There is, of course, an important difference in the attitudes of Wordsworth and Shelley at this point. For Wordsworth, this love always exists in the natural world, even though man becomes aware of it only in moments of heightened insight. For Shelley, it is less a natural state of affairs than something created in the contact with Intellectual Beauty, which leads "All things" to "put their evil nature off." [5] Moreover, Shelley does not always rely only on imagery drawn from nature to portray this love. He also tends to locate it in his paradisal bowers as a vague personification. In the garden of "The Sensitive Plant" the "Spirit of Love" was "felt everywhere" (line 6), and at the conclusion of the "Lines Written among the Euganean Hills" the poet described a bower or "healing Paradise" to which he would like to retire. There "the love which heals all strife" is "circling" and suffusing "All things . . . With its own mild brotherhood" (lines 355–369, *passim*).

But even when Shelley, like Wordsworth, employs nature imagery, the psychological processes involved are very differ-

5. *Prometheus Unbound*, III, iv, 77.

ent. Wordsworth, as was said, projects his own emotions into the natural scene. The reader never questions the actuality of the forms of nature observed; it is only in the emotions read into them that he detects the work of the imagination. Shelley's verse, however, does not encourage one to believe that the bower was present to the poet's eye. One feels, instead, that he starts with a state of mind, a nexus of emotions created by the contemplation of Intellectual Beauty, and then imagines a natural scene or bower which would be the appropriate setting of such joy. In other words, he uses natural imagery, but he uses it in a purely imaginative way, constructing by means of it something correlative to human emotions and expressive of them. Hence the bowers and gardens should usually be regarded as, among other things, a metaphor of a state of mind. So with the garden of "The Sensitive Plant." While Intellectual Beauty is present, the garden is a "Paradise" pervaded by "Love," but with the eclipse or vanishing of Intellectual Beauty the garden becomes a place of foul desolation and decay. Thus the basic symbolism of "The Sensitive Plant" is an extension and elaboration of a metaphor which Shelley used repeatedly. In *Epipsychidion* Shelley brings together the metaphors of *Prometheus Unbound,* where Asia is compared to the sun, and "The Sensitive Plant." Here Emily is the sun, and the poet compares himself to a "passive Earth" whose "fruits and flowers" will be awakened by the sun (lines 345–347), and to a plant whose fruit will be "made perfect" by the "sunny eyes" of Emily (lines 385–386). Again, in *Adonais,* Keats is hideously compared to a "pale flower by some sad maiden cherished" (line 48), and the sad maiden seems to be equated with Urania, or Heavenly Love and Beauty.

"The Sensitive Plant" is constructed in several layers of symbolism, but the symbolism at each layer suggests more or less the same thing. On one level of symbolic reference, the garden, as I said, is equated with the human mind when it touches transcendence. In this context, the sun seems vaguely to suggest Platonic reality. At least, it is present to the garden through spring and summer, and it calls the flowers into existence. Spring "arose on the garden fair,/ Like the spirit of Love." At its coming "each flower and herb . . . Rose" from the earth like a child awakening at the "singing sweet" of its mother, and, as was said, music and singing are often a metaphor of transcendence in its effect on the soul. Throughout summer the flowers "shared joy in the light of the gentle sun." The poem emphasizes the joy of the flowers, for it represents, of course, the ecstasy always felt in the immediate contact with transcendence. Hence throughout the summer the garden is an "undefilèd Paradise" (Pt. I, lines 5–8, 59–60, 65, 58). But "Swift Summer" flows into autumn and finally winter. The sun ceases to warm the earth, and the flowers die. Thus the symbolism of the seasons suggests the inevitable fading of the vision, and of the ecstatic joy it creates.

But the flowers themselves are not only a metaphor of a human state of mind. They are at the same time, as Carlos Baker remarks, also vaguely symbolic of Platonic reality,[6] and are associated with Shelley's usual transcendence symbols. The "hyacinth . . . flung from its bells a sweet peal . . . Of *music*" (Pt. I, lines 25–27); the "rose . . . *unveiled* . . . the soul of her beauty and love" (lines 29–32); the "lily . . . lifted up . . . the *fiery star*, which is its eye" (lines 33–35); and "*starry* river-buds glimmered by" (line 46).[7] In the context of these vague associations, the Sensitive Plant represents the human soul in rapt communion with

6. *Shelley's Major Poetry*, p. 199.
7. Italics mine.

Heaven. The Sensitive Plant is distinguished from the other plants in that it "has no bright flower;/ Radiance and odour are not its dower." Instead it is a Platonic lover, and "desires what it has not, the Beautiful" (Pt. I, lines 25–27, 29–35, 46, 74–77). Hence it passively receives emanations from the flowers around it, and feels the "sweet joy" or delight created in man by the presence of Platonic reality.

Like the garden itself, the Lady who presides over it has a double symbolic function. In part, she represents mortality. Like the "companionless" Sensitive Plant, she has "no companion of mortal race," but is in contact with Eternity. For in her dreams she knows "some bright Spirit" who "for her sweet sake/ Has deserted Heaven." Hence she experiences ecstasy, and "her dreams were less slumber than Paradise" (Pt. II, lines 13, 16–18). At the same time, however, she is a version of Asia or the Witch of Atlas and represents the unseen Power which Shelley called Intellectual Beauty. She is a Power, a "ruling Grace" whose footsteps leave no print on the "grass" and whose "glowing fingers" sustain the flowers (lines 26, 32). As she tends the garden, it is her presence which makes it a Paradise. Thus both the death of the lady and the process of the seasons represent the fading of Platonic reality from human experience.[8] While it is present, the mind knows the ecstasy or delight of which the skylark is probably Shelley's most memorable symbol. After it has vanished, a profound melancholy invades the human spirit, and the lengthy description of the blasted garden may be, despite the somewhat strained, charnel-house imagery, Shelley's most vivid representation of this state of mind. The Conclusion of the poem advances the thought in which Shelley usually seeks consolation for the loss of vision. Al-

8. See Baker, p. 199: "The death of the lady signifies the withdrawal of the spirit of love from the apprehensive powers of the sensitive mind."

though concealed by the "veil of daylight" the bright Spirit the Lady saw in dreams may be still "lingering" by her (Pt. II, lines 17–20). The star grows invisible as day spreads through the sky, but it still continues to shine. Mortal man, from the weakness of his own nature, cannot hold the vision of heaven for more than a brief time, but nevetheless the Paradise described in the garden of "The Sensitive Plant" has not passed away:

> That garden sweet, that lady fair,
> And all sweet shapes and odours there,
> In truth, have never passed away:
> 'Tis we, 'tis ours, are changed; not they.
>
> For love, and beauty, and delight,
> There is no death nor change; their might
> Exceeds our organs, which endure
> No light, being themselves obscure.　　(lines 130–137)

— 4 —

One of the principal insights a study of Shelley's symbolism provides is that most of his poetry gravitates about a rather small set of themes and attitudes. We have been tracing a variety of different symbols, but have found that the diverse symbols always return us to the same central preoccupations. Each excursion into a new set of symbolic equations may add nuances and ramifications to our apprehension of these basic preoccupations, but inevitably an exploration of Shelley's symbols entails frequent repetition. In fact, one of the things demonstrated by such an exploration is that Shelley himself was what Santayana called a "finished child of nature," having, like a cricket, his "own natural note" which no cannonade of fact and experience could ever change.[9] Of course, for as long as a finished child of nature with a natural note continues to sing, he can only re-

9. "Shelley," *Winds of Doctrine* (New York, 1912), p. 159.

peat what he has done before. Needless to say, the vivacity of Santayana's metaphor oversimplifies the problem, but pious Shelleyans, who have marked the vicissitudes of his intellectual history by concentrating on his formal philosophic beliefs, may have erred in the opposite direction. For the comparative lack of change in what he symbolizes suggests that behind superficial changes of creed lie the same assumptions, preoccupations, and needs, incapable, as it seems, of assimilating experience and growing on the basis of it. Critics have often pointed to the increasing pessimism of his later years as an indication of development, but this does not much contradict what we have said. By itself disappointment need not be called growth unless it marks a transition to other premises and modes of thinking.[10]

One of Shelley's central symbols is the child or some version of it such as the winged seraph, and in his poetry the child is often a guide to the cave or island paradise. In general the child seems to represent an angle of vision, a state of mind. For one thing, these child figures exhibit the gladness Shelley attributed to the skylark. To cite one example, in

10. The question of Shelley's development is somewhat vexed. It is an irony of Shelley scholarship that one of the romantic poets who developed least as far as his fundamental beliefs are concerned, has been repeatedly studied from the point of view of his intellectual development. Numerous studies of Shelley's "ideas" have been published. Usually the framework of these studies has been chronological, and, by reference to Shelley's readings and writings, the attempt has been to focus on changing attitudes and beliefs from year to year. The effect of all this scholarship is to obscure the central and important fact that Shelley's fundamental preoccupations changed relatively little. As one of the most energetic of Shelley scholars, Carl Grabo, states, *The Meaning of the Witch of Atlas* (Chapel, N. C., 1935), p. 21: "Any reader of Shelley will remark the consistency of his ideas . . . Shelley grows greatly in poetic skill in the ten or twelve years of his creative life, but the ideas and beliefs of his youth remain the preoccupations of his maturity." Cf. Mrs. Olwen Campbell, *Shelley and the Unromantics* (London, 1924), p. 279: "His real philosophy lay deep down in his imagination; and though it developed as he learnt wisdom, its main tendency was never changed."

Prometheus Unbound the Spirit of the reborn earth is Asia's child, and it is wrapped, "like an atmosphere of light," in joy, delight, and gladness (IV, 319–323). The child also embodies the love depicted in the garden of "The Sensitive Plant," a love not called forth by the beauty of particular objects, but flowing out to all things in an undiscriminating way and having in it a strong power to convert or transform things evil or ugly. In *The Revolt of Islam,* Cythna's child, "bold with love," pleads for Laon's life before the tyrant, but the child also loves the tyrant, and when he is overthrown only the child stays by him. The kind of outgoing love which the child represents involves a spiritual rebirth, and hence, as in Wordsworth, the mood of these child figures can be presented as an ideal toward which men should strive.

On the whole, Shelley was more fortunate than Wordsworth in his use of the child as a symbol. In the first place, his children are seldom presented in a naturalistic way, and as a result, being obviously but metaphors and symbols, they do not imply a regressive desire to return to one's own childhood. In the second place, the children in Shelley's poetry, as in Wordsworth's, have no notion of the painful sides of human experience, but in Wordsworth this state of mind seems simply to rest on children as a natural accompaniment of their stage in life. In Shelley, however, the course of the narrative often lends some more obvious dramatic probability to this way of picturing the child. For children in Shelley's poetry are often born or at least described in a social context which excludes pain and guilt from their experience. Thus in *Prometheus Unbound,* it is only after the regeneration of all living things that the Spirit of the Earth is presented as a child. Or when there has been no widespread rebirth, the child's state of mind can appropriately be thought of as an ideal because the child has lived

155

LIBRARY ST. MARY'S COLLEGE

apart from the contaminations of adult human life. In *The Revolt of Islam*, Cythna's child is reared in a cave knowing only its mother. Again classical Greece is described in *Hellas* as having been a "hermit-child" which, because of its seclusion, "knew not pain or guilt" (lines 996–999). To put the point another way, one could accept most of the premises of the romantic syndrome and still believe Wordsworth's symbolic use of the child to be unsatisfactory. But apart from local failures in expression, a critic who objected to Shelley's use of the symbol would probably do so from hostility to what Shelley had to say. For to take the child, as Shelley does, as an image of a desired state of mind, implies a wish to ignore or even to deny the inevitability of suffering in human life and of a disposition to wrong as a factor in human nature. It was this kind of optimism which armed Irving Babbitt for his rhinocerine attack on virtually all romantic literature. One of the differences between Wordsworth and Shelley seems to be that Shelley, being somewhat less capacious or inclusive in his attitudes, had a more clear-cut awareness of what he was saying. He might have welcomed precisely those implications of the child symbol which Babbitt attacked.

Yet in justice to Shelley some further remarks should be made. For one thing, it is always difficult to distinguish to what extent a poet is speaking through a symbol and to what extent he is imprisoned by it; for any given symbol will allow some things to be said and will block the expression of other notions which the poet may feel to be equally true. Hence we can remind ourselves that the child is only one expressive device occurring in a vast body of poetry, and in *Prometheus Unbound* Shelley qualifies what is implied in the child symbolism. The attitudes embodied in the child still remain an ideal, and that is why, at the end of the drama, Prometheus and his retinue of female abstractions will henceforth live "like human babes in their brief innocence" (III, iii, 33). But in *Prometheus Unbound* the intention, however crudely accomplished, was to show the childlike state of mind resulting from a process of suffering and regeneration. If there is the optimistic assumption that human nature can be purged of its less desirable qualities, there is also the more sober recognition of qualities which must be purged. Here Shelley aligns himself with a more profound and winning side of romantic thought. Though the romantics were often haunted by dejection and melancholia, they did strive to sustain a point of view optimistic in its fundamental premises, and, in their greater poetry, this optimism displays qualities of sternness and justice more often than Irving Babbitt and his followers have been willing to admit. Certainly the romantics wished to believe that "all life is holy," as Blake put it, but they also recognized that such a faith is little more than an assertion unless it takes into account aspects of human experience that would seem to belie it. Thus in Coleridge's "Ancient Mariner," the perception of the beauty of the sea-creatures comes at the end of a process of guilt and redemption; and even afterwards the burden of guilt cannot be wholly put aside. Again the great lyrics such as "The Tiger" in Blake's *Songs of Experience* have a depth and power lacking in the *Songs of Innocence* partly because they are able triumphantly to restate the faith of innocence broadened by a full recognition of the counter claims of experience. Thus if the child in its loving innocence suggests what is fundamental in human nature, it does not imply that such an attitude is easy to maintain.

But the child as a symbol does not merely represent man as he essentially is or man as he should be. Even if one agrees with Irving Babbitt that the romantic reading of human nature was optimistically inadequate, it cannot be denied that the great romantics possessed a rather sophisticated understanding of psychological processes. From this point of view, the child figure can be used to suggest what man must become in order to be either decent or happy. As Shelley phrased it, "The great secret of morals is love; or a going out of our own nature." [11] Self-concern of any kind, whether it be a strong sense of personal injury and a desire for revenge, or simply the egotism of an over-active conscience, leads to an unawareness of what is outside. Certainly the conscience can become morbidly sensitive and oppressive, and a strong sense of guilt can dry the fountains of love. In some sense, as Yeats said, "repentance keeps" the "heart impure" in its reaction to what is outside, and to "cast out remorse" is to be born anew into a state where "We are blest by everything,/ Everything we look upon is blest." [12] Thus the theoretic rejection of guilt which characterizes many of the English romantics need not be related solely to a sentimental view of the goodness of human nature, or to an expansiveness that denied all restraint. It is also related to their recognition of the need to escape from self-involvement — a recognition which is a persisting theme in the thought and literature of the English romantics. It received one prose ramification in the criticism of Hazlitt, with his praise of Shakespeare's capacity for sympathetic identification, and his strictures on Wordsworth as an example of "egoistic" genius which is "the reverse of the chameleon." Keats's early remarks, influenced by Hazlitt, on *Negative*

11. "Defence of Poetry," *Works*, VII, 118.
12. W. B. Yeats, *Collected Poems* (New York: The Macmillan Company, 1951), pp. 232, 250.

Capability, and his ideal of the "chameleon poet" make up another strand in the same pattern.

— 5 —

The need to escape from the prison of the self in an act of love is one of the central themes of *Prometheus Unbound.* The drama has been the subject of exhaustive as well as conflicting explication, and there is no need to take it up in detail. Or, if there is need, I have not the space or boldness for such an attempt, but, omitting all the social and millennial aspects of the play, will mention only what relates to the theme at hand. In the play, Jupiter is the principle of evil in the heart of man and in the human world. It should be noted that his rule is associated not only with conventional representations of evil such as war and cruelty, but also with such human qualities as "self-love or self-contempt," and "self-mistrust." In short, he is a symbol for whatever, withering the sources of affirmation and love, "makes the heart deny the *yes* it breathes" (III, iv, 134–152, *passim*).

Prometheus is the foe of Jupiter, and he has been "eyeless in hate" (I, 9). At the beginning of the poem he is chained to a rock and tormented by furies who are "foul desire round" his "astonished heart" (I, 489). His situation may be interpreted as symbolic of the human soul when instead of escaping from itself through love, it is shackled and tormented by its own hostility. As Demogorgon says, "All spirits are enslaved which serve things evil" (III, iv, 110) and the notion — so contrary to what is overtly said — may even be that in his calm hate Prometheus is in effect serving Jupiter. In his opening speech Prometheus seems to be on the way to a spiritual regeneration. "I hate no more," he says, and he announces that he now pities his foe. But in his earlier

159

"calm hate," Prometheus had cursed Jupiter, and he now demands to have the curse repeated. For although he claims that he now has no "memory . . . Of what is hate," he also desires that his former words should not lose their power, thus indicating either some remnant of hostility or a certain mental confusion (I, 69–72). On hearing the curse, however, he withdraws it, saying that he wishes "no living thing to suffer pain" (I, 305). This act of love represents the culmination of his spiritual regeneration, and it displaces Jupiter and frees Prometheus.

Thus if one takes a bird's eye view, the theme of the drama seems sufficiently obvious. But as soon as the reader descends to a closer look, difficulties loom in the way of any clear-cut interpretation, and these difficulties suggest that Shelley himself harbored conflicting attitudes toward his subject matter. For one thing, Prometheus is described in a tone of awe-struck admiration. Of course, he represents, Shelley tells us, "the type of the highest perfection of moral and intellectual nature," but the admiration seems to be directed especially to his persevering defiance and calm hate. As Shelley euphemistically phrased it in the Preface, Prometheus exhibits a "firm and patient opposition to omnipotent force," [13] but in the end it is not his opposition but his capacity to learn forgiveness through suffering that overthrows Jupiter. In other words, the poet's admiration seems to focus on what would logically appear to be secondary virtues. Also it might be noticed that Prometheus' gesture of forgiveness — "I wish no living thing to suffer pain" — is rather limited in its fervor. These words do not imply a very generous or active change of heart. Moreover, it is not altogether clear that Prometheus's forgiveness is specifically responsible for the downfall of Jupiter. For one thing, if

13. Preface to *Prometheus Unbound*, p. 201.

his words "I wish no living thing to suffer pain" precipitate the catastrophe, they do not exert their magic virtue immediately. For as soon as Prometheus has made this declaration the minions of Jupiter inflict upon him a prolonged series of mental torments. It is only later that Demogorgon drags Jupiter from his throne. Also there is much talk in the play of fate, of the "destined hour" of Jupiter's overthrow, as though it were a matter of necessity in time and not of the enlightenment of Prometheus's will. These and other difficulties one might mention can, of course, be woven together and smoothed into a consistent interpretation, but if one seeks consistency in the poem, the more one takes account of detail, the more ingenious and labored interpretation must become.

With the downfall of Jupiter, Prometheus attains the state of mind which Shelley represented in the child. In the speech of Panthea to Asia, the inward regeneration of Prometheus is represented by his changed appearance: "his pale woundworn limbs/ Fell from him" (II, i, 62–63) and

> the overpowering light
> Of that immortal shape was shadowed o'er
> By love. (II, i, 71–73)

By this inward regeneration, all things are "somewhat changed." Throughout the poem, the earth itself sometimes seems to be a metaphor of Prometheus's state of mind, although it also functions as a separate character — in fact, as his mother. At least, the "blue thistles," "toads," and "poisonous weeds" which grow on it while Prometheus is chained to the rock are the result of its grief and hate (I, 170–178). In the atmosphere of love which now pervades the earth, even "toads, and snakes, and efts," as in the "Ancient Mariner," become beautiful, and "All things . . . put their evil nature off" (III, iv, 74–77). What has changed fundamentally in the poem is the spiritual attitude of man, represented in Prometheus. Hence it is at least uncertain that the change described in all things must be interpreted as a literal transformation (although there are strong reasons for believing that Shelley conceived it as such). Rather what has altered is the eye which looks at the earth, and it is to an eye of love that all things are "somewhat changed." [14]

— 6 —

Although Shelley's social ideas are a large topic, they relate to the present theme only as an illustration of the extent to which Shelley's various preoccupations are all approached with the same fundamental attitudes and habits of mind. For as Yeats said, Intellectual Beauty and Liberty are more or less equivalent in Shelley's poetry. When Intellectual Beauty is present to one human soul, it creates the state of mind Shelley called ecstasy; if it were present to all men, a social utopia would be created. Thus the symbols employed in *Prometheus Unbound* can function in both an individual and a social context. From the point of view of the individual, the union of Prometheus, the human mind, with Intellectual Beauty or Love involves a withdrawal from the world to a cavern-bower. But in the poem, the same union creates a utopian society among men.

The important thing that Shelley's symbolism suggests, in contrast to some of his more abstract formulations, is that the new social order for which he yearned will not be

14. Cf. on this point Knight, *The Starlit Dome,* p. 217: "the new state [is] not so much a change of objective fact as a new dynamic relation where fact ceases to be wholly objective: that is, a state of artistic insight, the in-seeing of love . . . The eye having altered alters all." Knight suggests a parallel here with Coleridge's "Ancient Mariner." A correspondence between the themes of the two poems has also been noted by other critics, among them Maud Bodkin, *Archetypal Patterns in Poetry* (London, 1934), p. 252, who finds that both poems are types of the "Rebirth Pattern."

achieved by patient labor and continuing progress. His socialism was not of a Fabian variety. Although in *Prometheus Unbound* Shelley speaks of the dawning of love in the soul of Prometheus as a gradual thing, he is unable to dramatize the process. The conception of gradual change is simply not sufficiently central to Shelley's imaginative vision of things for him to portray it. Hence in *Prometheus Unbound* Shelley's imagination seizes only upon the sudden moment of conversion. For social revolution and the utopian order will result from the descent of numinous force into human life, and, in this context as in others, man is passive to the sudden visitations of transcendence. This, indeed, is the theme of the "Ode to the West Wind."

For the West Wind symbolizes something more than a spirit of social revolution. As Fogle remarks, "The West Wind is an absolute and hidden power which informs all things." [15] It is akin to the unseen Power which occasionally visits the mortal world. As the poem begins the west wind is apostrophized in language appropriate to divinity. With many "O's" and "thou's" it is addressed as an "unseen presence," a "Wild Spirit . . . moving everywhere," a "destroyer and preserver." Moreover, in a manner closely paralleling the beliefs of primitive peoples, the process of the seasons is portrayed more as depending on the arbitrary will of the winds than as an inevitable natural phenomenon. The west wind drives the dead leaves like "pestilence-stricken multitudes," and "chariotest," — an image of militant and irresistible force — "the wingèd seeds" to their grave. It seems almost to be a primitive Jehovah, a war god. Similarly,

---

15. Richard H. Fogle, "The Imaginal Design of Shelley's 'Ode to the West Wind,'" *ELH*, XV (1948), p. 224. Cf. Stewart C. Wilcox, "Imagery, Ideas, and Design in Shelley's 'Ode to the West Wind,'" *SP*, XLVII (1950), p. 637: "the implicit proposition that it is the Power of the Universe . . . runs like an undercurrent beneath the flow of poetical variation."

the spring is not so much an inevitable process as a resurrection willed by a succeeding wind and proclaimed by its "clarion." These images of irresistible, numinous force, of frenzy and destruction, are intensified in the second stanza. The wind is a stream — often in Shelley's poetry an image of forward compulsion. The clouds are "Angels of rain and lightning" heralding the coming divinity, and the maenad, in classical mythology an attendant upon Dionysius, is an image of similar implications. The west wind brings in the destructive violence of the storm — "Black rain, and fire, and hail" — and the storm will completely inform the vast "dome" of the atmosphere.

These opening stanzas are expressed at an extreme pitch of rhetoric. The speaker seems almost to be beside himself, caught up in a state of impetuous and wild emotional excitement which parallels what is said of the wind and anticipates the final identification of the speaker with it. The excitement is expressed in the volume of sound released, in the rhetorical structure of the stanzas, in the imagery of violence, and most of all, perhaps, in the dramatic situation. For the speaker invokes a destructive power which is unfriendly to ordinary and safe human pursuits, and to call thus on the daemonic and "uncontrollable" implies a state of mind beyond all restraint, beyond any fear or tenderness for the common ways of life. It is neither accidental nor merely fanciful that the dead leaves, "yellow, and black, and pale, and hectic red," are compared to "pestilence-stricken multitudes." The force which the wind represents as it brings "black rain, and fire, and hail" may well mean pestilence and death to multitudes, but the speaker nevertheless prays to be identified with it. And the third stanza makes clear the reason of this prayer. Burke once wrote of radical political reformers that "they never see any way to their projected good but by the road of some evil," and the wind now begins to become the symbol of a force making for liberation in the human world. For in some vague way the blue Mediterranean, the age-old center of human civilization, which has been lulled and is now wakened, and the "old palaces . . . overgrown with azure moss and flowers/ So sweet the sense faints picturing them" seem symbolic of the legacy of the past, conceived as sweet and still abiding in the present, to be shaken by the storm. Similarly the "sea-blooms and the oozy woods" which, hearing the voice of the wind, "suddenly grow gray with fear,/ And tremble and despoil themselves," behave rather like Shelleyan tyrants hearing riots in the streets. Being both "destroyer and pre-server," the wind symbolizes the destruction and regeneration which are twin aspects of any sudden revolution.

Having thus implicitly converted the wind to a symbol of a numinous force making for change in the social order, the poet can pray to be identified with the wind. In so doing, he finds a symbolic ground for optimism. His principles must triumph because they are urged by its irresistible violence. The symbolism of the seasons tends in the same direction, stressing the inevitability of the new earth — "O, Wind,/ If Winter comes, can Spring be far behind." Shelley had previously used these symbols in a similar context in *The Revolt of Islam*, where Cythna tells Laon that "the whirl-wind of our spirit" has "driven/ Truth's deathless germs to thought's remotest caves." Though winter has come "and here/ We die," yet "Behold! Spring comes, though we must pass, who made/ The promise of its birth" (lines 3669–3689, *passim*). In the Ode the poet, having identified himself with the wind, would at the same time be as the waves, leaves or clouds impelled by the wind, or as the forest, the lyre through which the wind expresses itself. In the dense network of identifications at the close of the ode, the poet would have the wind drive his "thoughts over the universe/ Like withered leaves to quicken a new birth," or, changing the figure, like "ashes and sparks" to raise the conflagration and destruction which must precede the renewal of the earth. At the same time, it is not his thoughts which would cause it. Rather he would have the wind speak through him, he being, like the cloud-angel or maenad, the "trumpet of a prophecy," the herald of the approaching storm and the "clarion" through which the wind rouses the "dreaming earth." If there is some confusion of thought here, it may not trouble the reader; for he may be lifted from the thorns of logic by the wind of Shelley's emotion.

In the "Ode to the West Wind," then, Shelley allies himself with a numinous violence which in creating a new golden age brings death and destruction into the old world. But this fanaticism is not merely political. If the ode implies a relative unconcern for the individualities to be abolished, this abstract, social frenzy is symptomatic of a more general attitude toward all concrete life. For Shelley was seldom able to focus on the particular. Hence there was little recognition of the complex entangling of good and evil in human nature. As one result, an earthly utopia seemed easy to imagine and not impossible to achieve. Of course, as he grew older he experienced a gradual loss of hope, but these dreams were never wholly relinquished. There was no real sense of the obstacles in the way. A strong dose of moral castor oil is all that human nature requires; or, to shift the metaphor, the poet has only to pipe his vision of "the beauty of true virtue" and mankind will fall into step. There was, in fact, a tendency in Shelley's imagination to construct processions. In *Adonais* there is the parade of mourners, in "The Witch of Atlas" the procession of animal and mythological creatures to view

the witch, and, of course, there is "The Triumph of Life."
A variant of the procession occurs in the last act of *Prometheus Unbound* with the choir of different voices all singing the same song. For these scenes suggest something totalitarian in Shelley's manner of governing his materials and ultimately in his vision of life. A diversity of particular reactions had no appeal for him, nor does he defer to the complexities of individual character. Instead, he wishes to compel everything to respond in the same way. He would put all things into uniform and set them marching in one direction. There is, however, some thematic fitness in these processional movements. The helpless forward march is usually a metaphor of the overwhelming attraction of what it proceeds toward. It is the tendency of the fanatic to inflate his own conceptions and then to require all to bow down before them. This creates genuine difficulties in reading Shelley's poetry. More often than not, the reader is himself expected to join the choir or procession, at least to the extent of sharing the emotions of the marchers. In other words, the poetry demands a complete empathic involvement and a sharing of ecstatic feelings. This is difficult to obtain in any case and the more difficult because the poetry itself is so little qualified in its expression. Keats, for example, in his much more tentative flights up or out from the mortal world, usually subsumes whatever in human experience or feeling works as a bar to the escape. With Shelley, however, this is seldom the case, and as a result the reader becomes aware of a lack of justice or discernment in the poetry, and, perceiving this lack, is liable to withhold assent.

Another variant of the choir or procession is the indiscriminate catalogue. Often, as in "To a Skylark," it is a catalogue of metaphors referring to the same object. Often it is simply a miscellaneous list of items in the concrete world. For the suggestion conveyed by these catalogues is that from the perspective of Shelley's obsessions all earthly objects are more or less the same, at least in the one respect that matters. Little distinction need be made among them; for since they are neither identified with the transcendent world nor a corridor to it, they are inconsequential. To put it another way, in comparison with the One, concrete individuations seem virtually to lack identity. The beauty of the Witch of Atlas, to take one example, was such that it "made/ The bright world dim," and beside her "everything . . . Seemed like the fleeting image of a shade" (lines 137–139). This statement, however, does not pertain merely to what is said in Shelley's poetry about the visitations of transcendence. It applies to Shelley's own sensibility as well. It is his earnest pursuit of Intellectual Beauty that partially accounts for the want of interest in the concrete. It explains, for example, his frequent resort to an imagery lacking in individuation. Even more, it explains his incredibly high-handed use of metaphor. For it sometimes seems in Shelley's poetry that virtually anything can be compared to anything else. The skylark is like a rose, the "carved lamps and chalices" of the Witch are "each like a flower," and the "busy dreams" which play over the countenance of Hermaphroditus are "thick as summer flies" (lines 205–206, 363–364). If one brings a visual imagination to bear, such metaphors become far-fetched not to say grotesque, and the fact that Shelley used them suggests that there was little awareness of the identity of the things compared.

Thus one may even feel that there is a moral liability at the heart of all Shelley's moral earnestness. It is, perhaps, unfair to employ an *ad hominen* argument, but his intention to introduce Mary Godwin into his household, believing that he, his wife, and his mistress might live harmoniously together, certainly suggests that his imagination was directed more to an ideal of what should be than to the actualities of human nature. But if we confine ourselves to his poetry, the liability still remains. For Shelley has the hatred of the oriental mystic for whatever impedes the dissolving of all into the One. Thus when Intellectual Beauty invades the soul, it is, in effect, a tyrant. The human will stands helpless before it, inevitably attracted, like the moth to the taper, and then, like the moth, annihilated in the moment of union. And if the annihilation does not, as at the conclusion of *Adonais,* involve a literal death, it at least means an extinction of consciousness as the individual is temporarily lost in the One. What is lacking, in other words, is what has always been central to western traditions of moral belief — the prizing of individuality and of free choice. What is lacking, from the point of view of literary success is the possibility of a solid realization of particulars, of drama, of conflict, and hence of tragedy. There is no possible process of doubt, exploration, or reconciliation to be made the subject of poetry. On the other hand, from Shelley's own point of view, matters of individuality, choice, and doubt are irrelevant. In a poetry of mystical experience, his premises are probably unassailable; and the loss of individuality is desired.

❦ VI ❦

SHELLEY

The Earthly Analogue

In comparison with Wordsworth, Shelley was in a rather ironic dilemma. For if he made a more open and acknowledged use of symbolism, he did so with much less confidence. Wordsworth, as I said, seems to have felt that a symbol itself takes part in the reality it represents. But for Shelley it is simply an analogy, a representation in human terms, although the sole means available for speaking, at least in poetry, of the transcendent world. But more is involved than simply the effort to make poetry out of conceptions essentially abstract. There is also the human and personal need for reassurance — the reassurance which comes from being able to conceive clearly and feel deeply. As Shelley put it, the mind is almost compelled to seek "in a mortal image the likeness of what is perhaps eternal":[1] the "mortal image" can be apprehended in a more immediate way, and it arouses emotions which could hardly be generated, even by Shelley, in a direct flight to abstraction. For example, we mentioned earlier that one of his habitual ways of suggesting Intellectual Beauty was through the image of a surpassingly beautiful woman or goddess. The symbol was not accidental or arbitrary. Instead it draws upon immediate personal experience, joined with a quasi-philosophic tradition. It would seem

1. Letter to Gisborne, *Works*, X, 401.

that sexual love, as Shelley conceived it, could offer a close analogue to the ecstatic emotions described in the "Hymn to Intellectual Beauty." In fact, the lover may respond with such intensity that the beloved seems no mere mortal but instead an incarnation of the ideal. When this is felt to be the case, human love is not regarded as a symbolic but as an actual approach to transcendence, and, as Carl Grabo puts it, "sexual completeness is identified with the attainment of intellectual beauty." [2] Of course, the notion of the soul rising to a union with the eternal through an intense reaction to what is mortal has a long tradition in Platonic thought. But Platonists, particularly when they are also poets, have rarely been able to keep the categories distinct. They have tended, instead, to see their earthly loves as a direct union with the ideal rather than a step in the ascent to it. Shelley was especially prone to this type of confusion, but the confusion itself served a real psychological need in helping him to flesh out, so to speak, and to vivify his preoccupation with the transcendent. The crucial instance here is *Epipsychidion*. Critics have frequently noted that *Epipsychidion* is Shelley's most ardent presentation of the quest for Intellectual Beauty, and the fervent emotion expressed in the poem does contrast strongly with the colder, more abstract raptures of the "Hymn to Intellectual Beauty." What happens in *Epipsychidion* is that the poet's emotion is directed both to a mortal woman and to Intellectual Beauty, for "Emily" is

> a mortal shape indued
> With love and life and light and deity,
> And motion which may change but cannot die.
>
> (lines 112–114)

Hence the abstraction is being pursued with an ardor generated in earthly experience.

2. *The Magic Plant*, p. 242.

171

In *Epipsychidion* Shelley imagines what is in some ways foreign to his fundamental attitudes. For he assumed, more often than not, that the transcendent and the concrete did not coalesce. The mind could know one or the other, but not both together. Yet in *Epipsychidion* he is seeking to know mortality and eternity in one presence. The combination is highly unstable, as the history of Shelley's personal reactions to Emilia Viviani also illustrates. For she quickly became dissociated from the ideal, and was reclassified as a "mortal shape"; and even in the poem the coalescence can scarcely be maintained. If Emily is regarded as Intellectual Beauty, the union with her would take the poet out of the natural world; if she is a "mortal shape," he must make a place for her in his human life. The result is a disunity almost grotesque, with Shelley leaping from one side of the fence to the other.

The first twenty lines of *Epipsychidion* address Emily as a mortal woman, and refer directly to her confinement in a convent school. But at once the poem makes an about-face, and Emily becomes another symbolic representation of Intellectual Beauty. She is "too gentle to be human," and, like Asia or the Witch of Atlas, veils "beneath that radiant form of Woman . . . light, and love, and immortality." Being "Youth's vision . . . made perfect," she is associated with Shelley's usual transcendence symbols. She is the "Veiled Glory of this lampless Universe," a "Moon beyond the clouds," a "Star above the Storm" (lines 21–42), and "from her lips" sounds emerge "sweet as stops/ Of planetary music." As always, the vision of Intellectual Beauty absorbs and extinguishes consciousness of anything else, "vanquishing dissonance and gloom," and "killing the sense with passion" (lines 83–86, 60). And, of course, as in the "Skylark," the effort to express in words the impact of her presence fails. The "dim words" simply obscure the reality:

> I measure
> The world of fancies, seeking one like thee,
> And find — alas! mine own infirmity   (lines 69–71)

Having established Emily as a mortal incarnation of Intellectual Beauty, the poem proceeds to take note of some of the complexities involved in such an encounter. To meet the "Vision" in a mortal form at a time when one has made other earthly commitments leads to difficulties. As Shelley says, it might have been better if his spirit had moved beside that of Emily from its birth, or alternatively, if they had met "in the fields of Immortality . . . But not as now" (lines 133–138). For the next two hundred and fifty lines, roughly the central section of the poem, the poet tries to deal with the situation created by meeting Emily now. In this section, she is primarily regarded as a mortal woman, and he attempts to reconcile his love for her with his love for Mary. The effort proceeds along two avenues. From a theoretical point of view, Shelley seeks to justify what he calls "True Love" by arguing that "to divide is not to take away" (lines 160–161), and that it is quite possible, in fact desirable, to love two women at once. But the effort has also a more immediately practical aspect in that, through an obscure autobiography, Shelley seeks to find a place in his personal life for Emily. The solution is finally discovered in a metaphor — perhaps the only way it could be found. The poet is the "passive Earth" ruled by "Twin Spheres of light," Mary as the moon and Emily as the sun (line 345). As in *Prometheus Unbound*, the force of gravity is a metaphor of the loving harmony in which they will dwell.

173

But even while he is trying to incorporate Emily in his household, as it were, Shelley also speaks of her as Intellectual Beauty. He describes the youthful contact with transcendence in terms reminiscent of *Alastor* or the "Hymn to Intellectual Beauty," recounts the continued effort to recapture this experience, and finally recognizes Emily as "the Vision veiled from me/ So many years" (lines 343–344). In *Prometheus Unbound* the unveiled presence of Asia transformed the earth into a paradise of love, and the situation is repeated here in a personal rather than a social context. Shelley is a "world of love," and the twin regency of Emily and Mary will "Awaken all its fruits and flowers . . . And lull its storms . . . luring to faint bowers/ The armies of the rainbow-wingèd showers" (lines 345–354). This section ends with a comparison of the poet to a plant. His poetry is the fruit which, ripening under the sun of his Lady's eyes, "Will be as of the trees of Paradise" (line 387).

The concluding section of the poem attempts to give some impression of the union with Emily.[3] As always, the union takes place in a natural bower or paradise, and in

3. White, *Shelley*, II, 268–269, has argued that the section of the poem which now begins — what he calls the "imaginary elopement" — was an afterthought added when the poem had been already completed at line 387. Professor White also argues that the concluding section of the poem is inconsistent with what has preceded it because Mary "is ignored in a manner contradictory to the sentiments expressed earlier in the poem." Joseph Barrell, *Shelley and the Thought of His Time* (New Haven, 1947), p. 169, agrees with Professor White, adding that the concluding section contradicts not only the sentiments but the thought expressed earlier in the poem. There is a point to these objctions. But the concluding section will seem contradictory only if Emily is primarily thought of as a mortal woman rather than a vision of Intellectual Beauty like the Witch of Atlas. For it is only when Emily is viewed as a "mortal shape" that it becomes necessary to take account of Mary. In so far as Emily is presented as a vision of Intellectual Beauty, the union with her is what the poem has been striving to conceive. Both the withdrawal to an island-bower and the erotic language are, as we have seen, entirely characteristic of Shelley when he seeks to symbolize the contact with transcendence.

describing the paradise, in this case an island, Shelley encounters the same sort of difficulty that has dogged him throughout the poem. If Emily is thought of as an Italian school girl, then the island must have a geographical location and a concrete existence, and the retreat to the island becomes something wishful and sentimental. It is the projection of a daydream, and recalls Shelley's letter to Mary in which he said that his "greatest content" would be to "retire with you and our child to a solitary island in the sea." [4] He notes, to begin with, that in order to make the voyage Emily will have to be freed from her "prison" or convent. He explains that because "the harbours are not safe and good," the island is uninhabited except for "some pastoral people native there." He locates the island "under Ionian skies" and says that the "blue Aegean girds" it (lines 395, 422–430). He also remarks that this isle and house has been prepared for their occupancy. Some chambers have been fitted up, books and music have been sent, and because "our simple life wants little" he has not disturbed or attempted to adorn the natural surroundings (lines 513–527). Certainly, this concern with the details of housekeeping tends to give a tone of outright wish-fulfillment to the description.

At the same time, however, if Emily is conceived as the incarnation of Intellectual Beauty, a permanent union with her would take the poet out of the physical world. From this point of view, the island must become not simply a place of escape from whatever is painful in human life; it must also be an escape from life itself, just as the union of Prometheus and Asia involves a withdrawal into a cavern-bower. Hence the island begins to acquire supernatural qualities which dissociate it from the mortal world. Instead of being surrounded by the "blue Aegean,"

4. *Works*, X, 315.

> It is an isle 'twixt Heaven, Air, Earth, and Sea,
> Cradled, and hung in clear tranquillity;
> Bright as that wandering Eden Lucifer,
> Washed by the soft blue Oceans of young air.
>
> (lines 457–460)

Nothing is more characteristic of Shelley's imagination than the descriptive passage which now begins. In a fever of longing he has been envisioning an earthly paradise, but since the island, being a home for Emily, must like Emily combine the mortal and the eternal, Shelley need not confine himself to mere earthly delights. Instead, he is free to join together all that excited him most, and the island even begins to become a symbolic representation of the transcendent world. At least, Shelley's usual transcendence symbols are associated with it. The island itself is eternal, its "fields and woods" possessing a "green and golden immortality" (lines 458–459). It is compared to the morning star, "that wandering Eden Lucifer." In the island there is the utter harmony and reconciliation of all things always created by the presence of Love or Intellectual Beauty; for music can be heard throughout the island,

> And every motion, odour, beam, and tone
> With that deep music is in unison.   (lines 453–454)

Moreover, with a wild defiance of poetic tact, the island itself even begins to seem a version of Asia or Emily. It is veiled by "exhalations" from the sea and sky, but as "veil after veil" is lifted by "Sun or Moon or zephyr"

> the isle's beauty, like a naked bride
> Glowing at once with love and loveliness,
> Blushes and trembles at its own excess.   (lines 474–476) [5]

5. Cf. Neville Rogers, *Shelley at Work* (London, 1956), p. 103: "In his excitement Shelley's symbols run more and more into each other. Ariadne,

Up to this point in the poem, Shelley has not been able to manage his verse in such a way as to suggest the coalescence of mortality and the transcendent world. In fact, in the descriptions of Emily and of the island the poem seems simply to contradict itself. The shores of an island "hung" like a star in the sky cannot be washed by the "blue Aegean." Only in the symbolism of the tower, which stands on the island, is he able to suggest the desired synthesis, and even here, perhaps, it is necessary to remember other Shelleyan towers in order to grasp the full significance of what is said. Since Shelley's poems often involve a circular or repetitious approach to a theme through multiple symbols, it is not surprising that the tower seems to recapitulate the description of the island. If the island itself is the setting of the union with Emily, the tower is the particular location within the island where the union takes place. It is a "pleasure-house" built of old by some "Ocean-King" for "his sister and his spouse" (lines 488–492). But the tower is a peculiar one. The product of human art, it seems to have grown in an organic way,

> in the heart
> Of Earth having assumed its form, then grown
> Out of the mountains, from the living stone,
> Lifting itself. (lines 494–497)

It had once carried "antique and learnèd imagery," but this has been erased and "in the place of it/ The ivy and the wild-vine interknit." Here artifice has been lost in nature, but the reverse also takes place; for through the winter tracery of stem and bough the sky shines into the hallways, "Working mosaic on their Parian floors," and the natural

who had just become identified with Love-the-Pilot, is now identified also with the Isle," and Rogers goes on to cite the lines quoted above.

becomes an abstract design (lines 498–500, 504–507). Perhaps one should not build too much on these slight details, but in so far as they count at all, they suggest the resolution of antinomies, the bringing together of the mortal and the eternal, the incorporation of nature with what is permanent.

Previously in the poem Shelley had asserted that the desired union with Emily was not sexual in character:

> To whatsoe'er of dull mortality
> Is mine, remain a vestal sister still;
> To the intense, the deep, the imperishable,
> Not mine but me, henceforth be thou united.
>
> (lines 389–392)

But when in the concluding lines of the poem Shelley speaks of the actual coming together, he describes what every reader would recognize as intense physical experience. The language is concretely detailed, and as heavily weighted with erotic suggestion as any passage in Shelley's poetry. At the same time, however, these lines reach out to something more than a sexual contact. Through the senses, the poet hopes to achieve a union in which

> The fountains of our deepest life, shall be
> Confused in Passion's golden purity.   (lines 570–571)

In fact, the focus of this passage is not primarily on the physical experience itself, though that is vividly presented. For immediately after implying a sexual union, the poem proceeds to metaphors which act as a filter, removing the vivid impression of physical contact. The lovers will come together like "mountain-springs under the morning sun," a metaphor that dissolves erotic associations and dwells only on the process of union itself as an abstract thing (line 572). Then the lovers are compared to two "spheres" or "meteors of expanding flame" which become one sphere as they

> Touch, mingle, are transfigured; ever still
> Burning, yet ever inconsumable:
> In one another's substance finding food.   (lines 578–580)

Of course, these lines are in keeping with the astronomical imagery used throughout the poem, but a strict application of the metaphor might suggest that in colliding the meteor figures would be mutually destructive. In fact, the metaphor is used in this sense in "The Triumph of Life," where "Maidens and Youths . . . Bending within each other's atmosphere,/ Kindle invisibly" and go to their "bright destruction" (lines 149–154). But at the end of *Epipsychidion,* Shelley seems to deny the implications of his symbolism. The burning, meteoric lovers are "ever inconsumable" (line 579). Thus if the double conception of Emily has created difficulties for Shelley within the structure of the poem, it has important advantages in this concluding section. In the first place, it permits him to use the language of erotic experience without recognizing or at least admitting the sexual implications. At the same time, the union with Intellectual Beauty can be felt and described with great emotional intensity, because the poet actually has in mind a living woman.

— 2 —

Since the object of man's quest is outside his habitual experience, he either passively receives intimations from another world, or seeks to find within his own environment some image or analogue through which the remoter world can be conceived. But man is not merely passive; he also builds in accordance with his intimations or aspirations. The most satisfying of sense analogues to abstract reality is that constructed by man himself. We are dealing with the role or function of art; but we have in mind not so much the sophisticated psychological explorations of romantic theory, as the extent to which art itself, or a work of art, could be regarded and used in poetry as a symbol. For obvious reasons, sculpture especially represents and evokes the attitudes clustered about art. This is plainly true of Keats and of Yeats, but Shelley also employed sculpture in a similar way. In the first place, sculpture suggests the permanence of art, and Shelley notices sculptured tombs

> Of whose pure beauty, Time, as if his pleasure
> Were to spare Death, had never made erasure;
> But every living lineament was clear
> As in the sculptor's thought.[6]

Similarly, in *Prometheus,* he describes a temple overwrought with carved figures,

> Praxitelean shapes, whose marble smiles
> Fill the hushed air with everlasting love.
> (III, iii, 165–166)

Moreover, the human artist creates something better formed than life itself. As Yeats puts it, the sculptured creations of man which "keep a marble or a bronze repose" are "mockers of man's enterprise"; for despite all his "enterprise," man cannot himself achieve their perfected and eternal "repose." The conception is as characteristic of Shelley as of Yeats, for in *Prometheus* Shelley too notices the paradox that

> human hands first mimicked and then mocked,
> With moulded limbs more lovely than its own,
> The human form, till marble grew divine.   (II, iv, 80–82)

And elsewhere he speaks of "forms that mock the eternal dead/ In marble immortality." [7]

6. "Ode to Naples," lines 13–16.
7. "Ode to Liberty," lines 73–74.

The unchanging perfection created by the artist is not thought to be something abstracted from the imperfections of actuality. Thus Shelley, like Blake, emphasizes that in creating "beautiful idealisms" the poet draws upon thought itself proceeding independently of the senses. The poet described in *Prometheus* "nor seeks nor finds"

> mortal blisses,
> But feeds on the aereal kisses
> Of shapes that haunt thought's wildernesses.
>
> (I, 741–743)

In other words, the object of art is not "memory," as Blake called it, not the creation of a naturalistic counterpart to human experience. Instead, the artist works in accordance with intimations of ultimate truth, and so creates "forms more real than living man" (I, 748). The work of art is an attempt to mediate between man and transcendent reality, to make the "remoter world" palpable to human senses, or, putting it differently, to symbolize what Yeats called "all heavenly glory."

Thus in creating a perfected and unchanging world, strongly contrasted with life as it actually is, the artist is not merely wishful. He is, as Shelley seldom doubts, elaborating an image of truth. The work of art, therefore, becomes a reliable analogue of the transcendent, and the more satisfying as an analogue in that it is always available to human senses. But in some ways art, or at least such varieties as painting and sculpture, may seem an analogue not altogether usable. For man desires to cross into the transcendent world, to merge himself with it, and no analogue can offer much reassurance which does not permit him to enact such a retreat, at least in a symbolic way. Now it is not easy to conceive escaping into a work of painting or sculpture. It is, in fact, difficult to imagine man except as a spectator of such art. This, indeed, as Keats's famous ode gradually discloses, is one of the liabilities of the Grecian Urn as a symbol. It does not readily allow the poet to join the figures on the frieze. Hence Shelley makes relatively little use of a symbolism of painting or sculpture in his poetry. He turns instead to other forms of human artistry in which the notion of a retreat, being more naturally suggested, makes the symbolism more reassuring.

— 3 —

What does have a large place in Shelley's poetry is a symbolism of architectural structures such as pyramids, domes, temples, obelisks, and especially towers.[8] In discussing this symbolism, it will be necessary to trace rather labyrinthine associations. In other words, there is no central poem to be exploited in quite the same way that one can recur to *Epipsychidion* in discussing the use of sexual love as an analogue. Instead, the imagery of architecture acquires its full symbolic value only gradually as the reader, becoming increasingly familiar with Shelley's expression, links one context with another. Starting with the obvious, one can say that architecture is a product of human thought. Now the transcendent world is, of course, abstract and immaterial, and there is a capability in man which corresponds to the transcendent and which expresses itself in endeavors of thought and spirit. Hence both the transcendent world and the human soul, man's "portion of the Eternal," are symbolized in terms of fire, and, anticipating a bit, it is suggestive that architecture itself is often described as "flame transformed to marble" — an image which incorporates the fiery

8. G. Wilson Knight in the *Starlit Dome*, pp. 179–257, discusses the architectural symbolism at length. Despite the difference in treatment here, I am indebted to his discussion for many suggestions.

thought of the artist with the permanence of stone.[9] Architecture, then, resembles sculpture in that it embodies human
thought and especially suggests the notion of permanence.
Thus equally with sculpture it could become an analogue of
the transcendent world. But, of course, the symbolism has
a further advantage in that it is possible to imagine a retreat
into the architectural structure.

In the fixed equation between human thought and architecture the symbolism suggests the permanence which only
thought can achieve. To cite one example, in *Hellas* classical
Greece is conceived less as a geographical or historical entity
than as an outpouring of the human spirit. It exists not in
material forms which "must decay" but as a timeless and
indestructible synthesis of particular attitudes and ideals.
Hence it can be compared to an architectural structure:

> Greece and her foundations are
> Built below the tide of war,
> Based on the crystàlline sea
> Of thought and its eternity.　　(lines 696–699)

As the play proceeds, it dramatizes a defeated effort to
make the spirit of Greece dominant in human life in time.
Thus the theme of the play is the failure of millennial hopes,
a theme which appears frequently in Shelley's poetry, notably
in *The Revolt of Islam*. But as in "The Sensitive Plant,"
Shelley finds consolation in the thought that what does
not persist in a concrete form does not therefore cease to
exist in the universe. Ultimately Greece is thought, and
"Thought/ Alone . . . cannot die" (lines 795–797). Hence

> If Greece must be
> A wreck, yet shall its fragments reassemble,
> And build themselves again impregnably
> In a diviner clime,

9. *Adonais,* line 447.

183

> To Amphionic music on some Cape sublime,
> Which frowns above the idle foam of Time.
> (lines 1002–1007)

But architectural structures and especially towers are also associated with the permanence of thought in a more literal way. It is not simply that creations of thought may be compared to a temple, nor simply that the architectural construction is the product and hence the perpetual embodiment of it. Occasionally in Shelley's poetry the tower is an actual repository of thought, either because it bears "antique and learned imagery" carved upon it, or because it is, in fact, a library or museum. In *The Revolt of Islam* the temple to which poets and sages withdraw at death is described as having "on every side,/ Sculptures like life and thought" (lines 584–585). Moreover,

> on the jasper walls around, there lay
> Paintings, the poesy of mightiest thought,
> Which did the Spirit's history display.   (lines 599–601)

Again in *The Revolt of Islam* or *Epipsychidion* the temple or tower contains "many a tome" of antique lore, "books . . . and all/ Those instruments" which call

> The future from its cradle, and the past
> Out of its grave, and make the present last
> In thoughts and joys which sleep, but cannot die,
> Folded within their own eternity.
> (*Epipsychidion*, lines 521–524)

Thus the tower may verge on being a Shelleyan version of Yeats's "Byzantium," a retreat "out of nature," an "artifice" or made counterpart of "eternity," in which the mind or soul, "studying/ Monuments of its own magnificence," may engage in a pure intellectual activity.

In the two previous chapters it was pointed out that the

transcendent world was often suggested by imagery of stars and fire, and the world of flux and generation by water imagery — by dew, mist, and cloud. Once developed, these symbols could be exploited to express a pattern of inter-relation and contrast between the two realms of experience. In view of this, architecture emerges even more strikingly as an analogue of the ultimate permanence; for the juxta-position of water and architecture, as Shelley describes it, produces tensions very similar to those generated in the conflict between fire-star and water imagery. Shelley's towers, to begin with, usually overlook a body of water. In *The Revolt of Islam*, the "Temple of the Spirit" stands on an island surrounded by ocean, and the hermit's tower rises beside a lake whose waters "play/ Even to the threshold of that lonely home." Similarly the marble ruin to which Laon and Cythna retire is on the top of a "rocky hill which overhung the Ocean," and "From that lone ruin . . . might be heard the murmur of the motion/ Of waters." Elsewhere Shelley speaks of "Cyclopean piles, whose turrets . . . frowned/ O'er the bright waves which girt their dark foun-dations round." [10] All the instances just cited have been taken from *The Revolt of Islam*, an early poem, but throughout his life Shelley continued to imagine towers impending over water, and the architectural monument which "frowns above the idle foam of Time" at once suggests a contrast between permanence and change.

Moreover, as the above citations would suggest, the body of water usually reflects the shadow of the architectural con-struction. Thus in "The Witch of Atlas," Shelley says that the Witch enjoyed going "adown old Nilus"

> where within the surface of the river
> The shadows of the massy temples lie,

10. *The Revolt of Islam,* lines 1436–1437, 2530–2536, 4762–4764.

And never are erased — but tremble ever
Like things which every cloud can doom to die.

(lines 513–516)

A poem composed about a year later, "Evening: Ponte al Mare, Pisa," describes the same thing in language parallel to that used in the "Witch":

> Within the surface of the fleeting river
>   The wrinkled image of the city lay,
> Immovably unquiet, and forever
>   It trembles, but it never fades away.   (lines 13–16)

One might also cite here the description of the tower in *Prometheus Unbound*. It stands beside a "crystalline pool," and its image ever lies on the "unerasing waves" (III, iii, 159–161). These descriptions derive symbolic significance from the perception — used by Wordsworth in a very different way in the final River Duddon sonnet — that although what it contains at any given time is fleeting, the river itself is constant. The shadows of the temples are endlessly reflected in an endlessly different mass of water. The reader is obliquely reminded of the familiar Shelleyan mysteries, that the individual is evanescent and resistlessly hurried along, that concrete life, on a large scale, is, like the stream, uniformly repetitious and hence unchanging, and that, though it may be clouded or veiled, the transcendent forever remains above the concrete. Moreover, not reality, not the tower itself, but only its shadow can be seen "within the surface of the river," and even the shadow is "wrinkled" or distorted. There is even a suggestion of conflict between the unchanging permanence of the architecture and the fluid change of the river. The river, if it were sufficiently agitated, must naturally be expected to erase or at least break up the reflection, and the cloud, another water image, coming between the reflection and the sun, would obscure or possibly eclipse it.

— 4 —

There is, of course, a further implication of the tower symbolism which makes it especially reassuring as an analogue. For the tower ascending toward the sky may suggest that man by his own energies and within his own context can build in imitation of the more naturally soaring lark, achieving a height from which — and here Shelley brilliantly exploits the just implications of his symbol — "Earth and Ocean seem/ To sleep in one another's arms." [11] From the tower, in other words, "Earth and Ocean" display the same loving harmony and smiling, dreaming calm which, at the end of *Prometheus Unbound,* was figured in the childlike spirit of the Earth. Sometimes these works of man are described as having "pierced that serenest sky," the "dome of many-coloured glass" which encloses the concrete world and "stains the white radiance of Eternity," so that from the point of view of one standing on the level earth, the tower, like the lark, may seem actually to attain the transcendent world suggested by star and fire imagery. Thus Shelley speaks of "many a star-surrounded pyramid," and he often compared architecture to fire, thus bringing together two of his habitual thought or intellect symbols. "Towers far and near," the sunlight playing on them, "pierce like reposing flames the tremulous atmosphere," and he similarly speaks of "column, tower, and dome, and spire," which "shine like obelisks of fire," or of "pinnacles" which "point from one shrine like pyramids of fire." [12]

---

11. *Epipsychidion,* lines 509–510.
12. "The Witch of Atlas," line 518; *Adonais,* lines 461–462; "The Witch of Atlas," line 350; *The Revolt of Islam,* lines 4493–4494; "Lines Written

But in the instances cited, when the tower appears "star-surrounded" or when it looks like flame, the point is that the poetry describes an appearance. Even when the word "like" is not used, the poetry does not allow the reader to imagine that the tower actually rises through the atmosphere into the starry heavens, or that it has been literally transformed into flame. It is only in relation to the observer, and to the circumstances in which he sees the tower, that it appears to merge into the transcendent world.

But a symbol can be so apt and fully satisfying that the person who employs it may seem to lose his grip. He may, that is, fail to remember or realize that he is speaking in symbolic terms and confuse his symbol with the reality for which it stands. Wordsworth, as we said, was especially prone to this type of literalism. Shelley was not. But the symbolism of the tower seems to have been so deeply entrenched that it occasionally, perhaps inadvertently, becomes something more than an analogue. In other words, the retreat into the tower must sometimes be read not merely as a symbolic enactment of the desired escape into the transcendent. It also becomes a direct way of establishing contact. For the most part, this is admitted only very indirectly through association with other symbols, but one can start by pointing out that towers in Shelley's poetry often stand on the crest of mountains where they are open to glimmerings from the "remoter world." In these buildings Shelley sometimes describes a "cloven roof" or some other opening through which shines the light of stars. For example, the temple to which Laon and Cythna retire is a marble ruin which crowns the crest of a mountain. It is first seen gleaming "in the ray/ Of the obscure stars," and within it

among the Euganean Hills," lines 106–107; "A Summer Evening Churchyard," lines 13–14.

there is a "shattered portal" which "looks to the eastern stars" (lines 2529–2570). Again in *Epipsychidion* the "sky/ Peeps" into the tower

> With moonlight patches, or star atoms keen
> Or fragments of the day's intense serene. (lines 505–506)

One of the important symbolic figures in *The Revolt of Islam* is the hermit who, in so far as it is possible for a living man, has retired from the concrete world into a life of thought and contemplation. His home is appropriately the tower; for the withdrawal of the hermit to a tower constitutes a symbolic dramatization, an imitation within the human world of the desired escape to a transcendent permanence. In this context, we are dealing only with an analogue. But it is not only hermits who retreat into towers. In *Epipsychidion* the architectural structure provides a setting for the union of the lovers, and the same thing takes place in *The Revolt of Islam*. On first reading, one may be surprised to find that instead of the expected bower, the sexual union of Laon and Cythna takes place within a marble ruin. But as with Blake or Yeats, the conduct of an action or the interrelation of images in Shelley's poetry often functions primarily on a level of symbolic propriety. Hence the withdrawal to a tower and the sexual union within it bring together two of the most important analogues, within the realm of human experience, of the flight to the transcendent, immaterial One. But the analogue may also be a bridge to the transcendent, and on this occasion, Laon says, a power which "like light beyond the atmosphere . . . doth ever flow,/ Came on us." [13]

13. *The Revolt of Islam,* lines 2600–2603.

❦ VII ❦

KEATS

The Eternal Present

In his *History of English Literature,* Taine approached
the romantic period with more sympathy than he had dis-
played for earlier epochs. But even the romantics, he felt,
were "fettered" by a national defect: they were "too moral."
Only Byron achieved the state of mind, so "difficult . . . for
a modern man," so "impossible for an Englishman," of being
"enfranchised from reflection." But Shelley and Keats,
"thanks to . . . their sickly or overflowing imagination,"
verged towards this "divine youth and simplicity." The remarks are patently inappropriate to Byron and Shelley, but
when applied to Keats they represent what was, at one time,
a widely held view. Many nineteenth-century critics, stressing
the sensuous relish and mazy enchantment of Keats's verse,
felt that he lacked what Arnold called "the matured power
of moral interpretation." The opinion is largely discredited
today, but it is still helpful to consider the qualities of
Keats's poetry which may have fostered it.

In the first place, there is an obvious tendency in Keats
to use the imagination in a purely escapist way. Especially
in the early poetry, he creates what he himself describes as
"trains of peaceful images," a "store/ Of luxuries" elaborated
merely that both the poet and his readers may enjoy them.[1]

1. "Sleep and Poetry," lines 340, 346–347.

They may, of course, have the relevance Santayana found at large in Shelley's verse: that it expresses the "unadulterated instincts" of the heart, not "warped by familiarity with the perversities of real things." [2] Hence, like most wishful dreams, they may tell us something about the poet who created them and about ourselves to the extent that we share them, but they make no attempt to reconcile these desires with the world of limited possibilities in which we live. As a result, such passages will inevitably seem sentimental — if it is sentimental to wish an impossibility — and any reader who believes that art is, or ought to be, an interpretation or "criticism of life" is bound to regard them with suspicion. Of course, Keats himself shared this suspicion, and even in the early work escapist wanderings of the imagination are usually enjoyed in a nostalgic, valedictory way. The poet knows and says that he will have to give them up. But this fact does not deny what we have said about the attraction to an escapist art: it confirms it. The attraction is so strong that in moments of "Sleep and Poetry," "I Stood Tip-Toe," *Endymion,* and elsewhere throughout his career, he is willing to indulge himself despite serious doubts, both aesthetic and moral, of the value of such indulgence. And if the doubts, which later become outright condemnation, are strongly expressed, it is because the tendency which they oppose was also powerful. In "Sleep and Poetry" the conflict is blunted by a conception, characteristic of Keats, of human life as a process of growth proceeding by stages. Hence it becomes almost legitimate to revel in fanciful delights; though ultimately they must be put aside, they can be tolerated for a while as an early stage in the development of a poet.

This good-humored, rather objective view of life, in-

2. *Winds of Doctrine,* p. 175.

cluding his own life, as process recurs in Keats's attitude towards the weaknesses of his own early poetry. Except when he is startled by the thought of death, there is little genuine impatience, nor is there any desire to nag each of his poems into perfected shape. Instead, to put the matter simply, he seems to have felt that he need only continue to write and increasing experience would turn him into a poet. "It is not," he said of *Endymion*, "in my nature to fumble . . . I have written independently *without Judgment* — I may write independently & *with judgment* hereafter." [3] One need only await the harvest of time. The metaphor of organic growth may also remind us that as Keats developed, no major tendency of his imagination was dropped. So with the movement toward a poetry of escape. It does not disappear but rather changes its character by being coalesced with other claims. Even in *The Fall of Hyperion*, where the escapist dreamer is reproached, the form of the poem is still a dream vision. And if in this poem Keats confronts the pain and tragedy of life, he does so through symbols — the fallen Titans and especially Moneta — which idealize, universalize, and at the same time make it more agreeable to contemplate. It is significant that the sordid and pathetic characters who inhabit Eliot's *Waste Land* are absent in Keats, and indeed, in romantic poetry as a whole. Of course, there is no reason why a poet need attempt this sort of thing. The point is merely that it is characteristic of Keats, as of other romantic writers, that when dealing in poetry with sickness, sorrow, and the like, he should transmute it into forms which openly offer pleasure and release to the imagination.

Throughout his brief career, Keats, like most poets, continued to meditate the function of poetry. Such speculation, at least when practiced by the poets themselves, usually in-

3. *The Letters of John Keats,* I, 374.

volves the search for direction, the effort to square one's own writing with a conception of the function of poetry, and in Keats one finds this especially in the later condemnation of the dreamer as compared with the true poet. Here, in other words, the notion would seem to be that wider ethical concerns may govern poetic composition, channeling it towards a certain subject matter and form which the poet seeks for the accommodation of instincts more obviously moral than poetic. If the ethical ideal is itself capacious, and the poet multitudinous in his resources, this may be healthy for his poetry. But like other forms of medicine, moralistic concerns can be unhealthy in excessive doses; they may lead to an enclosing of sympathies, and they may make one more fearful of offending than brave in adventure. When Yeats spoke of Wordsworth as a "great poet who, after brief blossoms, was cut and sawn into planks of obvious utility," [4] the example, I think, was less sound than it might have been, but there are plenty of poets to illustrate the danger Yeats had in mind. These considerations are not irrelevant to Keats. If he moved toward a rejection of purely escapist poetry, he also knew that didacticism is hardly a better answer. But when poets theorize about poetry one often finds that, in addition to the search for direction, there is a wish to defend or rationalize whatever form of poetry the poet would find most agreeable to write. Keats was no exception, and in the letters and poems of 1816–1817 the desire to use the imagination in an escapist way is matched by a rudimentary aesthetic theory which seeks to justify it.

One finds, in the first place, a scattering of remarks about the mood in which poetry is written. The point seems to be that poetry, which consists of imagined delights luxuriously enjoyed, is conceived in moments when the poet has been

4. *Autobiography* (New York, 1953), p. 143.

led to forget his own cares and those of other people. This takes place in an intense, sensuous response to the beautiful in nature or art, so that it is some object or cluster of objects actually present to the poet — the Grecian urn or the nightingale, to anticipate a bit — which "charms us at once away from all our troubles" (though in the later poetry the charm is seldom entirely effective — nor meant to be) and allows the poet to "feel uplifted from the world." On such occasions, the poet flies "from all sorrowing" into a visionary trance. In other words, a vital response to the immediate and the actual triggers the imagination, which then departs from whatever object may have released it and mounts to catch or create visions of delight. The visions may be of "white coursers . . . Bestridden of gay knights," of the "dales of Arcady," and the like, or of a bowery world similar to that which stimulated the imagination, but idealized (or "etherialized," as Keats might say) and compacted into a denser unit of pleasure.

To the reader, presumably, such poetry may offer an enjoyment exactly like that of the poet. Hence a poem is a "bower" or "little Region" for pleasant wandering in which the reader may forget "real things." "The great end/ Of poesy," Keats said in "Sleep and Poetry," is "that it should be a friend/ To sooth the cares, and lift the thoughts of man," and in this context the phrase "lift the thoughts" does not imply moral elevation but refers instead to being "uplifted from the world." [5] The formula recurs again, of course, in the "Ode on a Grecian Urn" where the urn is said to be "a friend to man." Needless to say, there are various possible grounds of friendship — the friends, for example, who offer merely diversion and escape, and, on

5. "I Stood Tip-Toe," lines 138–139; "To My Brother George," lines 20, 25–27; "Ode on a Grecian Urn," line 7; *Endymion*, line 4; *Letters*, I, 170; "Sleep and Poetry," lines 157, 245–247.

the other hand, the friends who share our troubles and even strengthen us to bear them. In "Sleep and Poetry," the friendship is clearly of the former kind. The "kings" among poets are those who "simply tell the most heart-easing things" (lines 267–268), and the expression in the "Ode on a Grecian Urn" may still carry something of the same meaning, though with the additional emphasis that in telling heart-easing things the artist is also revealing "the invisible world." At least in the letters of 1819, Keats was liable to attribute friendship of the latter kind to "the human friend Philosopher" and to the "miserable and mighty Poet of the human Heart" who in *The Fall of Hyperion* is directly contrasted with the escapist dreamer and described as "a sage;/ A humanist, physician to all men" (I, 189–190).[6] It is, however, unnecessary to detail Keats's later aesthetic theories. They have been closely studied by many critics ever since Professor Thorpe wrote *The Mind of John Keats,* and Keats's mature position is well summarized by Thorpe: "The materials of the poetic imagination . . . are those of actuality as we know it, abstracted from its accidents of time and place," and "transformed into symbols of universal truth and life." It is significant, however, as Thorpe implies, that in these later views the notion that art offers an escape, "a world of its own," still lingers, however modified by the assumption that the world of art must reflect and lead back into "actuality as we know it." [7]

— 2 —

If the escapist tendencies in Keats's early verse might be expected to arouse suspicion in a Victorian, there are other,

6. *Letters,* II, 139, 115.
7. Clarence D. Thorpe, *The Mind of John Keats* (New York, 1926), pp. 101–102.

more formal or technical procedures in the later poetry which might also contribute to the view that Keats was an amoral creative artist "enfranchised from reflection." This is especially true when the demand for a moral interpretation of life converts itself, as it is all too likely to do, into a search for moralistic statements about life, though one hastens to add that this type of erring criticism is less characteristic of Arnold than of his disciples. The point is that Keats's approach was essentially dramatic rather than didactic. In many of his poems, Keats does not come forward in his own person in any direct way; he merely presents or narrates. Even in the lyrics, a form in which by definition and convention the author directly expresses his own feelings and reactions, Keats often remains in the background. He establishes symbols, their latent significance is unfolded, and the poet seems to be largely passive to the implications of the symbol adopted. That is, he allows his own attitudes to take on the tincture or bent of the symbol. Where this is not the case, the poet often appears in the poem not as a manipulator directing his symbols, or as a direct commentator, but in a dynamic and changing relation to the controlling symbols, reacting differently to them through the course of the poem as their fuller potential significance is gradually disclosed. In this way as in so many others Keats, as compared with Wordsworth or Shelley, is concrete rather than abstract, and, in this sense, oblique rather than direct. Consequently, one does not find in him a clear-cut or obvious moral interpretation which can be pinned down in the language of abstraction. Less with him than with most poets of the last century and a half can we rely on abstract comments in the poetry to disclose its over-all significance or meaning.

Like all major poets, Keats brings to bear a considerable

range of typically human feelings, desires, and attitudes. Obviously some poets are more inclusive than others, and one may feel that, as compared with Wordsworth or Shelley, Keats was more generous in his preoccupations, and had a wider range of sympathies. Using more limited and manageable notions to speak of larger tendencies, we have observed that what Wordsworth and Shelley especially stressed in concrete nature provides an index or springboard to their more general attitudes, and the same thing is true of Keats. The point is that he saw not simply flux and decay, though that is taken into account, nor permanence and stability, though that too has its place, but a process in which change is potentially meaningful and orderly. But this fact at once indicates a major bias of his imagination. For he tended to resolve the large, unanswerable perplexities that afflict us all by constructing myths of process. A number of contexts might be cited. In the great myth, in the *Letters,* of human life as a "vale of Soul-making" there is the conception of the gradual forming of a human identity or "Soul" by means of a "World of Pains and troubles";[8] in *Hyperion* there is a rather similar myth of the cosmos progressively evolving forms more complex, aware, and beautiful. The consequence of this view of life as process can be felt everywhere in Keats's poetry. It means, for example, that time itself is not finally regarded with a blind, Shelleyan hostility and longing to escape; for it is only in and through time that things can work out their latent potentiality. For the same reason, his poetry does not display the lingering nostalgia which one finds so pervasive in Wordsworth, the sense of glory slipping into the past as the poet strives to hold, regain, or replace it with something else. In the last analysis, the perception of process implies, at least in Keats,

8. *Letters,* II, 102.

a trust in the cosmos. He was, of course, very much aware of all the ill and evil that might seem to belie trust, but he seems to have been potentially ready to subsume it within a wider, more hopeful vision of things. No more than other romantic writers can he be numbered among those whom William James described as the "second born." Throughout his very brief career, he retained the optimistic *élan* of youth, and with all his brilliant awareness, there was little bitterness.

What Keats observes in external nature, then, can be described as an extension or working into detail of an over-all imaginative bias. Or perhaps one should put it the other way around, and say that the organic processes of nature provided a metaphor or clue to the interpretation of life as a whole. In either case, probably no poet since Shakespeare has had so firm a sense of process in the natural world. Even in the early verse, he stresses things budding, growing, and ripening — "new buds unfolding," the year that "grows lush in juicy stalks," "swelling leafiness," "the creeper, mellowing for an autumn blush." [9] Any number of such images might be cited. In them one observes a pronounced reliance on the present participle, a stylistic mannerism characteristic of Keats throughout his career and serving to vivify and dramatize the sense of process taking place, re-enacting it, so to speak, in the texture of the poetry. Often he presents the whole process of the seasons in a series of images, as in the passage in "Fancy" (lines 55–66) which begins with the field-mouse emerging from "its celled sleep" and moves by a series of evocations through spring, summer, and fall with its "acorns ripe down-pattering." One might also cite the sonnet "After dark vapours," where

9. "Sleep and Poetry," line 169; *Endymion,* I, 45–46; "Calidore," line 34; *Endymion,* II, 416.

> The calmest thoughts come round us; as of leaves
> Budding — fruit ripening in stillness — Autumn suns
> Smiling at eve upon the quiet sheaves,

a progression which, significantly, ends in death. For the steady commitment to process is one of the elements entering into the peculiarly passive and serene acceptance of death sometimes found in Keats's poetry.

The sense of process also reveals itself in an imagery which seems to contain the past and future of whatever object it describes. For one casual example we can turn to "The Eve of St. Mark." The action of the poem takes place in April, and "on the western window panes" of Bertha's room

> The chilly sunset faintly told
> Of unmatur'd green vallies cold,
> Of the green thorny bloomless hedge,
> Of rivers new with spring-tide sedge.   (lines 7–10)

Even though the green vallies are now unmatured, the hedge now bloomless, the epithets carry the imagination forward to the time of maturing and blooming. This sense of seeded potentiality is already strong in Keats's early verse, and, what is perhaps equally significant for Keats's over-all attitudes, there is also the suggestion that the type of imagination it implies represents something of an ideal. Just as in the "Ode" the nightingale can sing in mid-May of summer, in the "Hymn to Pan" the god is one

> to whom
> Broad leaved fig trees even now foredoom
> Their ripen'd fruitage; yellow girted bees
> Their golden honeycombs; our village leas
> Their fairest blossom'd beans and poppied corn;
>
> .   .   .   .   .
>
> pent up butterflies
> Their freckled wings; yea, the fresh budding year
> All its completions.   (*Endymion*, I, 251–255, 258–260)

199

Pan is, of course, a benevolent nature deity, but he is also a patron of poetry, and the complete intuitive and empathic sense of things here attributed to Pan was also discovered in Shakespeare. "He has," Keats writes, "left nothing to say about nothing or any thing." In the same context, speaking of the *Sonnets,* he remarks that "they seem to be full of fine things said unintentionally" and quotes four lines:[10]

> When lofty trees I see barren of leaves
> Which erst from heat did canopy the herd,
> And Summer's green all girded up in sheaves,
> Borne on the bier with white and bristly beard.

It is, of course, not possible to say with certainty just which of the many "fine things" in these lines Keats had in mind, but what seems to be most distinctive in them, and might therefore have especially led Keats to quote them, is the condensed expression of the entire life of the trees or the corn as a process occurring through time. It is also characteristic that the summer trees are seen in relation to the herd. Shakespeare, as Hazlitt once said, "had only to think of any thing in order to become that thing, with all the circumstances belonging to it," [11] and in these four lines one finds an illustration in which the "circumstances" include both the past and future of the object and also whatever other objects might naturally be associated with it.

Precisely because his style is less mannered, the influence of Shakespeare is seldom so obvious in Keats's verse as is that of Hunt, Spenser, Milton, Dryden, or other poets one might mention. Yet we know that Keats read and reread Shakespeare. It is scarcely possible that a poet so quick to imitate and so various in his resources as Keats would not

10. *Letters,* I, 188–189.
11. *Complete Works,* ed. P. P. Howe (London, 1930–1934), V, 48.

pick up something, and it seems to me that he shows a Shakespearian influence especially in the imagery I have been attempting to describe. Of course, it need not be a matter of direct imitation, but rather of a parallel habit of mind reinforced by admiration, for a Shakespearian sense of things is already present even in the early verse. For example, in *Endymion* (II, 397) Keats speaks of "ripe October's faded marigolds." The point is that in this casual phrase he does not simply see the marigolds "faded," but faded as part of a process which also permits October to become "ripe." As with Shakespeare, in other words, there is both the feeling for process and the habit of seeing objects in relation to other objects or events. Certainly Keats's more mature nature imagery at times attains an almost Shakespearian completeness of reference. "To Autumn" is one extended example, and there is also the brilliant metaphor in the "Ode on Melancholy" of "Aching Pleasure nigh/ Turning to Poison while the bee-mouth sips" where there is an intense, empathic sense of process taking place within the body of the bee. Or, for a final instance, one might turn to the "Ode to a Nightingale" where Keats speaks of

> Fast fading violets cover'd up in leaves;
> And mid-May's eldest child,
> The coming musk-rose, full of dewy wine,
> The murmurous haunt of flies on summer eves.
>
> (lines 47–50)

The time is mid-May. Keats describes the musk-rose "coming" as the violets fade, but his imagination also darts ahead to summer when the musk-rose will be "full of dewy wine."

— 3 —

This constant perception of inevitable and universal process — of things gathering to a fulfillment, fading, and dying — might lead either to an aroused desire to participate or to a desire to withdraw from concrete experience, depending partly on whether one concentrates on the fulfillment or the dying. Of course, there is no need to go to either extreme. One can adopt an attitude which subsumes both within a larger context, and, on the whole, this is what Keats did. For example, like Wordsworth, he certainly felt the attraction of whatever might deaden feeling and awareness and so mitigate the pain of loss. Throughout his poetry such symbols as Death, Sleep, Lethe, and Wine suggest the pull of "forgetfulness divine," of an "age so shelter'd . . . That I may never know how change the moons." [12] Symbols of this sort are not only frequent but powerful; and in the slow movement of the odes especially they show a gravitational strength that potentially, perhaps actually, appeals more than the Wordsworthian stasis. On the other hand, the context of other desires remains consistently strong in Keats — indeed it becomes stronger as his poetry matures. In the presence of this context, symbolic expressions that merely suggest forgetfulness become rhetorical flourishes, although they still remain functional. As in the beginning of the "Ode to a Nightingale," they indicate feelings or states of mind that are temporary: they are quickly caught up and used as a springboard for other desires. On other occasions they serve as a supplement or afterthought. Where they are actually developed and continue to contribute directly and functionally, they undergo a metamorphosis, so to speak, and become shifted in such a way as to lead at once to something very different from oblivion. We may here be possibly touching on a distinctive quality of Keats that appears to have tantalized his readers for over a century — a quality

12. "Ode on Indolence," lines 48–49.

that has suggested, to so many different people, another similarity with Shakespeare in kind if not degree. It is the extent to which a variety of human feelings (including the natural desire for tranquillity and repose that Wordsworth builds upon) are taken into account; yet no one complex of desire is compartmentalized, pursued separately, and made into a fixed object or aim. Instead, while being shared, the various desires are carried further, led around under their own force, and made to re-enter again the arena of common experience in which one desire, however strong, gives way to another, and in which the craving for change, for variety and interplay is still stronger than the fixed compulsions that dominate only special types of people.

In Shakespeare, both the sympathy and also the reabsorption back to the more general interests of experience take, of course, an openly dramatic form. The centrifugal concern with character and with particular states of feeling in individual characters is unparalleled. The nineteenth-century tendency to equate Shakespeare with human life builds upon it. This sort of thing can naturally be overdone; and we can fall into the habit of speculating about "How Many Children had Lady Macbeth," yet in general this tendency is innocent. It is a state of exuberant interest that is one extension of "dramatic illusion." It is one side or result of our participation. But the reader not only shares in the quick sympathetic grasp of diverse states of mind and the presentation of them with fairness, genuineness, and integrity; he also participates in the large honesty of the centripetal use of them in the over-all structure of Shakespeare's dramas. It is an honesty that works toward no specific doctrine, no one set of static criteria. Doctrines and criteria may be plucked out by the critic. But if the critic is "hot for certainties," he may feel, as Eliot did, that Shakespeare, in lacking a fixed centrality, suffers when compared, for example, with Dante.

The centrality, it is true, cannot be quickly systematized. Any quick or abstract schematization would involve a distortion or flat interpretation of human motives and actions as they exist in actual interplay. The immediate sense of this is apparent throughout Keats's own remarks on Shakespeare (as when he speaks of Shakespeare's delight in conceiving an Iago being as great as in conceiving an Imogen; and his feeling that Shakespeare is to this extent a "chameleon" as distinct from the "virtuous philosopher"). What is cherished here is a capacity to remain open and to use our empirical sense not to make platforms from which we can "dispute or assert" but rather to understand and to "whisper" or tentatively communicate our insights to each other.[13] The insistence on this is one of the first premises of Keats's thinking, from the startling insight of the Negative Capability letter that he wrote at the age of twenty-two through the next three years until his death. For though Keats's later writing is deeply concerned with the need and struggle of the soul to obtain "identity," the identity desired is anything but exclusive or self-sealed. To apply Keats's vivid sense of the fluid variety of human feeling to his own poetry is not to shackle the verse with biographical criticism and a flat idea of "intention." It is to use biography and what we know of his own hopes and interests intelligently to enlighten our study of the brilliant writing of this period.

— 4 —

Even, however, if Keats had been capable of intense and limited preoccupations or obsessions, we may feel very sure

13. *Letters,* I, 232.

that they would not have been similar to those of Wordsworth or Shelley. The poetry of Keats is everywhere invested with an eager appetite for a full, vivid, and concrete experiencing. This open receptivity is, perhaps, as fundamental in Keats as any of his attitudes. Certainly it remains as a basis and groundwork throughout his life, and other, more particularized, and changing attitudes are often simply attempts to carry it out. Together with the range of sympathetic awareness and the refusal to compartmentalize desires, it especially characterizes and distinguishes him from Wordsworth and Shelley; for it would be impossible for Keats to turn his back upon concrete human experience by a flight into abstraction or even by a withdrawal into whatever may promise a "pure" repose and stability. Poetry, said Keats, should "surprise by a fine excess." [14] Any study of the development of Keats's poetry will focus on the progressive fineness of the excess. For the excess, at least the potentiality for it, seems present from the beginning. The exuberance and quick willingness to carry almost anything to an extreme are so ready that Keats's early poetry, for squeamish tastes, is perhaps the most embarrassing of all the early poetry we have from any of the great English poets. It seems ready to throw itself, without reserve, into almost anything that can be vividly enough felt. What saves it is the self-corrective strength that is a part of its own energy. "The Genius of Poetry," as he said in speaking of the chaos of *Endymion,* "must work out its own salvation." [15] More, perhaps, than any other English poet, Keats exemplifies Johnson's dictum that "activity" carries within itself its "own reformation," and that excess, as Johnson said, is always "a fairer object of hope" than deficiency.

14. *Letters,* I, 238.
15. *Letters,* I, 374.

With a Marlovian gusto, the poetic conception of Keats habitually seeks

> more plenty than the fabled horn
> Thrice emptied could pour forth, at banqueting
> For Proserpine return'd to her own fields.[16]

This persistent imagery of fullness is perhaps the most obvious single expression, at least in the texture of the poetry, of the desire for intense experience. Indeed, the imagery is so pervasive that it suggests a delight in the very notion of fullness, and the suggestion is further reinforced by the fact that these images are usually associated with eating or drinking. Sometimes it seems that the fullness of the objects promises a vivid and prolonged experience. Here one might think of such characteristic phrases as "rich brimm'd goblets," or, in the "Ode to a Nightingale," the "beaker full of the warm South . . . With beaded bubbles winking at the brim," or of such variants as "honeysuckles full of clear bee-wine," the "coming musk-rose, full of dewy wine," or of the fruits in the ode "To Autumn" which are filled "with ripeness to the core." Or sometimes it almost seems that the objects themselves have been glutted and satiated. Thus the immensity of the sea is projected in the fact that it "gluts twice ten thousand Caverns," and in "To Autumn" a very similar image suggests the prolonged quality of autumn by the fact that it has "o'erbrimm'd" the "clammy cells" of the bees.[17] One might also cite a passage from *Endymion* (III, 30–40) in which "Powers" in water, fire, and air are "filling" human senses "with spiritual sweets to plenitude,/ As bees gorge full their cells."

In fact Keats characteristically conceived a fullness of

---

16. *The Fall of Hyperion,* I, 35–37.
17. "To My Brother George," line 39; *Endymion,* IV, 698; "Ode to a Nightingale," line 49; "On the Sea," line 3.

pleasurable experience so complete and glutted that it becomes straining and painful, or, becoming insupportable, ends in loss of consciousness. Since our point is that this was true of Keats at all periods of his development, we may again mention a few examples chosen at random. He speaks of

> A butterfly, with golden wings broad parted,
> Nestling a rose, convuls'd as though it smarted
> With over pleasure,

and conceives a sweetness

> Sweeter by far than Hybla's honied roses
> When steep'd in dew rich to intoxication.[18]

Similarly, the lovers in Keats's poetry, especially in his earlier years, either faint like Henry Mackenzie's "Man of Feeling," or else come close to it from sheer intensity of emotion. Endymion is a chronic offender, especially when Keats portrays him "swoon'd/ Drunken from pleasure's nipple" (II, 868–869).

In several places Keats uses the word "intensity" to suggest the process of experiencing he had in mind as an ideal. The term, as Keats employs it, has special connotations. To explore these connotations is one way of trying to understand what he valued both in art and in the wider possibilities of life. At least two contexts are especially important for any discussion of the term, one from the *Letters* (To George and Tom Keats, 21 Dec. 1817) and the other the rather vague "Pleasure Thermometer" passage in *Endymion* (I, 775 ff.). In the "Pleasure Thermometer" lines, he speaks first of events in nature which serve as stimuli to the imagination. These, he adds, are "entanglements" or "enthralments," that is, they capture and enslave attention. Then

18. "Sleep and Poetry," lines 343–345; "Had I a man's fair form," lines 10–11.

in the letter, he remarks that West's paintings have "nothing to be intense upon; no women one feels mad to kiss; no face swelling into reality." Hence the notion of "intensity" implies, first of all, a reaction, both passionate and imaginative, to some external object or event. The significance of this becomes apparent when one contrasts the views of Wordsworth and Shelley; for in both these poets, though in different ways respectively, man's most vital and intense experiences are construed as "fallings from us, vanishings," moments, in other words, when there is a blank withdrawal of sensory stimuli, a consciousness without content except of the "sentiment of Being." But in connection with West's failure to paint women one feels mad to kiss, the phrase "swelling into reality" seems especially significant. It suggests that the women might have been depicted in such a way that for the moment and for the imagination they would almost seem real, or at least to have some life more than the cold endowment of a face in a painting. It also suggests a process taking place in the mind of the spectator whereby he would become increasingly conscious of the object and absorbed in it.

We seem, then, to be dealing with a sympathetic use of the imagination. This implication receives some support from the fact that the letter quoted also contains the famous discussion of Negative Capability, so that one can easily suppose some connection between the two ideas. Moreover, it seems to me that the controversial Pleasure Thermometer is mainly an account of the possibilities of sympathetic identification. "Human happiness," Keats says, lies in a "fellowship divine,/ A fellowship with essence." These lines have been variously interpreted. Some critics have maintained that they refer to a fellowship with Essential Being or Divinity. More recently it has been urged, on the basis of other contexts of the word "essence" in Keats's poetry, that the term refers to the essential being or "identity" — what Hopkins called "inscape" — of concrete presences, and that "fellowship" denotes a coming together or participation.[19] Certainly Keats was more an Aristotelian than a Platonist (if we want to adopt Coleridge's hasty and, as Babbitt said, rather flattering mode of distinguishing all human beings); and in view of his general habits of mind we may prefer the second interpretation to the first. The remainder of the passage seems to carry out and justify this interpretation. Keats goes on to instance a number of sources of intense experience. This first of these involves, as I said, a strong sensitivity to natural beauty. To "Feel . . . these things" is to share sympathetically in their identity, and in doing so we achieve "a sort of oneness," a phrase which implies both a oneness with the object and a personal integration created in us as the object draws our total capacity for attention. These "enthralments" are "self-destroying," destructive to the self or ego, and at such moments "our state Is like a floating spirit's." This phrase must be read in connection with the previous statement that in "fellowship with essence . . . we shine,/ Full alchemiz'd and free of space." What Keats seems to have in mind is a sympathetic participation so strong that we lose all sense of distinct or personal identity and become totally merged with something else, conscious of nothing but the object of our identification, a state in which, as Eliot says, "you are the music/ While the music lasts." Groping for an expression which, he said, "was a regular stepping of the Imagination towards a Truth," [20] the young Keats put it with less precision, but,

19. Newell F. Ford, "The Meaning of 'Fellowship with Essence' in *Endymion*," *PMLA*, LXII (1947), pp. 1061–1076.
20. *Letters*, I, 218.

like Eliot in the line quoted from the *Four Quartets*, he
seems especially to imply that in this identification we begin
to lose the haunting awareness of time and mortality, momentarily seeming to become "immortal" or "divine." For there
are "richer entanglements" and of these the "chief intensity"
is love. At its apex of intense feeling, this "earthly love has
power to make/ Men's being mortal, immortal." Here one
may recall the line from *Antony and Cleopatra* which Keats
underlined in his copy of Shakespeare: "Eternity was in our
lips and eyes."

But the demand for "intensity" can also be applied to
works of art: "the excellence of every Art is its intensity,
capable of making all disagreeables evaporate, from their
being in close relationship with Beauty & Truth — Examine
King Lear & you will find this exemplified throughout."
As W. J. Bate has pointed out, the word "disagreeables"
does not refer to whatever might conventionally be considered unpleasant — the use of Lear as an example would
bar such a sentimental interpretation — but to whatever
would not be agreeable or in harmony with the work of
art itself. "Intensity," then, can be defined as a sympathetic
participation so massive that it obliterates consciousness not
only of self but also of anything other than the object
focused upon. Hence intensity, or the object that permits
it, can offer an escape, and Keats writes to Haydon, for
example, saying "I know not you[r] many havens of intenseness," [21] but the escape is not into tranquillity or dead
calm, as with Wordsworth, nor a flight into abstraction, as
with Shelley, but rather a passing into a vivid and massive
process of experience. The drama of such poems as the
"Ode to a Nightingale" or the "Ode on a Grecian Urn"

21. *Letters*, I, 265.

partly lies in the frustrated effort to achieve exactly this kind of intensity.

— 5 —

The ideal of intensity implies, then, a process working through time; and if time permits the process to occur, it also limits it and causes its dissolution. Even if the objects themselves persist, the capacity to experience fades as the mind and senses become cloyed. Much of Keats's poetry thus involves the effort, familiar and traditional in poetry, to reconcile the desire for a full and lasting intensity with the inevitable fact of decay. That the theme is perennial in most great poetry does not stale its urgency. On the contrary, the familiarity simply indicates how universal and how central the problem is in human experience. Furthermore, it is capable of as many resolutions as there are people, and through the course of any one life attitudes toward it will probably change. Keats, of course, did not come to any fixed answer, but it is possible to discover an over-all tendency in his poetry, a direction, so to speak, in which any resolution would be found, even though the resolution itself seems to exist more as a wish than a possibility.

Once again we can start with certain characteristics of his imagery. Keats's stylistic habits have been exhaustively studied, and the intention here is not once again to traverse familiar ground, but rather, taking for granted the results of previous studies, to attempt to show that these devices of style reflect his more general attitudes carried into poetic practice. For example, the quick impressionism of Shelley's poetry, in which all is fleeting, darting, and only momentarily impressed on the attention, offers the strongest possible contrast to Keats's leisurely fingering of detail, as one finds it in the description of the sleeping figure in the ode "To Autumn," or of the wine in the "Nightingale," or, to take something very different, in the slow picturing of Hyperion's palace swinging open:

> his palace-door flew ope
> In smoothest silence, save what solemn tubes,
> Blown by the serious Zephyrs, gave of sweet
> And wandering sounds, slow-breathed melodies;
> And like a rose in vermeil tint and shape,
> In fragrance soft, and coolness to the eye,
> That inlet to severe magnificence
> Stood full blown, for the God to enter in. (lines 205–212)

These lingering descriptions, so intrinsic to Keats's poetry, surely reflect a desire to draw out the enjoyment of concrete experience, to slow it down and give it a more massive persistence. Again the stylistic habit of what he called "stationing" — of vividly bringing an image before the reader by locating it in relation to its surroundings — joins with his unusually active sensuous grasp of things to give weight, solidity, and an almost marmoreal repose to his images. So also with his pictorial and sculpturesque effects — the description of Cybele's chariot in *Endymion* (II, 641 ff.) or the figure, in the "Ode on Melancholy," of "Joy, whose hand is ever at his lips/ Bidding adieu!" The effect, however, is not of mere absence of motion, but of things poised on the brink of action, their motion briefly arrested and ready to continue. The description of Cupid and Psyche in the "Ode to Psyche" is an instance:

> They lay calm-breathing on the bedded grass;
> Their arms embraced, and their pinions too;
> Their lips touch'd not, but had not bade adieu,
> As if disjoined by soft-handed slumber,
> And ready still past kisses to outnumber. (lines 15–19)

The over-all result of Keats's characteristic imagery is to render the concrete with unusual solidity, making it seem both vital and imperishable and so holding it in what Kenneth Burke rightly calls an "eternal present."

— 6 —

Whatever permanence Keats might be expected to seek, then, would never involve a drawing away from vivid and immediate concrete experience. Instead it would offer a lasting participation in some moment of fulfillment. The desire, as Keats phrased it, would be to "annihilate" time at a pitch of intensity and "keep our souls in one eternal pant." [22] The "Bright Star" sonnet is one example of this wish expressed in poetry — "Still, still to hear her tender-taken breath,/ And so live ever" — though there is little here to suggest that the wish might become a reality. But desires felt with much strength and persistence may virtually compel one to believe that they can be satisfied. That is, if we must relinquish either an obsessive desire or a firm grip on actuality, it is not always possible to predict which will win out. The conflict, however, presents itself less sharply to romantic poets, for whom a transcendent world is always available to redeem the shortcomings of earthly existence. Hence nothing was more natural for the young Keats than to feel that desires frustrated in this world would be fulfilled in another. The world which stands beyond present life, and which, perhaps, we enter at death is one in which earthly pleasures will be immortally repeated "in a finer tone." One should add at once that this postulate, which was never more than a "speculation," as Keats would call it, was only one of the many themes weaving into the drama of his poetic expression, and that towards the end it plays a distinctly minor

22. "To J. R.," lines 6, 12.

rôle. To speak of this world Keats uses Christian terms such as "heaven," terms drawn from pagan or mythological sources such as "Elysium," and terms without much specific reference such as "paradise." In mentioning this scrambled phraseology, the point, of course, is to stress that whatever vocabulary Keats may use implies no particular pattern of religious or philosophic belief. Such terms are used simply as symbols to refer to the transcendent world and to imply that it would (or will) be a happy place.

In *Endymion* Keats seems to depict a successful movement into the transcendent world, though it is difficult to feel certain of any interpretation of this scattering of wild oats. The point to be stressed, however, is that the escape is not accomplished, as with Shelley, or, in a different way, with Wordsworth, by shrinking from the world of human experience. Instead, one must abandon visionary mountings and seek happiness on earth. Until the end of the poem, however, Endymion does not turn to the concrete. He has "within his stedfast aim" a love frankly directed to an immortal goddess. In his desire to achieve a permanent state of aroused experiencing, he is seeking to bypass concrete intensities ("I can see/ Naught earthly worth my compassing"). Throughout Keats's poetry, such an effort rarely succeeds. Endymion is only gathered to "Immortal bliss" in his union with Cynthia after he has accepted an earthly love. He feels that his dream meetings with Cynthia have been illusory:

> I have clung
> To nothing, lov'd a nothing, nothing seen
> Or felt but a great dream!   (IV, 636–638)

Consequently he renounces Cynthia in favor of the Indian Maiden.

There never liv'd a mortal man, who bent
His appetite beyond his natural sphere,
But starv'd and died
         . . . One human kiss!
One sign of real breath.   (IV, 646–648, 664–665)

And he runs on in the same vein, ending up with "no more of dreaming." But the Indian Maid turns out to be Cynthia in disguise. In other words, the "endless heaven" can be won only by turning to the breathing world.[23]

As our discussion has implied, what Keats conceived as an ideal — an endless sharing in some concrete fulfillment — was not simply an arbitrary projection of his own wishes without any basis in experience. Instead, we may regard it as the lengthened shadow of a common psychological reaction — a reaction which helps to explain why Keats insisted so strongly that one can become "free of space" only by turning to the concrete. For at the apex of intense experience one is often conscious only of what is being experienced, and the moment seems not immortal or everlasting, perhaps, but timeless. Thus a paradox is involved. The desire is to get outside of time, but ultimately the only satisfaction of this desire which is at all possible derives from the momentary sense of timelessness arising during intense experience in time. Keats's poetry presents frequent examples of the kind of reaction I have been trying to describe abstractly. Though I shall have to anticipate a bit, it might be helpful to cite one of them here in order to clarify the point. In the "Ode on Melancholy" the poet urges that "when the Melancholy fit shall fall" one should "go not to Lethe." Instead,

Then glut thy sorrow on a morning rose,
Or on the rainbow of the salt sand-wave,

23. I am indebted here to Douglas Bush, *Mythology and the Romantic Tradition in English Poetry* (Cambridge, Mass., 1937), pp. 93–95.

Or on the wealth of globed peonies;
Or if thy mistress some rich anger shows,
Emprison her soft hand, and let her rave,
And feed deep, deep upon her peerless eyes.

Here everything experienced — the morning rose, salt sand-wave, and the anger of the mistress — is by nature short-lived or evanescent. The act of experiencing, however, is prolonged. The poet would not sip but glut, and the phrase "deep, deep" lengthens out the feeding. The lines thus express a paradox: the brevity of the objects themselves, but an experience so massive and intense that it seems long enduring, and potentially almost timeless. The paradox is resolved, in other words, by the nature of experience itself, in which the experiencing imagination is able to cooperate with its object. The resolution need not, for that reason, be wholly subjective. There is no real attempt here to dodge the claims of time, or recast the facts of existence in some more arbitrarily ideal fashion. All that is happening, in this slowing of numbered moments, is that creative habits, developed in the light of other experience and retaining the acknowledgment of it within them, have come into a harmonious union with what is being experienced, supplementing only by prolonging, and prolonging only for the imagination and only because the experience is massive. At this point, where "all disagreeables evaporate," the union is satisfying to human demands while remaining honest to the interests of what exists outside them.

❦ VIII ❦

KEATS

The Uncertainties of Vision

Our understanding of the psychology of art probably received its greatest single step forward in the romantic study of the imagination. Realizing this, we are sometimes tempted to minimize one side of the romantic interest in the imagination which we rightly feel used to be loosely overstressed — that is, its interest in what we may call the "visionary" imagination as something that either supplements our empirical understanding or even takes precedence over it. This is natural enough. Like Keats himself, in his later poetry and letters, it is not easy for us to take visions seriously or to find much solace in them. In this positivistic age most people would feel that the romantics put their best foot forward when they were thinking of the fluid, imaginative use of the immediate and concrete. But the hope reposed in the "visionary" imagination is still an important aspect of English romanticism, at least to the extent that we are concerned primarily with their poetic accomplishment. Of course, the fact that this hope sometimes seems to loom larger than empirical experience does not mean that the romantic poet of "vision" was deliberately willing, more than anyone else, to fly in the face of "truth." From his own point of view, he naturally regarded the act of imaginative vision as far from a mere projecting of human wishes. It was conceived as a revelation of what would actually exist, either unapparent to the senses, or at some place beyond the concrete world, or at some future time. If he rejected these alternatives, he might still find protection in the notion that what the imagination envisioned came into some "real" being in virtue of the fact that it had been envisioned; that the imagination is a power which transcendentally creates or helps to create "truth" — "whether it existed before or not," in Keats's phrase.

In the chapters on Shelley, the poetry of vision was described mainly by referring to the way it handles symbols, though the technical procedure rests upon a particular nexus of belief which appears in its most emphatic form in Blake. Man, in Blake's view, stands between two worlds which he calls "Nature" and "Eternity." "Nature" includes whatever can be known by the senses, whereas the imagination penetrates and lives in "Eternity." Because it deals with events experienced in our day-to-day world, the poetry of Wordsworth, according to Blake, proceeds from "memory," and for that reason he would assign it a lesser value. The true artist dwells in his imagination and hence in "Eternity," and his work is but a copying of what he sees there. A very similar scheme of things might be discovered in Shelley. With Wordsworth, of course, one would have to make substantial alterations to the doctrine before it could be applied. When one comes to Keats, however, the situation is confused. At times he sounds much like Blake, as when in *Endymion* (II, 438) he says that the poet "presents immortal bowers to mortal sense," or in "I Stood Tip-Toe" (lines 185–191) that having "burst our mortal bars" and gone "into some wond'rous region," the poet returns "bringing/ Shapes from the invisible world." At other times he more modestly implies that the poet "guesses at Heaven" rather than winging into it. And again he sometimes seems to hold a still more sober view: that poetry does not deal with "Presences," to use Yeats's word, plucked or copied from "Eternity," but rather with symbols drawn from the poet's own life and personality. "Almost any Man," he writes, "may like the Spider spin from his own inwards his own airy Citadel," and he goes on to speak of the "fine Webb . . . full of Symbols" which a man may "weave" and through which he may express his "Soul." [1]

But despite gestures in the direction of Blake, Keats's trust in vision was never very secure. As a result, he writes less a poetry of vision than a poetry about the human need and use of it. Hence his verse is obviously capable of development into drama in a way that Shelley's is not. Like any other drama, that of the human desire for vision must, of course, start by feeling the attraction of opposite points of view, each of which can be shared. Drama does not begin to give credit to the complexity of life, or even to hold much interest (as Aristotle saw when he mentioned the need for a "flaw" in the character of the tragic protagonist) if sympathies are from the start entirely on one side. This commonplace applies directly to the appeal of Keats. Especially in his youthful verse, there is a hope, sometimes strong, though frequently wavering, that the heart's desires can in some way be satisfied through vision. So the poem "Fancy" begins with the injunction that man should "ever let" his "fancy roam" — should attempt to live, that is, in the visionary imagination — since, in the world of process, all fulfillment decays and even the enjoyment of it cloys. But even in this relatively early poem, the confidence in vision seems more a graceful pose than an earnest faith. The tripping meter and tumbling presentation of detail suggest a *jeu d'esprit* in

1. *Letters,* I, 231–232.

which the injunction to live in vision is advanced without much conviction. For Keats's overall approach to the visionary imagination is beset by doubts and hesitations. Can man derive any genuine satisfaction from what he envisions? And if he seeks to do so, is he in fact embracing a reality caught by the imagination, or an illusion projected from his own desires? To jump ahead to the distinction Keats makes in *The Fall of Hyperion,* the question is whether the visionary is a "dreamer" or a "poet" — whether, indeed, "Beauty is truth." On the whole, as has long been recognized, Keats's poetry dramatizes an increasingly negative answer to these questions. Indeed, the over-all course of his development might be partly described as a periodic, though gradually cumulative, loss of confidence in the merely visionary imagination.

— 2 —

Nevertheless, the early poetry often implies a faith that in picturing a world conformable to the desire for endless and intense experience, the imagination is reliable or even anticipatory in its constructions. A remark frequently cited in this connection occurs in a letter of 1817: "The Imagination may be compared to Adam's dream — he awoke and found it truth." [2] The statement may serve to remind us that the most frequent example of the kind of intensity one would wish to render permanent, though it is by no means the only example, is sexual experience, and one can think of *Endymion,* "The Eve of St. Agnes," "La Belle Dame Sans Merci," "Bright Star," *Lamia,* and, among the odes, "Psyche," the "Grecian Urn" and "Melancholy" which at least touch the theme. In *Endymion,* "The Eve of St. Agnes," and, with a different mood, in *Lamia,* the sexual union is prefigured in

2. *Letters,* I, 185.

the mind of one of the partners by a dream. In the earlier poems, the dream represents the vivid imaginative conception of the desired state, and the union authenticates the dream, showing that it was not an illusion. Hence, in presenting the situation dramatically, there is a tendency not to separate the visionary conception from the waking experience, but to permit them to melt into each other. An almost comic instance occurs when Endymion, feeling himself "endued/ With power to dream deliciously," seeks a "mossy bed" where he can enjoy his dream, and, "stretching his indolent arms," suddenly finds himself clasping, "O bliss!/ A naked waist" (II, 707–713). So, in another episode, he "beheld awake his very dream" (IV, 436). Again in "The Eve of St. Agnes" Madeline is in a confused state between dream and waking while Porphyro woos her, and she awakens to find that the dream was also a reality.

In Keats's poetry the visionary imagination, the paradise it conceives, and the poetry which embodies this conception are all associated together; for a work of art — the Grecian urn is the most obvious example — mirrors the visionary intuition of the artist. Because of the uncertainties clustered about the visionary imagination, Keats's poems often become reflections about art or poetry, critical exercises in which a young poet meditates his task, seeking to resolve perplexities and find a path for his talent. Among the great odes three especially question what sort of art a poet can or should create — "to Psyche," "on a Grecian Urn," and "to a Nightingale." The question primarily resolves itself into a measuring of what one would like to believe against what it is possible to believe. The poet would like to maintain that "Beauty is truth," and thus to render legitimate a purely visionary art, but he is less than sure. Or he would wish to sing like the nightingale, and singing to "fade far away," but it turns out that this cannot be done. Hence each of these odes contain moments of ambiguous phrasing which reflect doubts in Keats's own mind. Within the ambiguity there are, of course, differences in emphasis, but this does not suggest Keats making up his mind in a step-by-step, chronological way. Even if one could list the poems in precise order of composition, the time involved is so short — probably no longer than six weeks — that one must suppose a ferment of conflicting attitudes toward the central themes. Each poem, while mirroring the conflicts, is also the expression of a slightly different mood, and the mood or attitude involved is itself biased by the symbol adopted. Hence there is no compelling reason for discussing these odes in any particular order.

We can, however, start with the "Ode to Psyche" which was the first written and which approaches the claims of the visionary imagination with a relative hopefulness and optimism. Keats had referred to the myth of Cupid and Psyche in "I Stood Tip-Toe" — "Their woes gone by and both to heaven upflown." Psyche was a mortal maiden loved by Cupid. After many vicissitudes the lovers were united, and Psyche was made immortal. In Keats's poetry there are a number of such couplings of mortal and immortal lovers. Cynthia and Endymion, the elfin lady and the knight of "La Belle Dame Sans Merci," Lamia and Lycius, are the primary examples, but there are also minor episodes of this type in *Endymion*. It is easy to see, in a general way, why these pairings are symbolically appropriate to the preoccupation Keats explores in his poetry. In the "Pleasure Thermometer" Keats had spoken of love as the "chief intensity." That the love is directed to an immortal suggests the hope to go beyond time into an intensity that is timeless. Moreover, as we shall see, the immortal goddess also symbolizes the visionary imagination which permits or lures man to conceive such a state. For example in *Endymion* Cynthia, or the moon, represents many things and among them poetry creating its "mazy world/ Of silvery enchantment" (I, 460–461). Within the machinery of the "Ode to Psyche," to assert as an undoubted fact that in some way and in some realm of experience one has seen the "winged" or deified Psyche would seem to be a way of saying that such a desire can be fulfilled. But this premise at once becomes qualified when one considers that, as a mythological figure, Psyche herself may be regarded as only an imaginary creation, and the first stanza of the poem may imply simply that the poet can successfully envision a life which corresponds to his wishes. But this by itself is significant; for one of the main liabilities of the Grecian urn as a symbol is that it does not even permit the poet to envision such a "happy" world. In this connection it is important to notice that in contrast to *Endymion* the "Ode to Psyche" does not depict the lover in the act of escaping from the human world of time and process. Psyche is already a "Goddess" or "vision," and the problem is whether to regard the vision as something illusory or real, whether or not to offer belief and worship, and further whether if trusted the visionary imagination can itself offer a substantial happiness.

"Surely I dreamt to-day," the poet says, "or did I see/ The winged Psyche with awaken'd eyes?" The question poses what is probably the central perplexity in each of the three odes — "Was it a vision, or a waking dream?" In Keats's later poetry up to *The Fall of Hyperion* the verb "to dream" can suggest either a valid or an illusory process of imagination, but in this context it seems to imply something merely fanciful or even false. And then there is the ambiguity surrounding the phrase "awaken'd eyes." Does it imply wakeful-

ness rather than sleep and dreams, referring to sensory perception, to what Blake called the "vegetable eye," and so
going as far as possible to express a literal trust in vision?
Or does it rather imply eyes especially "awaken'd" beyond
the usual power of mortal sight? The vision itself was seen
"on the sudden" as the speaker "wander'd in a forest." This
sudden jump into a visionary realm contrasts strongly with
the much more gradual approach in the odes "on a Grecian
Urn" and "to a Nightingale" where the poet crosses into
"faery lands" only by means of a continuing sympathetic
absorption in a concrete object. In other words, in the
"Grecian Urn" and "Nightingale" the visionary realm becomes available only through special stimuli, whereas in
the "Ode to Psyche" it seems to be much closer to the day-to-
day world and the poet is liable to slip into it at any moment.

As in the "Ode on a Grecian Urn," the vision is of figures
from the Arcadian golden-age of classical mythology. The
poet saw Psyche and Cupid lying together in a bower:

> 'Mid hush'd, cool-rooted flowers, fragrant-eyed,
>   Blue, silver-white, and budded Tyrian,
> They lay calm-breathing on the bedded grass;
>   Their arms embraced, and their pinions too;
>   Their lips touch'd not, but had not bade adieu,
>   As if disjoined by soft-handed slumber,
>   And ready still past kisses to outnumber.

The attitude of the lovers suggests the timeless intensity
desired. Whereas "breathing human passion," to quote the
"Ode on a Grecian Urn," often

> leaves a heart high-sorrowful and cloy'd,
> A burning forehead, and a parching tongue,

the love of Cupid and Psyche is uncloyed, and their almost

slumbering posture expresses a repose amid intensity contrasted with the frenetic passion of mortals. It is the attitude Keats usually attributes to lovers who have transcended the world of process. One thinks of the "Bright Star" sonnet where the poet wishes to be for ever "pillow'd" upon the breast of his love; of "La Belle Dame Sans Merci" where the lovers "slumber'd on the moss"; and of the repose of the almost sleeping lovers in *Lamia* (II, 22–25). But this repose does not involve simply the absence of motion. Instead it is kinetic. In fact it is this ready potentiality and poise that allow the union to seem permanent; for, as the Grecian urn illustrates, one can only envision immortal passion in terms of potential fulfillment.

The poet addresses Psyche as the "latest born and loveliest vision far/ Of all Olympus' faded hierarchy." The fact that Psyche "was not embodied as a goddess" until after the Augustan age, and consequently "was never worshipped or sacrificed to with any of the ancient fervour" provides the imaginative frame of the ode, the metaphoric vehicle which allows it to be written.[3] The ode, that is, posits two periods of time. The first would be the past mythological age of animistic faith, "When holy were the haunted forest boughs,/ Holy the air, the water, and the fire." There was then no question or reservation of belief but only the "altar heap'd with flowers" and the "believing lyre." But this time of "happy pieties" has passed, and in the present age of unbelief the hierarchy of Olympus is "faded" or "faint." But the poet, by his "own eyes inspir'd," can still see the faint Olympians, and because Psyche never enjoyed worship or a temple, can himself offer to build a fane or temple and to worship. He seems, then, to display a complete confidence in the process of vision through which Psyche is glimpsed,

3. *Letters,* II, 106.

and the suggestion is that as a devotee of Psyche he can himself dwell happily in a visionary world. The faith in the goddess or vision creates the state of mind which Keats habitually described as "paradise," and in picturing the "rosy sanctuary" the poet will create in his own mind, the ode now develops Keats's usual paradise symbols. The mind becomes a place where Dryads — creatures of the golden age — will "be lull'd to sleep," and, like other paradises in Keats's poetry, this will be uncloying; for "Fancy . . . breeding flowers, will never breed the same."

But if the ode expresses trust in the visionary imagination, it also necessarily implies a particular direction for poetic endeavor. In other words, the poet presenting himself as a worshipper of Psyche is also making a statement about the kind of poetry he will write. Moreover, he has promised to be a "choir" singing hymns to the goddess, and the ode he writes, itself a hymn to Psyche, is a direct example. This is particularly true of the last stanza. He not only promises to build a "rosy sanctuary," but in the richly imaginative ornament he actually does so, at least in the medium of poetry. For the last stanza, with its "wreath'd trellis," its flowers, its "buds, and bells" duplicates the bowery atmosphere with which the poem began. In the scheme of the ode, however, the first stanza describes something external to the poet and envisioned by him, whereas the final stanza describes a subjective creation. The premise, then, is that the poet can recreate the visionary world in his own mind and in the medium of poetry.

At the same time, a different movement has been working throughout the last stanza, gathering and intensifying ambiguities present throughout the ode. The doubts suggested by the question "Surely I dreamt to-day, or did I see" have already been mentioned. There is also the word "fond" in the "fond believing lyre." It seems to hover between "affectionate" and the older meaning of "foolish" or "doting," suggesting a tenderness wishful and possibly indulgent. Again in the last stanza a reservation may be implied when Psyche is promised "all soft delight/ That shadowy thought can win"; for with Keats delight is more usually associated with particular, concrete experience than with what thought — particularly "shadowy thought" — alone can give. Similarly the stars that Fancy supplies are "without a name." This may imply merely that they will be stars other than those we know, or it may more ominously suggest that these stars lack concrete identity, just as with the Grecian urn the poet asks "What men or gods are these" and gets — and expects — no answer. One should also note that the paradise will hold all that "the gardener Fancy e'er could feign," and the word "feign" recalls the partial disillusion at the close of the "Ode to a Nightingale": "Adieu! the fancy cannot cheat so well/ As she is fam'd to do, deceiving elf." But most of all one wonders about the frank recognition that the visionary poet must work subjectively, that because the poet worships Psyche in an unbelieving world, the worship must be private. It can exist only in the mind, and even in "some untrodden region" of the mind, a place set apart and secluded where other processes of cognition will not intrude. In other words, the visionary and the mortal worlds cannot be known simultaneously or in juxtaposition, and, like Madeline withdrawing to dream in her chamber, the poet must protectively isolate the vision in order to enjoy it. To the extent that he consecrates his own mind as a "shrine" to Psyche he retreats from confronting "the agonies, the strife/ Of human hearts." The very clear recognition of this which the ode expresses later became one reason for rejecting an openly visionary poetry. In the ode itself, however, these implications seem to be more than acknowledged; they are welcomed, and the poet expresses a firm resolve to protect his vision from the withering touch of actuality.

— 3 —

In his few theoretical statements about the imagination, Keats seems to distinguish between at least two kinds of imaginative response. One, indicating his affinities with Blake and Shelley, would involve the capacity of the imagination to conceive a form of life independent of the limitations of actual earthly existence. But at the same time, one cannot forget that the larger emphasis in his letters is on the need for a sympathetic or empathic response, and that a strong empathic grip is indeed one of the distinctive characteristics of his poetry. Through the process of empathy, the imagination comes to the concrete world and experiences it, if the empathic sharing is sufficiently strong, with an aroused intensity and gusto. Through the process of vision, on the other hand, the imagination compensates for the frustrations inherent in earthly existence. What might be required, then, in any approximate realization of the intense, timeless experiencing Keats posited as an ideal, would be the simultaneous working of both sympathetic and visionary processes in a single response. Hence in the "Ode to Psyche," the primary symbol does not go all the way in offering the sort of experience desired. Throughout the poem Psyche remains more a concept than a concrete presence. As a result, the symbol becomes wishful, an assertion of what the poet would desire rather than a means of imaginatively taking hold of it, and hence there is not the same passionate arousal and commitment that one finds in the "Ode on a Grecian Urn" or "Ode to a Nightingale." The fact that "all is cold Beauty" seems to me to be a weakness of "to Psyche," though only by comparison with the immense achievement of the other two odes.

One can make the point another way by briefly describing what seems to be the usual process of vision as Keats presents it. The point is that the odes "on a Grecian Urn" and "to a Nightingale" dramatize this process, whereas "to Psyche" does not. There is, then, an initial response to some beautiful object or event. This response is sensuous and sympathetic in character, and the sheer intensity of it brings about a trance or semi-trance (the "drowsy numbness" of the "Ode to a Nightingale"). In this state of mind, when the "dull brain" no longer "retards," the visionary power becomes active, moving into scenes suggested by the object. In the "Ode to a Nightingale" the stanza dealing with wine provides a miniature example. Because the "draught of vintage" offers both sensuous pleasure and intoxication, to drink it releases the imagination. Hence the description is not simply of the wine itself, but of the "country green,/ Dance, and Provençal song, and sunburnt mirth" associated with it. In other words, the object still serves as a stimulus, but less to the senses than to something else which, it is hoped, intuits the essential character of the object in a more satisfying and penetrating way. Thus in the "Ode on a Grecian Urn" there is the reflection that "heard melodies are sweet" and then the larger claim for the imagination in that "those unheard/ Are sweeter"; and in the "Ode to a Nightingale" there is the parallel statement — "I cannot see what flowers are at my feet" — and then the revelation that with the imagination one can "guess" or intuit them just as well or better. A progress into the visionary world takes place in the "Ode on a Grecian Urn" where the poet's imagination moves from the original stimulus, the urn seen as a totality, to the "legend" or "brede" carved on the urn and finally into a close focus upon particular scenes in the "legend" which seem for the moment almost to be living. The "Ode to a Nightingale" follows a similar course: the imagination, aroused by the song, moves toward visionary glimpses such as the "Queen-Moon" on her "throne," the flowery retreat, or the "magic casements" in "faery lands." Again, in the ode "To Autumn" something very similar takes place. In the first stanza there is the strongly empathic and sensuous description followed in the second stanza by an allegorizing or personifying of autumn which corresponds, at least in some ways, to a vision. But the visionary flights always come to an end, and they are followed by a return upon the object *qua* object, now stripped of its visionary nimbus. There is, in other words, a waking out of the trance, and in that waking the nightingale is no longer thought of as an "immortal Bird" in an enchanted land, but simply as a bird flying away, and the scenes on the Grecian urn no longer seem almost living, but are recognized as "marble" carvings. Thus there is always some sadness in this return to actuality, and in it the poet meditates what took place during the visionary trance.

The essential structure, in other words, may involve the development of a symbol which at first seems to promise an immediate, felt knowledge of the state of mind desired. As one reads the poem, one then finds a dramatic movement in which the poet pursues, questions, and tests the symbol, hoping to find it adequate. The conclusion may then bring a recognition that the symbol does not completely express what the poet would wish. The cause of this recognition lies in the massive commitment which the poet brings to bear; he explores the symbol with an honesty and completeness which end in partly undermining it. One finds, in other words, a mode of poetry in which the symbol is something more than a tool of expression. With Shelley, for example, symbolism provides a way of translating the abstract into the concrete. His attitudes are already formed and simply await a vehicle for poetic expression, and, as a result, he directs attention to the symbol only so far as it can be made relevant to what he wants to say. But with Keats a poem is more likely to be a dynamic process of cognition carried on by means of symbol. At the same time, because the symbol is not so much an expressive device as a means of thinking, it becomes only one element in the poem. As the poet gradually discovers that the symbol does not suggest what he had hoped it might, he withdraws from it, or may even appear to derive implications which the symbol does not permit, as it seems to me Keats does with the Grecian urn. Or if he adheres more strictly to the symbol, he may abandon the hope which had led him to it, as in the "Ode to a Nightingale." Or he may simply state his wish in open contradiction to the symbol, as in "Bright Star."

For if the two odes are Keats's most impressive achievement in this mode of poetry, the "Bright Star" sonnet shows the typical structure or method more briefly and clearly. Throughout Keats's poetry stars often appear as a metaphor of the desired permanence. Psyche in the "Ode" is compared to "Phoebe's sapphire-region'd star,/ Or Vesper, amorous glow-worm of the sky"; for the star suggests more or less what Psyche represents. For one thing, the star is outside process and immortal — "Thou dost know of things mysterious,/ Immortal, starry," Peona says to Endymion (I, 506–507) — and at the same time stars are frequently imagined as intensely experiencing, dwelling in "one eternal pant." Thus Apollo, in *Hyperion,* says

> Point me out the way
> To any one particular beauteous star,

231

And I will flit into it with my lyre
And make its silvery splendour pant with bliss;

(III, 99–102)

and Lamia began to sing

A song of love, too sweet for earthly lyres,
While, like held breath, the stars drew in their panting fires.

(I, 299–300)

Moreover, the starry heavens are traditionally associated with order and repose. By retaining this suggestion of repose amid intensity, Keats's star symbolism parallels the dynamic and taut stasis of the lovers in the "Ode to Psyche" or the "Grecian Urn." In "The Eve of St. Agnes" Porphyro, at the crest of feeling, is lifted above process — "Beyond a mortal man impassion'd far" — and he becomes

Ethereal, flush'd, and like a throbbing star
Seen mid the sapphire heaven's deep repose.

(lines 318–319)

The "Bright Star" sonnet, then, is a closer look at a frequent symbol. In the first line the star begins to represent the state to which man aspires — "Bright star, would I were stedfast as thou art." Moreover, the star is eternal, sensuously aware ("watching"), and sleepless just as the poet would like to be. It is, however, alone and an "eremite." In this context, the patient eremite is one who does not experience human passions, having made a withdrawal for religious purposes. Hence the star watches the sea in its "priestlike task/ Of pure ablution" as it purifies "earth's human shores," or the snow which, like the sea, seems to purify or at least hide the earth. The star, in other words, is part of an order of cold, chaste, pure, and eternal things — of sea, snow, and mountains — existing in an immense sweep of space, and this order is felt to be unresponsive or even unfriendly to earthly and human qualities which it seeks to purge or conceal. In contrast to this, the sestet describes a warm, sensual, and intimate human situation. Because the star almost immediately reveals aspects or characteristics which make it inadequate as a symbol, the poet begins his withdrawal from it almost at the same time that he takes it up ("Not in lone splendour . . ."). In the drama of the poem, he discovers that his wish is not to be like the star after all, but rather to transpose the potentiality of the star for eternal awareness into the realm of human life and feeling, and that of the most intense variety. Yet it might also be argued that the contrast in the sestet is not as thoroughgoing as it may seem at first. By means of irrational and almost subliminal correspondences, feelings of religious purity associated with the star are partially carried into the sestet, modifying what might have been a wholly erotic situation.

— 4 —

In the Grecian urn Keats might seem to have found exactly the symbol he was seeking. With its "brede" or bas-relief carving, the urn could be viewed as uniting vitality and passion with the enduring repose of art, holding the intensity of sensuous life in a stillness potentially immortal. Thus the adjectives "sylvan," "flowery," and "leaf-fring'd" suggest the transitoriness of growing things. Yet they are solid on the urn. Like the sonnet "Bright Star," the ode scrutinizes what is really a habitual symbol with Keats — the symbol, in this case, of plastic, sculptural art. Special studies have been made of Keats's poetic exploitation of sculpture, and there is no need to go in detail over the same ground. In *Endymion* (I, 318–319) there is the suggestion that sculpture preserves some sort of life or vitality: the heroes of Thermopylae are "not yet dead/ But in old marbles ever beautiful." In "The Eve of St. Agnes"

> The carvèd angels, ever eager-eyed,
> Star'd, where upon their heads the cornice rests,
> With hair blown back, and wings put cross-wise on their breasts.
>
> (lines 34–36)

Here the angels are almost incorporated into the human world. Their hair is blown by the wind and they stare "ever eager-eyed" upon the scene of human revelry. Thus the carving presents a life and activity similar to that of man, but ever poised and immortal. In *Hyperion* Keats describes the Titans in terms of sculpture: Saturn and Thea "were postured motionless,/ Like natural sculpture in cathedral cavern"; Hyperion, turning to the stars, "Lifted his curvèd lids, and kept them wide" (I, 85–86, 350–351). These sculpturesque effects in *Hyperion* are far from being a casual habit of style. Instead they are entirely functional in the poem, characterizing the life of the Titans — "solemn, undisturb'd,/ Unruffled" (I, 330–331) — as contrasted with "men who die" in "the mortal world beneath."

But in the ode, the sculptured urn does not finally offer itself as a satisfactory symbol. Instead it remains teasingly silent. Of course, the implications of this silence change during the course of the poem. The urn, it is said, can express a tale, and it can speak "more sweetly" precisely because it is silent and does not embarrass or interrupt the imagination: with its "unheard" melodies it communicates "not to the sensual ear" but by simply suggesting to the aroused imagination. As the ode proceeds, however, it is recognized that the urn cannot really tell its tale at all. The poet is repeatedly compelled to ask questions — "What men or gods"; "What little town" — which the urn cannot answer. Here

Keats brilliantly pursues the implications of his symbol. Owing to the silence of the urn, all the uncertainties implied in the poem remain "mysterious," shrouded in ambiguity and enigma. One perplexity, for example, revolves about the identity of the figures on the urn. Are they "deities or mortals," are they "both," or are they rather, as the last stanza suggests, mere "marble men and maidens" — creatures having no genuine identity? If the figures on the legend can be regarded as mortals, they are also held in the repose of art, and so express the union of human passion with permanence. If, on the other hand, they are simply "marble men and maidens," "cold" figures wrought in stone, lacking vitality and identity, they become a kind of mockery; for they present permanence without the warm and living fervor man wishes to preserve.

One can phrase these questions another way. If the figures are "marble men and maidens," they are endlessly arrested and imprisoned — "Fair youth, beneath the trees, thou canst not leave/ Thy song." On the other hand, if the urn expresses an immortal intensity or fulfillment, then, considering the poised about-to-kiss of the second stanza, in some sense there must be movement in the legend. If there is no fulfillment, the urn cannot be said to disclose or symbolize what Keats would wish. The problem is not simply that the life of vision may be impossible, or that the vision itself may be an illusion. These things are, of course, debated, but the poem also probes more deeply. For art embodies man's "guesses at Heaven," and if the guess turns out to be largely a mockery of the permanence he seeks, then the imagination cannot even conceive what the poet would adopt as his heart's desire. It is not that the ideal exists only as an illusion, but that it cannot be imagined even as an illusion. Of course, the poem offers no clear-cut resolution of these questions, and we are simply exploring the range of possible implications. But within the enveloping uncertainty, the poet drifts toward a less optimistic attitude.

For as the ode begins the urn is seen to depict "mad" sexual "pursuit" and "wild ecstasy" paradoxically rendered all but immortal. Moreover, the description of the figures on the urn is ambiguous, suggesting that they may not be simply carved in marble but alive in those "immortal bowers" which the urn presents "to mortal sense," borrowing Keats's phrases from *Endymion,* and which the poet can hope to enter by contemplating the urn. The tale or "legend haunts about" the "shape" of the urn, and the verb "haunts" suggests both the elusive mystery of the legend and also a life or movement more than that of figures on an urn. Again the word "legend" conveys an ambiguity precisely appropriate to its context. It means, of course, something inscribed or stamped as on a coin, and hence would be "leaf-fring'd" or bordered with leaves. But it also refers to a mythical story which is not solidly fixed on the urn but "about" it as a nimbus or aura to be known by the imagination. In asking "What men or gods are these?" the poet may, among other speculations, be wondering to just which myth (or myths) the urn alludes, information which as a "historian" the urn presumably possesses and which the poet must obtain in order to share the life of "Tempe or the dales of Arcady." Without a definite object the empathic imagination cannot stir.

As the poet continues to contemplate the symbol, it still seems to disclose a life of immortal intensity. Yet in contrast to the quiet assertion of the first stanza, qualifications of a slightly melancholy nature seem to be suggested by the urn itself. The symbol raises questions which trouble — though not yet overtly — the poet's serene acceptance of it:

> Fair youth, beneath the trees, thou canst not leave
> Thy song, nor ever can those trees be bare;
> Bold Lover, never, never canst thou kiss,
> Though winning near the goal — yet, do not grieve;
> She cannot fade, though thou hast not thy bliss,
> For ever wilt thou love, and she be fair.   (lines 15–20)

The trees are an instance of Keats's habitual symbolism of the seasons. They would be bare at the end of autumn, and as soon as they become bare winter or death is imminent. The lover, of course, represents Keats's usual way of suggesting the intensity one wishes to enjoy forever. The object of his love cannot fade in the sense of losing her beauty and also in the sense of fading from his eye as the nightingale "fades," or as, in the "Ode to Psyche," "Olympus' hierarchy" is now "faded." The situation of the lover, then, is to be forever poised and arrested. He is "winning near the goal," but he cannot kiss. If there is no fading or death, there is also no fulfillment. Significantly the lover is not thought of as happy. Instead, he is simply urged not to grieve. In spelling it out so tediously, one loses the effect of these lines. But as they are read, one feels a balancing reflected even in the "Though . . . yet" sentence structure. It is not evident, after all, that unheard melodies are really sweeter, and the poet's attitude has become less certain than it was initially.

Previously the world of process had been implicitly contrasted with the life of the urn. Now the contrast becomes explicit:

> Ah, happy, happy boughs! that cannot shed
> Your leaves, nor ever bid the Spring adieu;
> And, happy melodist, unwearied,
> For ever piping songs for ever new;
> More happy love! more happy, happy love!
> For ever warm and still to be enjoy'd,
> For ever panting, and for ever young;

All breathing human passion far above,
That leaves a heart high-sorrowful and cloy'd,
A burning forehead, and a parching tongue.

In making this comparison, the poet also reveals that he has not been "uplifted from the world," as Keats put it in "I Stood Tip-Toe," and drawn into the carved legend or the Arcadian realms it discloses; for if there were a strong empathic participation, it would make "all disagreeables evaporate" to the point that the poet would be conscious only of the work of art or what it reveals. Instead the disagreeables are all too present. The poet does not share the happiness of the figures on the urn, but expresses the nostalgia of an outsider. The repetition of "happy," reaching a crescendo in the mere exclamatory line "More happy love! More happy, happy love!," jars a little less when it is read as this nostalgic envy and helpless retreat. But remaining, as he does, conscious of the mortal world, the poet also thinks of it largely in terms of aftermath and decay — the "heart high-sorrowful and cloy'd." In other words, he opposes the pre-fulfillment of the lover on the urn to post-fulfillment in human love, potentiality to death, spring to winter, if I may employ one of Keats's own symbols. In terms of this antithesis the boughs are "happy," but the antithesis is a false or partial one; for it neglects the fulfillment or summer possible in the world of process.

In fact, the sentimentality sometimes noted in this stanza may be the poem's own implicit comment on the falseness of the antithesis. It is the obvious sentimentality of directly assigning to things a greater value than they merit. It is an attempt to assert and defend a wish in contradiction to fact. For the poet has been pursuing the urn, as a symbol, with an ardor it cannot support, and the ardor can continue to be maintained only by what in the medium of poetry amounts to a lie. But if the ardor is still being maintained, the stanza that follows (iv) begins to right the perspective. It repeats the questions of the first with greater insistence: "Who are these coming to the sacrifice," "what green altar," "What little town." But as these questions become more urgent, the inscrutability of the urn is more clearly recognized: "thy streets for evermore/ Will silent be; and not a soul to tell." Because of this unfathomable silence, the poet can adopt no sure attitude towards his symbol. Even the lesser details of the stanza reflect the uncertainty. The priest, for example, is "mysterious" not only because his religion is a mystery, but also because the poet cannot be certain of his identity or of anything about him. Similarly, the altar is "green" or vital; but the flanks of the heifer are "silken," and the adjective perfectly reflects the ambiguity of the poem. "Silken" may picture the sheen of the living animal, or it may describe the pallor of the marble figure. It is precisely this sort of ambiguity that permits the poet to speculate about the little town. What takes place is an imaginative leap which results from thinking of the "folk" as alive and hence as having come from a town. Throughout the poem there is a confusing and melting together of scenes one feels compelled to imagine literally carved on the urn and of the pastoral world it represents and evokes to the poet. But one probably does not infer that the little town is depicted on the urn, and in speaking of it the poet openly moves into Arcady. At once there is a final fixation on the immobility of the figures. The town must "for evermore" be "silent" because the people cannot return. In other words, to think of the figures as too literally alive immediately compels an opposite recognition that there is no movement and hence no life on the urn. Thus the delicate sadness pervading the last three lines of the stanza is no mere sentimental pining over the little town. It expresses the poet's own regret that the urn presents but scenes in marble which, however beautiful, are cold, motionless, and not to be called either happy or unhappy.

The urn, however, still remains inscrutable: "Thou, silent form, dost tease us out of thought/ As doth eternity." Keats had previously used the phrase, or versions of it, in his poetry. In "To J. H. Reynolds Esq." he had written "Things cannot to the will/ Be settled, but they tease us out of thought" (lines 76–77). And the "Sonnet written in the Cottage where Burns was born" has the line "Yet can I think of thee [Burns] till thought is blind." The notion is of pursuing a question or intuition as far as one can, and yet coming to no definite view or settlement.[4] Thus the urn can appropriately be compared to "eternity" in that it is long-lived, silent, and, like the notion of eternity, not to be fully possessed by any act of mind or imagination. Instead, having gone as far as it can, thought becomes "blind" or inoperative, and the mind, having no clear conception, can be described as empty or vacant. Thus the "Hymn to Pan" in *Endymion* apostrophises Pan as

> the unimaginable lodge
> For solitary thinkings; such as dodge
> Conception to the very bourne of heaven,
> Then leave the naked brain.   (lines 293–296)

4. Of course, the line can be read in the light of Keats's common antithesis between "thought" and feeling or intuition. From this point of view, the line can be interpreted as meaning that the urn draws the poet into a full sympathetic experience of its life precisely because it does tease him out of thought. Thus Douglas Bush, *Mythology and the Romantic Tradition*, p. 107, points out the parallel to this line in the "dull brain" which "perplexes and retards" the poet in the "Ode to a Nightingale," and one might also mention that in the "Ode to Psyche" the poet saw the vision of Cupid and Psyche as he "wander'd in a forest thoughtlessly," which may mean "out of thought" and so ready for imaginative seeing. Both Earl R. Wasserman, *The Finer Tone* (Baltimore, Md., 1953), p. 52, and Cleanth Brooks in *The Well Wrought Urn*, p. 150, appear to follow Mr. Bush.

But if the urn teases "out of thought" by remaining silent to the questions asked of it, the poet has nevertheless unraveled the confusions of the first stanza. There he viewed the figures on the urn as "deities or mortals," "men or gods." He saw them as in some sense living creatures acting out a wild ecstasy, and he wished to share their life. The over-all movement of the poem has been to break down these expectations. Now, in the last stanza, the poet is incapable of reacting further to the urn and uncertain what to make of it. Within this uncertainty, however, he has an altered attitude to the urn, and a more reserved acceptance of it as a symbol. For the urn is art — a "shape," "attitude," or "form" — and not life. It is not warm with vitality, as the love was said to be forever warm, but "cold." The figures on it are not men or gods but "marble men and maidens." They do not exist in a legend but in a "brede"; and the legend does not haunt about the shape with a life of its own, but is "wrought" upon it by the hand of the artist. The urn is not a historian, a chronicler of truth or actuality, but a "Pastoral," an art form usually associated with direct and acknowledged wish-fulfillment. Finally, there is a progressive shift of emphasis through the poem from the capacity of the urn to speak to the fact of its silence.

The dramatic development traced in the ode might also have been described as a meditation on the use of art. It is especially from this point of view that one feels a conflict unresolved in the poem. The poet clearly wishes to make a statement similar to what one finds in the early verse. The urn is a "shape of beauty" of the sort Keats had mentioned at the beginning of *Endymion*. With its marble permanence it should be a "joy for ever," still keeping a "bower . . . Full of sweet dreams." It is analogous to the type of "eternal book" described in "Sleep and Poetry" from which man may

> copy many a lovely saying
> About the leaves, and flowers — about the playing
> Of nymphs in woods, and fountains.   (lines 65–67)

As such, it should offer an escape, dispelling "the pall/ From our dark spirits" (*Endymion*, I, 12–13), and permitting the spectator to enter and dwell happily in the world it depicts. But in the ode even if the urn does mirror a life of immortal intensity (which is doubtful at best), the poet has not been able to share it. Instead the overall movement of the ode has split the poet from that life. He can only stand on the outside and comment. So that if at the end of the ode Keats inserts a critical notion similar to his more youthful speculations, he does so without entire support from the immediate experience with a work of art. Of course, by an act of ventriloquism he has the statement that "Beauty is truth" come from the urn itself,[5] but it is still he who draws the inference, and the inference is, in effect, that imaginative constructions are valid glimpses of truth, and hence that the poet can commit himself to the visionary imagination. The unwillingness to relinquish the doctrine is significant, but so also is the inability to illustrate it when the attempt is made. At the time he wrote the great odes Keats was brooding a transfer of poetic intention, and the failure of a removed and pastoral art to live up to the claims made for it would presumably be one element leading to the shift, or at least a symptom of it.

— 5 —

In rhyme-pattern and the structure of the stanza, Keats's odes were an experimental development from the sonnet, as

5. One of the main sources of disagreement about the ode has been the question: who is speaking to whom in the last line and a half? I follow Douglas Bush, in his forthcoming edition of Keats, in believing that the whole of the last two lines should be enclosed in quotes.

both Mr. Garrod and Mr. Bate have shown.[6] It is tempting to extend the implication to other aspects of form less clear-cut and more general than versification. The fact that the sonnet, as Wordsworth said, provided only a "scanty plot of ground," meant that its subject had to be limited. Thus it encouraged concentration on a single dramatic situation, or on an object of a circumscribed, relatively definite character. Keats's sonnets are themselves examples: "On first looking into Chapman's Homer," "On the Grasshopper and Cricket," "To Homer," "On the Sea," "On sitting down to read King Lear once again." To mention the titles is to mark that they relate to specific events or circumstances. On the other hand, as distinct from the shorter odes of such writers as Akenside or Collins, the "greater ode," as either the true or false Pindaric was called in the eighteenth century, had for a century and a half revealed the disadvantages of "too much liberty," to borrow once again a phrase from Wordsworth. It had tended to be a ruminative, discursive, often declamatory expression of an exalted theme. The somewhat roving organization many of these odes display results from a very general subject matter which provides neither a starting point or a boundary. Wordsworth's majestic "Intimations of Immortality" can be viewed as the natural descendant and the culmination of the genre, and in it he puts, or attempts to put, virtually all that he had to say.

But Wordsworth could do this with considerable success. To this extent, he was aided by the relatively limited character of his preoccupations; the necessary exclusion was already present when he came to writing the poem. He could be direct and even hortatory because he was stabilized by

6. H. W. Garrod, *Keats* (London, 1926), pp. 85–90; W. J. Bate, *The Stylistic Development of Keats* (New York, 1945), pp. 126–132.

doctrine. Had Keats, however, possessing the skeptical, open, exploratory, and speculative turn of mind D. G. James describes so well — "to let the mind be a thoroughfare for all thoughts," and "not a select party" [7] — attempted a similar kind of lyric, one imagines that it would have expanded until it completely lacked shape. Or rather, it would not have been written at all; for Keats's critical tact was too fine to make such an attempt. The problem, then, is how, with such a temperament, to achieve a spacious lyric expression. It is resolved in the "Ode on a Grecian Urn" and "Ode to a Nightingale," as in many of the sonnets, by focusing on a particular object and staying with it — in other words, by use of a central symbol. If this is something of a technical innovation within the genre of the ode (though at times Shelley does a rather similar thing), it is, like most such innovations, accomplished not for the sake of mere novelty, but as a means of surmounting a personal dilemma. But the symbol does not dissolve the uncertainty, the openness to many points of view, which made necessary the resort to it. Instead it merely permits the lyric to be written by providing a field within which contrary attitudes may engage and seek a resolution.

Although the "Ode to a Nightingale" ranges more widely than the "Ode on a Grecian Urn," the poem can also be regarded as the exploration or testing out of a symbol, and compared with the urn as a symbol, the nightingale would seem to have both limitations and advantages. The advantage of the urn is that it does convey the notion of experience immortally prolonged, but it does not readily allow the poet to enter and share the life it portrays. He has to stand on the outside as a spectator. The nightingale, however, has a living identity and sings to the senses, thus allowing a mas-

7. *Letters*, II, 213.

sive sympathetic response. The liability is that unlike the urn the song of the nightingale does not suggest something potentially eternal. It is true that in his ardor the poet momentarily makes it immortal, but he does so at the cost of destroying any sympathetic union with it, and, in the logic of the poem, virtually compels it to fly away. Hence the same sympathetic grip that makes the experience vivid to the point that one would wish to prolong it, also forces the recognition that it must be short-lived.

The dramatic development that takes place in the ode lies partly in the gradual transformation of a living nightingale into a symbol of visionary art. By means of the symbol the ode explores the consequences of a commitment to vision, and as it does so, comes close to implying that the destruction of the protagonist is one of the results. In the verse previous to the odes, Keats had occasionally associated creative activity — whether visionary or not — with death. There is nothing surprising in this. Many artists have expressed themselves in a similar way; notions of withdrawal and self-immolation are all too readily suggested by creative enterprise. The distinction is partly that Keats makes poetry of the theme, and partly that he gives it an individual bias. In "Sleep and Poetry" there is the representative remark that in "the o'erwhelming sweets" of poetry he might "die a death/ Of luxury" (lines 58–59), and in a passage from *Endymion* which clearly anticipates the "Ode to a Nightingale," the shepherds were

> Such as sat listening round Apollo's pipe,
> When the great deity, for earth too ripe,
> Let his divinity o'erflowing die
> In music.   (I, 141–144)

Here Apollo reveals his divinity by letting it die. Similarly, the nightingale "pouring forth" its "soul abroad" is both declaring its identity or "soul" and dying. But, of course, the nightingale is not thought to be literally dying. The point is that the deity or the nightingale can sing without dying. But as the ode makes clear, man cannot, or, at least, not in a visionary way.

For Keats progressively tended to connect death with purely visionary excursions — in other words, with fantasy and dreams. We noted that the visionary flight usually begins with a partial loss of consciousness. In the more objective, narrative structure of *Lamia* and *The Fall of Hyperion* the equivalent to this "drowsy numbness" would be the "cloudy swoon" which overcomes both Lycius and the poet in *The Fall of Hyperion*. Thus when Lycius first meets Lamia he believes that she is about to "fade" and beseeches her to stay, saying "Even as thou vanishest so shall I die" (I, 260). But as Lamia still threatens to depart, Lycius swoons. Similarly, in *The Fall of Hyperion* the poet drinks of a "transparent juice" which is compared to poison and causes him to lose consciousness:

> No poison gender'd in close monkish cell,
> To thin the scarlet conclave of old men,
> Could so have rapt unwilling life away. (I, 49–51)

In both these poems, then, the swoon which precedes visionary activity is presented as a kind of death, and in *Lamia* it later leads to the actual death of Lycius. In *The Fall of Hyperion* the poet, having entered realms of fantasy, would also have died had he not been able to go through or beyond them by mounting the altar steps and confronting the tragic countenance of Moneta. In the "Ode to a Nightingale" a similar development takes place. It begins with the poet in a state of "drowsy numbness" which, he says, is as though he had taken poison (hemlock) and were dying ("Lethe-wards had sunk"). The further movement of the poet into the nightingale's world also involves a steady movement toward death and a momentary acceptance of it. Then at the beginning of the seventh stanza the nightingale stands revealed for what it is, or rather for what the poet, using it as a symbol, has made of it. No longer a part of the natural world, it is an "immortal Bird" living in a visionary realm. It is almost analogous to La Belle Dame Sans Merci or Lamia luring men to fantasy and death. But, of course, the attitude to the nightingale is quite different from that adopted to Lamia. Keats seems to feel the attraction of what both Lamia and the nightingale represent much more strongly in the ode, and as a result the conflict is not resolved to the extent that it is in the later poem. Or perhaps one should simply say that a different symbol would compel a different attitude.

As the poem opens, the poet hears the nightingale and participates in its life. The happiness he shares is so intense that for the poet it becomes the paradoxically "aching pleasure" of the "Ode on Melancholy," a pleasure felt as pain ("My heart aches, and a drowsy numbness/ Pains . . ."). But at the same time, this suspense or obliteration of conscious, waking faculties releases the imagination,[8] which is already turning upon the nightingale and seeing it as something more (or less) than a bird. It is a Dryad from the Arcadian world, like the "moss-lain Dryads" of the "Ode to Psyche." Its happiness is reiterated, recalling both the "happy, happy boughs" of the urn and also Psyche, the

8. One can here recall that, in the "Ode on Indolence," the "Masque-like figures" of Love, Ambition, and Poesy come to wake the poet from a numbing trance:

> The blissful cloud of summer-indolence
> Benumb'd my eyes; my pulse grew less and less;
> Pain had no sting, and pleasure's wreath no flower.

The three figures summon the poet to enterprise in the human world, but they are dismissed, and partly because the trance is favorable to visionary activity: "Farewell! I yet have visions for the night,/ And for the day faint visions there is store."

"happy, happy dove." And although the time is mid-May, the nightingale sings of summer, the time of fulfillment. But the nightingale, now singing from a "plot/ Of beechen green," is going to "fade away into the forest dim," and the poet wishes to fade with it. Of this desire the appeal to wine is the first symbolic expression. It is a necessary gesture because the poet in his numbness can scarcely respond to the song, and also because without a further drugging the song is not an unmingled pleasure.

Like many of Keats's finest passages, the description of the "draught of vintage" magnificently condenses a metaphor recurrent throughout his career. In "To Charles Cowden Clarke" wine is metaphorically linked with poetry:

> Because my wine was of too poor a savour
> For one whose palate gladdens in the flavour
> Of sparkling Helicon,   (lines 25–27)

he has never "penn'd a line" to Clarke, and in a prose passage he compared the "pleasures of Song" to "cups of old wine." [9] Near the beginning of *Endymion*, "All lovely tales that we have heard or read" are

> An endless fountain of immortal drink,
> Pouring unto us from the heaven's brink. (lines 23–24)

In *Endymion* (III, 801), Keats speaks of "a pure wine/ Of happiness," and wine is frequently associated with the ascent to what Keats termed "heaven." It makes man a Hermes, Keats said,[10] and in *Hyperion* Apollo cries that he is deified

> as if some blithe wine
> Or bright elixir peerless I had drunk,
> And so become immortal.   (III, 118–120)

9. *Poetical Works and Other Writings*, ed. H. Buxton Forman (New York, 1938–1939), V, 292.
10. *Letters*, II, 64.

And in *Lamia* wine has "every soul from human trammels freed" (II, 210). Thus wine was at one time or another explicitly linked with poetry, with imagination, with happiness, with "heaven," in short with all that the nightingale represents. Moreover, in the second stanza, wine resembles the nightingale in being associated with summer, happiness and song — "Provençal song and sun-burnt mirth." Like the "immortal Bird," the wine comes from a "long age," and the reiteration of the word "full," the fullness of the beaker, suggests a desire for an intense, glutted experiencing similar to the poet's deep reaction to the song of the nightingale.

But the impulse to leave the world leads inevitably to a recollection of actual human life. Mortal existence, as the poet thinks of it, has a distorted and ghastly resemblance to his own state of mind in the first stanza. As he hears the nightingale's song, so "men sit and hear each other groan." The poet has been drowsy as though drugged; men are weary. He has been glutted or "too happy" with the song of the nightingale; men are "full of sorrow." [11] In human life "Beauty cannot keep her lustrous eyes,/ Or new Love pine at them beyond to-morrow." There can be no actual prolonging either of what is beautiful in itself or of an intense response to it. Furthermore, except in moments of escape, life inevitably involves pain, for "but to think" (which I take as meaning to be fully conscious rather than in the numbed state favorable to visions) "is to be full of sorrow." At this point, then, the poet is firmly planted in the world of process — "Here." But his wish is still to "fade far away, dissolve, and quite forget," to enter a visionary world of immortal, unmingled bliss, and the wish seems to be reinforced by his recollection of "the weariness, the fever, and

11. Wasserman, *The Finer Tone*, p. 208, points out the contrasts between stanzas two and three.

249

LIBRARY ST. MARY'S COLLEGE

the fret" of mortal experience. For the fourth stanza opens by reiterating the will to escape with greater urgency and emotional force — "Away! away! for I will fly to thee." The vehicle of the flight is now no longer wine ("Not charioted by Bacchus and his pards") but Poesy, and in this context Poesy means visionary poetry, or one might even call it fantasy.

Supposing himself to be with the nightingale ("Already with thee!") and associating it with the forest and with darkness, the poet now thinks of a verdurous bower and luxuriously describes it. Like the earlier stanza about wine, the extended imagery of flowers represents a momentary release achieved through the imagination, and, indeed, the capability of the imagination is dramatized in the poetry. In the darkness the poet cannot see the flowers, but precisely for that reason he can see and describe them all the better. The song-haunted darkness stimulates the imagination to "guess each sweet." And the statement that the poet "cannot see . . . what soft incense hangs upon the boughs" is, of course, a typical example of Keats's use of synesthesia, but it is more than that: it is a vivid assertion of the power of the imagination to see more than the sensory eye can see. It converts the incense into something virtually solid so that, as one reads the line, it presents what is very close to a visual image.

One can repeat all this by referring to the overall metaphoric pattern on which the poem is constructed. The Provençal world suggested by the wine comes as an early anticipation of the realm into which one would wish to retreat. The continuing vehicle of escape is the song of the nightingale; for, as the poet in his trance contemplates the nightingale, he sees it withdrawing further and further from the human world. In stanzas iv through vi, through most of which the poet feels himself to be with the nightingale, the movement is not yet completed, and, as the poem proceeds, the nightingale finally crosses into a realm where the poet cannot follow. But there is a momentary union, and in it the poet, standing in the forest, is able, like the nightingale, to sing of summer even though the time of year is only mid-May. For process is actively taking place within the forest. The violets are "fast fading" and are being replaced by the "coming musk-rose," and as the poet, conscious of the process, thinks of the musk-rose, his imagination leaps ahead to the time of fulfillment and completion when the musk-rose will be "the murmurous haunt of flies on summer eves." Here, of course, under the spell of the nightingale and by means of the imagery of flowers, the poet is able to contemplate process with a serenity anticipating the ode "To Autumn," but as "To Autumn" makes clear, a strong commitment to process leads to the thought of death and even permits one to acquiesce in it. In this connection, one should note that the darkness is described as "embalmèd." The primary sense of the word in this context is "perfumed," but there is also the suggestion of death, as though to be in the forest were a scented, hushed burial.

Throughout the poem darkness has been gathering about the poet as he moves into the nightingale world — "there is no light"; "I cannot see"; "embalmèd darkness." Now the poet remains in the dark, still hearing the song of the nightingale:

> Darkling I listen; and, for many a time
> I have been half in love with easeful Death,
> Call'd him soft names in many a musèd rhyme,
> To take into the air my quiet breath.

Keats repeatedly used "easeful Death" as an escape symbol. Thus in *Endymion* after listing the ills of life, the hero says that they have "in themselves" a "good": they make us feel "How quiet death is" (II, 159). One might also cite the sonnet, "After dark vapours," where the poet speaks of a moment of release after the oppression of a "long dreary season" of bad weather. At such a time "calmest thoughts come round us," and the sestet goes on to list some of these in a series of images. The progression moves from images of hushed natural process — "Fruit ripening in stillness" — to a hypnotic sense of time running out and comes to an end with "a Poet's death."

But the release Keats meditated in death was not always conceived as merely quiet and easeful. It can also be "rich to die" in that the poet, groping for a symbol of fulfillment or intensity, thinks of death as a positive experience. The sonnet "Why did I laugh" even anticipates the phrasing of the ode as it concludes:

> Yet would I on this very midnight cease,
>   And the world's gaudy ensigns see in shreds;
> Verse, Fame, and Beauty are intense indeed,
>   But Death intenser — Death is Life's high meed.

So, in a loose moment, Keats wrote Fanny Brawne, "I have two luxuries to brood over in my walks, your Loveliness and the hour of my death." [12] Nor is it difficult to see how, for Keats, death becomes associated with fulfillment. In the first place, a massive intensity (as Keats envisages this impossible state) turn finally into oblivion — or at least into a suspended animation not unlike death. So Clymene, for example, describes for the assembled Titans in *Hyperion* the music of Apollo:

> my sense was fill'd
> With that new blissful golden melody.

12. *Letters*, II, 133.

A living death was in each gush of sounds.

(II, 279–281)

Secondly, in the world of process, fulfillment and death are often simultaneous. This perception receives a specifically sexual expression at the end of the "Bright Star" sonnet. Keats apparently had trouble with the last lines,

> Still, still to hear her tender-taken breath,
> And so live ever — or else swoon to death,

and it is difficult to know how they should be read. They might imply no more than a hyperbole which could be paraphrased, "If I can't have this forever, let me die before it fades." Or the phrase "swoon to death" might specifically refer to a sexual climax which would end the passionate, "sweet unrest." But especially if one takes account of the last line of the original version — "Half-passionless, and so swoon on to death"— the notion would also seem to be that experience so intense must end in numbness and death.

Throughout the ode the poet has been steadily relinquishing a grip on actuality until now, under the influence of the song, it has become possible to assert that death would be a climactic release and outpouring desirable in itself and the more desirable because it would bar a return to the human world "Where Beauty cannot keep her lustrous eyes":

> Now more than ever seems it rich to die,
> To cease upon the midnight with no pain,
> While thou are pouring forth thy soul abroad
> In such an ecstasy!

But if death represents a form of escape more final and complete than wine or Poesy, it does not suggest a further union with the nightingale, or a prolongation of hearing its song:

Still wouldst thou sing, and I have ears in vain—
To thy high requiem become a sod.

"Land and Sea, weakness and decline," Keats once wrote, "are great separators, but death is the great divorcer for ever." [13] The final lines of the stanza represent the speaker's sudden recollection of this fact and a return to actuality compelled by recognizing the direction in which he has been moving.

By the end of the sixth stanza, then, the human and nightingale worlds have been entirely sundered. At once the poet turns directly to the nightingale in a passionate apostrophe: "Thou wast not born for death." To the objection so often raised, that this particular bird will die, one can only reply that in its distance from the poet the nightingale has now been openly transformed into symbol. Indeed, the poem now largely parallels the last stanza of the "Ode on a Grecian Urn." Like the urn, which is compared to eternity, the bird is immortal, and its life is contrasted with the "passing night" or brief generations of man. Here, of course, Keats employs a brilliant poetic tact to justify the symbolic assertion. By referring only to the voice of the nightingale, he can identify it with all nightingales and so find a natural basis for claiming that, like the urn, it has remained "in midst of other woe/ Than ours, a friend to man." It has been heard by all men — "emperor and clown" (or rustic) — and "perhaps" its song "found a path/ Through the sad heart of Ruth."

But throughout the seventh stanza the nightingale, even as a symbol, continues to move farther away from the human world. It is heard first by "emperor and clown," figures presumably out of the historical past, then by Ruth

13. *Letters*, II, 345.

in a world of Biblical legend, and finally it is heard in "faery lands," and these faery lands may be the faery lands or "elfin grot" of "La Belle Dame Sans Merci" — a place which may represent a destructive illusion. The faery lands are "forlorn" because man cannot live in them. For the same reason the song of the nightingale is no longer happy. Instead it is a "requiem" or "plaintive anthem." And as the poet awakens from his trance, there is even the suggestion that the visions stimulated by the song of the nightingale may have been illusory; for the poet, bidding farewell to the vision, says

> Adieu! the fancy cannot cheat so well
> As she is fam'd to do, deceiving elf.

Finally, one may note that it is not the bird that "fades" but its song, and this does not happen until the poet has been tolled back to his "sole self." Thus if the departure represents the flight of a living bird, it is also presented as the fading of a vision. Moreover, the song does not merely fade. With a final, ironic reflection upon the theme of death, it is described as "buried," as if to imply the denial of any possibility of hearing it. And the poem ends with uncertainty and a question: was the process that has taken place a momentary glimpse of truth (a "vision"), or a musing subjective half-dream; and is the poet's inability to experience it now an awakening into reality or a lapse into insensibility:

> Was it a vision, or a waking dream?
> Fled is that music: — Do I wake or sleep?

The question is one that has haunted poetry ever since the romantic age, and poets, writing their own versions of Keats's great ode, have often used virtually an identical symbol. In Hardy's "Darkling Thrush," which employs direct verbal echoes of the "Ode on a Nightingale," the bird sings in a bleak, wintery scene, and the speaker, finding no cause for "carolings/ Of such ecstatic sound" in any visible object, is able to think that the thrush possesses some special insight denied to him:

> I could think there trembled through
> His happy good-night air
> Some blessed Hope, whereof he knew
> And I was unaware.[14]

With Robert Frost the romantic appeal is still felt, but he exploits the symbol to make an anti-romantic gesture. In "Come In" the speaker stands at dusk at "the edge of the wood." He hears the song of the thrush "far in the pillared dark" of the forest, and the thrush resembles Keats's nightingale singing of summer:

> The last of the light of the sun
> That had died in the west
> Still lived for one song more
> In a thrush's breast.

Like the song of the nightingale, the call of the thrush is felt "almost" as a lure "to come in/ To the dark and lament." But in the last stanza the speaker deliberately rejects the temptation, and, with a tough-minded naturalism, goes on to recognize that the thrush is not actually singing to him at all:

> But no, I was out for stars:
> I would not come in.
> I meant not even if asked,
> And I hadn't been.[15]

14. Thomas Hardy, *Collected Poems* (New York: The Macmillan Company, 1953), p. 137.

15. Robert Frost, *Complete Poems, 1949* (New York: Henry Holt and Company, Inc., 1949), p. 446.

And one might also mention Eliot's *Four Quartets,* where the thrush leads into the momentary happiness of the garden, and where the poet asks, "Shall we follow/ The deception of the thrush?" [16] To do so, he remarks, would take us "into our first world," and adapting the phrase to a different purpose, one might suggest that for much in contemporary poetry the "first world" is that of the great romantics, who, eager as they were to follow the thrush, also recognized that it might be but a deception.

16. T. S. Eliot, *The Complete Poems and Plays* (New York: Harcourt Brace and Company, 1952), p. 118.

❧ IX ❧

KEATS

The Affirmation of Process

If the great odes of April–May, 1819, spring from doubt and self-division, the uncertainty was continued through the next three months, but with a changing attitude. In Keats's early poems the visionary is often pictured as a heroic figure. On several occasions Keats presents him as a type of mariner, a common romantic symbolism which Keats develops in a personal and distinctive way. For instead of voyaging over the sea, the figure which corresponds in Keats to the romantic mariner may remain standing on the shore and merely look seaward. The stance suggests, of course, a desire to see beyond the "bourne" of earth into a truth transcending the immediate experience of process. Endymion, for example, says

> I can see
> Naught earthly worth my compassing; so stand
> Upon a misty, jutting head of land.　　　(II, 161–163)

But the stance also implies an inability, entirely characteristic of Keats, to leave the earth behind in an unreserved commitment to vision. Yet only the visionary dares even to look out to sea. One remembers the magnificent picture of Cortez, in the sonnet "On first looking into Chapman's Homer,"

> when with eagle eyes
> He star'd at the Pacific — and all his men
> Look'd at each other with a wild surmise —
> Silent, upon a peak in Darien.

Here, like Tennyson's Ulysses or Melville's Captain Ahab, Cortez is sharply distinguished from his followers. While the other men look at each other, as if seeking reassurance and security, he stares at the sea. "To J. H. Reynolds Esq.," closes with a powerful image of the danger of vision, although the danger here arises — and this is not characteristic of Keats — from the fact that the vision itself is morbid. It destroys human happiness by disclosing naturalistic struggle as the root principle of life. Keats pictures himself standing on the shore of the sea:

> [I] should have been most happy, — but I saw
> Too far into the sea, where every maw
> The greater on the less feeds evermore. —
> But I saw too distinct into the core
> Of an eternal fierce destruction.   (lines 93–97)

But as doubts about the visionary imagination began to accumulate, the visionary himself became less heroic. This changing attitude may possibly be reflected in the revision of "La Belle Dame Sans Merci" which converted the heroic "knight at arms" into a "wretched wight." At least, the poem expresses some hesitation about the life of vision. In speaking of "La Belle Dame" at this point, I am, of course, violating the order in which Keats's poems were composed, and it is significant that this ballad of uncertainty was written at approximately the same time as the more assured "Ode to Psyche." It suggests that if the major poems of this five or six months, the odes, "La Belle Dame," the revised *Hyperion,* and *Lamia,* involve a gradually shifting attitude to a central perplexity, the change was not step by step.

Poets, like other people, seldom achieve a firm commitment without many lapses and a rather eddying progression. Accordingly one can discuss "La Belle Dame" in connection with *Lamia* and so highlight parallels in theme and symbol. The union of the knight with La Belle Dame is one of Keats's many mortal-immortal pairings, and, as in *Lamia*, questions about the visionary imagination are posed in the equivocal character of the lady. The usual interpretation has been that La Belle Dame is a Circe, cruelly leading men to their destruction. Lately, however, it has been argued that, since there is no indication that she wilfully banished the knight from her "elfin grot," the union of the lovers is broken by the knight's own inability to retain the vision.[1] But the fact is that either interpretation may be maintained, or rather that the poem brings together both points of view as it mirrors a conflict in Keats's own mind.

The first three stanzas serve as an introduction, defining the tone of the poem and establishing the situation. It is a ballad with medieval trappings, but unlike the ballads of Scott, for example, it is an openly visionary poem. One feels that the action takes place not so much in some historical period as in a timeless realm of imagination. The speaker meets a knight at arms who is "haggard," "woe-begone," and even seems to be dying:

> I see a lilly on thy brow,
>> With anguish moist and fever dew;
> And on thy cheeks a fading rose
>> Fast withereth too.

He asks "what can ail" the knight, and the question expresses the naive character of the speaker, puzzled at the

1. Wasserman, *The Finer Tone*, pp. 74–77. Despite the disagreement here with the general tendency of his interpretation, I am indebted for numerous suggestions to Mr. Wasserman's searching discussion of the poem.

deathly appearance of the knight and assuming that in the approach of winter he ought not to be "palely loitering." And, of course, the naiveté helps to create the overtly simple, fairy-tale atmosphere of the ballad. The questions also serve as description, and the time of year has a loose metaphoric significance. Not only summer but autumn, the fulfillment of the summer, is now over. Only winter and death remain. The poem then goes on to resolve these questions. The pallor of the knight turns out to be that of the "pale kings," the "pale warriors, death-pale" he sees in his dream, and he is loitering on "the cold hill's side" in a vain wish to meet again the lady and re-enter her elfin grot.

After this introduction, the knight begins his tale. He "met a lady in the meads." She was an immortal, a "faery's child." He wooed her with flowers, and she him with song. She had all his attention so that he "nothing else saw all day long," thus indicating his entire and whole-souled commitment to a life of vision. And the lady, in turn, "look'd" at the knight "as she did love,/ And made sweet moan" — "as," of course, meaning "as if," implying the impossibility of being sure of anything about this strange being from other world. Again, no more than the knight can the reader feel secure in interpreting the sweet moan which the lady made. It may be similar to the "delicious moan" of the "virgin-choir" in the "Ode to Psyche," a song merely expressing her love, or it may also be a moan of sadness, implying, as the phrase "sighed deep" two stanzas later may imply, the lady's own recognition that their union must be short-lived. The lady, says the knight,

> found me roots of relish sweet,
> And honey wild, and manna dew,
> And sure in language strange she said —
> 'I love thee true.'

The food here recalls the "manna and dates" which Porphyro offers to Madeline in "The Eve of St. Agnes," but without going into nuances of symbolic implication suggested by this association, one need only point out that roots, honey, and manna might be appropriate for a "faery's child," but they would not provide much nourishment to a knight at arms. The lady's intentions may be loving, but the food she offers makes clear a radical difference in the character of the two lovers. The poem then suggests the consummation of their union in the elfin grot. The slumber of the mortal-immortal lovers at this point — "and there I shut her wild wild eyes/ With kisses four"; "And there she lulled me asleep" — represents the security and the paradoxical repose amid intensity Keats envisioned as an ideal.

To this point in the poem, everything has implied that the love affair cannot go on for very long, but there has been little reason to question that the lady's love is genuine. Even after having awakened upon "the cold hill's side," the knight does not deny that she loved him. He remarks that "she said — / 'I love thee true,'" and seems to believe it. But she said it in "language strange," so neither the reader nor the knight can really be sure about anything but the strangeness of the language. That is indeed the point. The lady is a "faery's child." One simply cannot be positive about her nature, for humanity cannot establish any certain contact with her. Yet even with this reservation in mind, the knight's account of the dream he had after being lulled asleep still remains puzzling.

> I saw pale kings, and princes too,
>   Pale warriors, death-pale were they all;
> They cried — 'La belle Dame sans Merci
>   Thee hath in thrall!'

I saw their starved lips in the gloam,
    With horrid warning gaped wide,
And I awoke and found me here,
    On the cold hill's side.

Whatever one makes of this dream, two things, at least, are reasonably certain. It breaks up the union of the lovers and the knight regrets it — "Ah woe betide!" Secondly, it has its pernicious effect by picturing the desolation which will come with the knight's return to actuality. Indeed, the warning might be no more than that man cannot hold visionary experience for very long, and that when he awakens he becomes starved for lack of it. What is puzzling, however, is that the warning seems to be about the character of the lady, that she is sinister, cruel, without pity or mercy, and the poem has scarcely prepared the reader for this interpretation. These "pale warriors" are exact equivalents of the pale "knight at arms." The phrase "starved lips" certainly suggests that they too have been with the lady in her elfin grot, and are in that "second circle of sad Hell" of the "pale" lovers described in Keats's sonnet "On a Dream," written the same month as "La Belle Dame." The very fact that there are many with starved lips suggests the victims of a Circe. We may also remember that, in *Endymion,* Glaucus is caught by the "cruel enchantress," Circe, in "a net" of "thraldom" (III, 427). The attitude toward La Belle Dame then, seems to shift during the course of the poem, so that at the end one is tempted to infer that the knight has been deliberately seduced and then banished to the cold hillside to die. But the inference does not necessarily follow; and the poem is not only uncertain but a poem about uncertainty.

— 2 —

In *Lamia* an analogous story also resulted in ambiguity. Lycius, of course, resembles the knight as he is briefly drawn

263

into an affair with a "lady elf" or demon, and if Keats describes his plight with sympathy, he can also make use of Apollonius to voice a withering contempt. As in "La Belle Dame Sans Merci," the attitude to Lamia seems to shift through the course of the poem, revealing an irresolution in Keats himself. But as compared with the odes, at least, both "La Belle Dame" and *Lamia* embody a more settled state of mind. The doubt concerns only what attitude to take in exposing the visionary imagination. The escape it offers may be sweet but impossible to possess for very long. Or, as in *Lamia*, the condemnation may be sterner in character, emphasizing that the vision deceives. The lover of vision may be only the innocent victim of his own quest for happiness, or he may be a fool as well. In any case, he is certain to become a "wretched wight." We may remember what Endymion comes to acknowledge:

> There never liv'd a mortal man, who bent
> His appetite beyond his natural sphere,
> But starv'd and died.   (IV, 646–648)

The very opening of *Lamia* is in marked contrast with the "Ode on a Grecian Urn" and the "Ode to a Nightingale." In these two odes, as in so much of Keats's earlier poetry, the desire or interest had been to bring together human life and the Greek pastoral or visionary world. Now, however, in the opening of *Lamia*, the over-all effect is to distinguish sharply between them. For the poem begins with a pretty love affair between the god Hermes and a nymph. There are elements, in this little prefatory idyl, that suggest the sort of ideal union represented or symbolized by the recurrent pairs of lovers in Keats's earlier poems. The difference is that now the whole affair is relegated to a nonhuman realm. With it, to some extent, is also relegated the issue that was a central concern in so much of Keats's earlier

264

poetry: the hope of waking from a dream to find it actual. There is almost the suggestion that this awaking to find it truth, this authenticating of the visionary imagination, takes place only in the realm of myth, where dream and actuality are interchangeable. So Hermes, desiring to find the nymph, at last sees her —

> It was no dream; or say a dream it was,
> Real are the dreams of Gods, and smoothly pass
> Their pleasures in a long immortal dream.   (I, 126–128)

Indeed, the significance of this episode, as Mr. Wasserman has said, is that the human world does not in any way participate in it.[2] By implication, the affair between Hermes and the nymph suggests the impossibility of any such fulfillment in the human world of process and mortality. This prefatory episode can have little purpose otherwise. It has no necessary, organic connection with the story that follows. In a rather artificial way, it is used to introduce the main story. But it is then dismissed.

We can only assume that this half-playful, slightly mocking idyl is to highlight, by contrast, the principal narrative. And the narrative that follows, whatever else can be said of it, is an exploration of the nature of illusion, and of the effect of disillusion on the human imagination. Significantly, none of the principal characters is a thoroughly desirable type. Lamia, the immortal serpent-woman, is no stable embodiment of the ideal: she is a shifting, evanescent thing, liable to vanish before the cold light of reason. Lycius, her mortal lover, is far from Shakespearean, to say the least; he has little to characterize him except an extraordinary capacity for wish-fulfillment, a desire to retreat with his vision, and a lack of flexibility. And the third principal

2. *The Finer Tone,* pp. 159–162.

character, Lycius' old tutor, Apollonius, whose sharp-eyed gaze penetrates to Lamia's true identity, makes her vanish by doing so, and thus indirectly kills his equally humorless pupil, has, aside from a certain dignity, only negative virtues to recommend him. He is free from illusions — at least of the visionary sort. But there is nothing positive; and he is almost as far as Lycius from approaching the ideal of the "mighty and miserable Poet of the human Heart," of which Keats spoke shortly before beginning *Lamia*. There is, however, this difference. Whatever Apollonius represents cannot be disregarded. It must in some way be faced and subsumed.

Lamia is not quite of the same order as the god Hermes. But she is able to take on some of the same properties; and similarities are suggested. The god is described in terms of astronomical or heavenly images — "star of Lethe" or "bright planet" — and possesses a "serpent rod." Lamia is equally associated with astronomical images — for example, her "silver moons," "mooned body's grace," "stars," and "starry crown." The fact that Hermes and Lamia can each grant the love aspirations of the other suggests another similarity. But Lamia desires a mortal. She thus becomes a revised model of a familiar symbol — the immortal lady whose sexual union with a mortal symbolizes the human yearning to retain forever the apex of passionate intensity. She is La Belle Dame Sans Merci, the "faery's child," and so is described as a "lady elf," as having "elfin blood," and as lingering "faerily" by the roadside. The moon imagery links her with Cynthia. But she is also a serpent, which is to say that Cynthia has now become a serpent. In view of the many Miltonic echoes scattered through the poem, we may feel that, as a serpent, Lamia even suggests Satan.[3] At least,

3. Cf. the phrase "serpent prison-house" (line 203) with Keats's marginalia in *Paradise Lost* (IX, 179–191): "Satan having enter'd the Serpent, and

the Lamia theme may have attracted Keats because the serpent would be associated, however unconsciously, with temptation. Also Lamia is a "cruel lady" (though kind to the woodland nymph) with a "Circean head," and the reference to Circe suggests that she lures and seduces men to their own destruction.

But at least in the first part of the poem, she is described in a tone tinged with mockery. Hermes, for example, addresses her as a "beauteous wreath" and the periphrasis certainly shades into satire. The poet describes her as a grotesquerie:

> Striped like a Zebra, freckled like a pard,
> Eyed like a peacock, and all crimson barr'd. (I, 49–50)

The quick, college-cheer movement of the verse, the incongruity of the menagerie, and the kaleidoscope of color all define an attitude toward her. Moreover, her array of patterns and colors, "golden, green, and blue," shifts, flickers, and dazzles as she breathes, and together with her overlavish collection of other ornament her "silver moons" and her "crest . . . Sprinkled with stars," it does not seem to be a highly tasteful display. She reminds one of a burlesque dancer. These wonders are topped by the bizarre absurdity of the mingling of woman and serpent.

> Her head was serpent, but ah, bitter-sweet!
> She had a woman's mouth with all its pearls complete.
>
> (I, 59–60)

This is not far from caricature if one tries to visualize it; and the mocking humor is delicately enforced by calling attention to the "complete" set of "pearls" or teeth in her

---

inform'd his brutal sense — might seem sufficient — but Milton goes on . . . whose head is not dizzy at the possible speculations of Satan in the serpent prison?" *Works,* V, 305.

mouth. On the whole, this tone is maintained throughout the first half of the poem. Significantly, Keats, in opposition to his earlier antipathy to the style of Dryden and Pope, is now taking Dryden as a model. The gusto of Dryden, and his gift for ridicule, are caught up here, and they accentuate the ironic detachment. At the outset, then, the poet pictures Lamia as altogether mixed with contrarieties, and her ultimate attractions as highly ambiguous.

In her "serpent prison-house" Lamia was able to dream "of all she list," and "once, while among mortals dreaming thus,/ She saw the young Corinthian Lycius." She "fell into a swooning love of him," and wants to make her dream a reality. Having adopted a woman's form, she is now "a maid/ More beautiful" than any human maiden. She is paradoxically

> A virgin purest lipp'd, yet in the lore
> Of love deep learned to the red heart's core:
> Not one hour old, yet of sciential brain
> To unperplex bliss from its neighbour pain.   (I, 189–192)

She seems to offer, that is, an escape from process to a pure bliss, unmingled with sorrow. Having stationed herself by the road side, she calls to Lycius as he walks by, and he turns to her, at once seized with wonder and passion:

> For so delicious were the words she sung,
> It seem'd he had lov'd them a whole summer long:
> And soon his eyes had drunk her beauty up,
> Leaving no drop in the bewildering cup.   (I, 249–252)

Here are the familiar symbols, song, summer, and wine, so frequently associated, as in the "Ode to a Nightingale," with the movement into the world of vision. In this case, of course, the "bewildering cup" of Lamia's beauty merely suggests the wine symbolism. Lycius recognizes her as a "goddess" or immortal. The situation now begins to repeat the established pattern. Lycius fears that instead of his becoming united with the vision it will fade from his human eyes, and begs Lamia to stay:

> For pity do not this sad heart belie —
> Even as thou vanishest so shall I die.   (I, 259–260)

But Lamia, "growing coy," reminds him that immortals cannot live in the human world "where no joy is, — Empty of immortality and bliss." And when she pretends to say farewell, Lycius, like the "pale warriors" of "La Belle Dame Sans Merci," turns pale and swoons away. This fit of oblivion, of course, represents the death Lycius prophesied if Lamia should vanish. So far the encounter has pursued the course of "La Belle Dame Sans Merci."

The difference is that Lamia has been "coy." The "cruel lady" now

> Put her new lips to his, and gave afresh
> The life she had so tangled in her mesh. (I, 294–295)

Lycius thus revived, Lamia "threw the goddess off," and declared herself to be a mortal lady dwelling in Corinth. It might seem that at this point Lycius has died out of process into an immortal bliss. Similarly, the goddess has put off immortality to become a woman. But one recalls the serpentine nature of Lamia and the delicate mockery with which she is described. Moreover, Lycius is not an immortal about to fade into the "green-recessed woods." Instead, he has only swooned; and he will shortly return to Corinth. Similarly, Lamia has put on only the shape and appearance of a woman, but her nature remains untransmuted. She retains her magical powers, and by a spell reduces the distance to Corinth to a few paces.

In other words, the union of Lamia and Lycius is not an actual experience of what is desired. Only in the subjective imagination of Lycius does the situation seem to enact the ideal permanence, just as the love of Hermes and the nymph exists only in the pastoral world, the age-old repository of human wish-fulfillment. When Lycius and Lamia come to Corinth, they take for their dwelling a house where "none but feet divine/ Could e'er have touched." Like the "unheard" melodies of the "Ode on a Grecian Urn," this house represents a withdrawal into purely imaginative activity; for it is known only by Lycius. Other human beings cannot see it, and when subsequently the wedding guests arrive, they

> enter'd marveling: for they knew the street,
> Remember'd it from childhood all complete
> Without a gap, yet ne'er before had seen
> That royal porch, that high-built fair demense.
>
> (II, 152–155)

As a mortal, Lysius must live in Corinth. He cannot escape to the Cretan Elysium where Hermes found his nymph. But he can live in Corinth wholly engaged with his own fantasies and without sharing the life around him, and that is what he does. In short, Lycius is a "dreamer," to borrow the vocabulary of *The Fall of Hyperion*, seeking to become thoughtless or unaware in the fond haven on an unreal paradise, and the poem explores the consequences of such a life. Now as long as the dream is at least partially recognized as only a dream, and in the privacy of the imagination cherished and protected from the intrusion of fact or truth, it can be maintained and enjoyed. As soon as actual human life is vividly represented, it exposes the falsehood of the dream and destroys it. At first, Lycius seems to half-realize that he is indulging a dream. As he enters Corinth with Lamia he endeavors not to be seen — "Muffling his face, of greeting friends in fear." In particular, he fears the sharp eyes of Apollonius. Even to look at Apollonius as he comes near makes Lycius uneasy; for "he seems/ The ghost of folly haunting my sweet dreams."

The character of Apollonius, the philosopher, has probably provoked most of the critical disagreement about the poem. A traditional view was that he represents science or "consequitive reasoning" dispelling imagination, and the passage beginning "Do not all charms fly/ At the mere touch of cold philosophy?" can be cited:

> Philosophy will clip an Angel's wings,
> Conquer all mysteries by rule and line,
> Empty the haunted air, and gnomed mine —
> Unweave a rainbow, as it erewhile made
> The tender-person'd Lamia melt into a shade.
>
> (I, 234–238)

But to interpret the poem in these terms is to make the unwarranted assumption that, if a poem contains a passage of abstract statement, this passage necessarily summarizes the poem. The same notion has vitiated much criticism of the "Ode on a Grecian Urn," in which the poem has been tortured to make it reveal how or in what sense the urn demonstrates that "Beauty is truth." More recently, critics have pointed out that, however harsh and crabbed Apollonius may be, he is not for that reason the villain of the poem, for Lycius himself is illuded and a dreamer. Both these interpretations are helpful but incomplete. The important point is that within the poem Apollonius is penetrating and Lycius deceived. Lamia is, after all, a serpent, and however loving she may be, she still preys on him, as Apollonius says, by absorbing him to the point that he is incapable of any wider concern. Hers is a frightened, selfish love that would keep its object from growing up in order to continue to possess it. And one might add that from the start Lycius has no chance against this "Virgin . . . in the lore/ Of love deep learned to the red heart's core." We know from the letters that Keats was increasingly tending to equate philosophy with truth at the expense of poetry:

> Though a quarrel in the Streets is a thing to be hated, the energies displayed in it are fine . . . This is the very thing in which consists poetry; and if so it is not so fine a thing as philosophy — For the same reason that an eagle is not so fine a thing as a truth.[4]

Again, at the very time he was writing *Lamia*, he said in another letter: "I am convinced more and more every day that (excepting the human friend Philosopher) a fine writer is the most genuine Being in the World."[5] But *Lamia* does not contrast the philosopher with the poet; it contrasts him only with the visionary poet or dreamer.

Apollonius, then, represents a clear though perhaps a single-eyed view of reality. In fact, symbolism of eyes is important in the poem. The vision of Lycius is filled and intoxicated by Lamia:

> his eyes had drunk her beauty up,
> Leaving no drop in the bewildering cup,
> And still the cup was full.   (I, 251–253)

Lycius is "blinded" (I, 347), or looks solely into Lamia's "open eyes,/ Where he was mirror'd small in paradise" (II, 46–47). "Ah, Goddess, see/ Whether my eyes can ever turn from thee," he says (I, 257–258). Her existence increasingly depends on the complete subjective commitment of his eyes to her, which also permits him to see himself mirrored. Only when at the feast he takes his eyes from Lamia to look at Apollonius does Lamia begin to vanish; for at this point, as we shall see, only Apollonius, of all the people at the

4. *Letters*, II, 80–81.
5. *Letters*, II, 139.

feast, remains fixed in the realities of mortal existence, refusing to enter or share the dream:

> By her glad Lycius sitting, in chief place,
> Scarce saw in all the room another face,
> Till, checking his love trance, a cup he took
> Full brimm'd, and opposite sent forth a look (II, 239–242)

to his old teacher. In contrast to Lycius, Apollonius has
"sharp eyes," or "quick eyes" or "eyes severe" (I, 364, 374; II,
157). To the dreamer they are "juggling eyes," or "demon
eyes" to be threatened with "blindness," for they banish the
dream with their unilluded gaze:

> the sophist's eye,
> Like a sharp spear, went through her utterly,
> Keen, cruel, perceant, stinging.   (II, 299–301)

It is true that Apollonius appears as a character of sour
disposition. Of course, one could argue that, if he is now
harsh to the dreamer, he had previously been a "trusty
guide/ And good instructor" to Lycius. Moreover, he is seen,
to some extent, through the dreamer's eye. But if he is
crabbed, that is also partly the attitude of the poem to what
he represents. The dreams are sweet, but they are still
folly, and however unpleasant, Apollonius' is the completely
unilluded perception. To quote from *Hyperion*, he to some
extent represents "the pain of truth, to whom 'tis pain."
Keats is posing an unhappy dilemma, but it is not the core
of the poem. Instead, the poem is largely about the consequences of being a dreamer.

The second part of the poem begins with a "doubtful"
conundrum. In keeping with the attitude to reality reflected
in the poem, the actual passion of mortals is "love in a hut,
with water and a crust." The love of "faery land" is "love
in a palace." Neither is satisfactory, but "perhaps at last"

the love of faery land is "More grievous torment than a
hermit's fast" (II, 1–5). The poem then presents Lamia and
Lycius enjoying their bliss. The time is summer and they
lie upon a couch, reposing

> Where use had made it sweet, with eyelids closed,
> Saving a tythe which love still open kept,
> That they might see each other while they almost slept.
>
> (II, 23–25)

This, of course, is the familiar slumberous repose of Keats's
mortal-immortal lovers. But Lycius hears the sound of trum-
pets, which carries his thoughts out of this "purple lined
palace" and "into the noisy world almost forsworn." Lamia,
"ever watchful,"

> Saw this with pain, so arguing a want
> Of something more, more than her empery
> Of joys.   (II, 35–37)

Having recollected the varied life of the human world,
Lycius begins to find the dream insufficiently satisfying by
itself. Inevitably, he wishes to convert the dream to an
actuality in his human life, where Apollonius walks. To
translate this into the symbolism of the poem, he and
Lamia have been living in "sweet sin," but he now wants
to marry her and to have her take a place beside him in
his mortal life, together with other companions and interests.
As this desire reveals, he has begun to confuse the dream
with reality. Up to now, he has not asked Lamia her name,
"ever thinking thee," as he says, "Not mortal, but of heavenly
progeny,/ As still I do." But he now treats her as a mortal
woman, brow-beating her, and asking whether she has "any
mortal name" or any "kinfolk." The questions are similar to
the questions addressed to the Grecian urn — "What men
or gods are these" — and bespeak the same state of mind; for,
as I mentioned, the poet, as the "Ode on a Grecian Urn"

begins, has confused "marble men and maidens" with "deities or mortals," and the initial confusion of imaginative vision with earthly reality tends, at the end, to make for a sharper distinction between them. In *Lamia*, however, Keats reaches further. By confusing dream and reality, the dreamer, who is to have an unhappy end, brings them together. Confronted with actuality, the dream is inevitably dispelled. By contrast with the heart's illusion, reality appears meager and crabbed. Meanwhile, the dreamer, having lived so long with his illusion, has become incapable of dwelling in the actual human world. He cannot bear mortal life as it really is, and crumples at the impact.

It is unnecessary to trace the further development of the poem in detail. Lycius decides on a wedding feast to which he will invite his fellow Corinthians. At the feast, things seem at first to go well. With the "wine at flow," the garlands, and the music of powerful instruments — all habitually associated with the paradise that is now viewed as an illusion — the guests seem to enter or share Lycius' state of mind. "Every soul" is "from human trammels freed," and Lamia appears "no more so strange." Only Apollonius remains surely fixed in human realities; but he is enough. When Lycius looks at him, as we have seen, the illusion begins to dissolve under the steady, withering eye of the philosopher. Finally it is destroyed, and Lycius dies.

Of course, Keats's early poetry had often depicted a similar situation. After his first dream-union with Cynthia, Endymion awakens into the life of process and is sore dissatisfied with it:

> all the pleasant hues
> Of heaven and earth had faded: deepest shades
> Were deepest dungeons; heaths and sunny glades
> Were full of pestilent light.   (I, 691–694)

Also, shortly after Endymion decides that he has been deluded, has "lov'd a nothing, nothing seen/ Or felt but a great dream" (IV, 637–638), he senses that he is going to die:

> Why, I have been a butterfly, a lord
> Of flowers, garlands, love-knots, silly posies,
> Groves, meadows, melodies, and arbour roses;
> My kingdom's at its death, and just it is
> That I should die with it.   (IV, 937–941)

Numerous similar instances might be cited. For example, in the early epistle "To My Brother George," Keats had written:

> Yet further off, are dimly seen their bowers,
> Of which, no mortal eye can reach the flowers;
> And 'tis right just, for well Apollo knows
> 'Twould make the Poet quarrel with the rose. (lines 43–46)

But if the conclusion of *Lamia* recalls these earlier passages, it does so in a sterner mood. The poet is no longer willing to "quarrel with the rose" for the sake of visionary bowers. We may also recollect that in *The Fall of Hyperion,* where Keats projects himself directly as the protagonist, he almost dies on the steps because he has been a dreamer. In a sense, *Lamia* may be regarded as Keats's version of Wordsworth's

> farewell the heart that lives alone,
> Housed in a dream, at distance from the kind!
> Such happiness, whatever it be known,
> Is to be pitied, for 'tis surely blind.[6]

— 3 —

The Fall of Hyperion shows the conflict of attitudes in Keats's mind more nakedly than any other of the poems he

6. "Elegiac Stanzas, suggested by a Picture of Peele Castle," lines 53–56.

wrote during this five or six months. There is the suspicion
that he has been a dreamer, the assertion that he ought not
to be, and the fear that poetry may inevitably involve illusion and make-believe. There is the notion that the poet
has special powers of vision beyond those of other men, and
the contrary premise that all men have visions like the poet.
There is the assumption that the poet stands apart from the
typical life of man, and the wish to see him as a humanitarian
actively engaged in promoting human welfare. Finally, there
is the desire to find some "haven," and the conviction that
it cannot be found, especially by the poet. Of course, *The
Fall of Hyperion* does not simply pose these questions: it
attempts to resolve them, but in doing so it partially abandons
an indirect, symbolic approach and proceeds more by statement and didactic assertion. The result is unfortunate. One
can scarcely hope to lead a forward march of argument until
a mass of contrary sympathies has been ordered, disciplined,
and purged. In *The Fall of Hyperion,* the ferment in Keats's
mind produced as much confusion as complexity.

Keats's intention nevertheless remains tolerably clear. At
the beginning of the dream the speaker pictures himself
in a visionary bower, surrounded by flowers. In it there are
"trees of every clime" and the produce of different seasons —
roses and grapes; for the imagination can enjoy these "all
together." "On a mound/ Of moss" he sees "a feast of summer
fruits," a paradisal banquet which "seem'd refuse of a meal/
By angel tasted or our Mother Eve" (I, 28–31). An "appetite,/
More yearning than on Earth" he "ever felt/ Growing
within," the poet "ate deliciously" (I, 38–40). In view of the
general subject matter of the poem, it is easy to infer that
this bower represents Keats's own early poetry, or the state
of mind which he felt it reflected. Having glutted himself,
the poet becomes thirsty, and drinks from a "cool vessel of

transparent juice" which stands nearby. Before drinking, he pledges "all the mortals of the world,/ And all the dead whose names are in our lips"; for the draught will take him out of the bower into a fuller experience of human life, though this will itself be represented as a vision, and both the strong sensuous response and the swoon are, as we noticed, usual preludes to visionary experience. He struggles "hard against/ The domineering potion," but falls asleep and awakens in a temple. It was, of course, inevitable that the poet should drink. The feeding or enjoyment of the bower creates the thirst. But in drinking the poet now dies into life, like the Apollo of *Hyperion*. The temple, with its mingling of classic, Egyptian and medieval motifs, suggests the age-old experience of humanity of which he must now become aware. It also represents a state of mind to which every artist must come; for in it he must resolve how to make use of the visionary capacity, what kind of poetry to write. He is alone in it because in creating every artist is alone.

In the disquieting dialogue with Moneta, the poet learns that once one has reached the temple no escape or haven is possible. The black gates of the temple are "shut . . . evermore." One cannot retreat. One has the choice of remaining on the pavement, momentarily enjoying the incense, and so dying. Or one can move forward to the altar, climb the steps, and share with Moneta her power to view the epic scene of struggle and pain. At this point it is helpful to recall Oceanus's remark in the first version of the poem:

> to bear all naked truths,
> And to envisage circumstance, all calm,
> That is the top of sovereignty. (II, 203–205)

And considering that Moneta is herself a Titan, it is at least suggestive that in "Sleep and Poetry," anticipating the future course of his poetic career, Keats wrote that at a later stage he would "seize" the "events of this wide world . . . Like a strong giant" (lines 81–82).

With regard to what has been said so far, the dialogue with Moneta and the action that takes place during it seem clear and explicit. But when one considers Moneta's remarks on "dreamers" and "visionaries," the intention seems confused — a confusion perhaps acknowledged in Keats's desire to omit much of the dialogue. It appears that, in a mood of self-flagellation, Keats wishes to exalt men of humanitarian action who "labour for mortal good" more directly and fruitfully than poets of any sort. Such men are "no visionaries" and hence would never come to the temple. The poet does, for he is "less than they." Moneta, that is, seems at first to include all poets in the term "visionaries." But she also seems to recognize two possible ways of employing the visionary imagination. The first is that of the poets who "find a haven . . . Where they may thoughtless sleep away their days." The other characterizes those poets to whom "the miseries of the world/ Are misery, and will not let them rest." The protagonist in *The Fall of Hyperion* is of the second kind, and hence he does not die on the pavement. Nevertheless, he can do no "benefit . . . To the great world," and, in addition, he "venoms all his days" by living in a state of restless agitation or fever. In order that "happiness be somewhat shared," Moneta says, the visionary is often "suffer'd in these temples"; for if the temple involves a threat it can also be a reward. The vision achieved in it creates a genuine understanding and knowledge which, though visionary in form, is applicable to actual human experience and so helps to ease "the burden of the Mystery."

The expression so far, apart from the remarks about humanitarians, may seem just and final. But apparently it

279

was not satisfactory to Keats, and if one can judge from what he goes on to say (in the passage he may have intended to omit), the liabilities would seem to have been, first, that, he was not really content that the poet should be ranked below the humanitarian activist, and, secondly, that in his growing distrust of the visionary uses of the imagination, he was neither able to make a significant place for vision nor willing to have all poets described as dreamers. Hence the protagonist recoils in self-defense and tries to suggest to Moneta that not all the poems

> sung into the World's ear
> Are useless; sure a poet is a sage;
> A humanist, physician to all men.   (I, 187–189)

Moneta's answer does not deny this function of poetry, but takes it for granted, and makes a distinction between it and all that can be included under the heading of dream or vision, stamping in the distinction with emphatic repetition. She simply responds:

> Art thou not of the dreamer tribe?
> The poet and the dreamer are distinct,
> Diverse, sheer opposite, antipodes.   (I, 198–200)

Behind this emphasis is Keats's own statement, in his letter of two or three months before, that the greatest writers of England have known intimately "the bye paths of life and seen the festerings of Society. They have not been treated like the Raphaels of Italy." So Boiardo, for example, was "a noble Poet of Romance; not a miserable and mighty Poet of the human Heart." [7] The response of Moneta certainly implies that Keats was seeking to develop a new mode of poetic endeavor. But despite his ambition to "write a few fine plays," it seems unlikely that he would

7. *Letters*, II, 115.

ever have completely abandoned a visionary approach. Hence the undiscriminating attack on all visionaries here implied may be regarded as a temporary reaction. Had he lived, Keats would probably have returned to the position expressed earlier in the dialogue, that the visionary imagination can be used in various ways, and that some uses are valid.

The ascent to the altar, then, may recapitulate the earlier movement of the poem. As the poet draws near, the incense conveys "forgetfulness of everything but bliss" — a bliss corresponding to the bower which preceded his entry into the temple. He is forced to climb the stairs by the "tyranny" of Moneta's "fierce threat," just as he was overcome by the "domineering potion." Finally, after he has reached the top of the altar, Moneta says

> Thou hast felt
> What 'tis to die and live again before
> Thy fated hour.   (I, 141–143)

In other words, like the "cloudy swoon," to mount the stairs may symbolize a dying into life, but with a wider range of implication. For the altar can be approached only "by steps . . . and patient travail/ To count with toil the innumerable degrees." In other words, the poet can see the face of the goddess only by a gradual, stage-by-stage progression. Keats, of course, was in the habit of conceiving imaginative perception as developing through stages. As early as "Sleep and Poetry" he outlined a poetic career. "First," he wrote "the realm I'll pass/ Of Flora, and old Pan" and he described this as a paradise. But "these joys . . . must" be abandoned "for a nobler life,/ Where I may find the agonies, the strife/ Of human hearts" (lines 101–102, 122–124). In a letter two years after "Sleep and Poetry," and a little more than a year before he wrote *The Fall of Hyperion,* Keats put the conception more clearly in the famous comparison of human life to "a large Mansion of Many Apartments, two of which I can only describe, the doors of the rest being as yet shut upon me — The first we step into we call the infant or thoughtless Chamber, in which we remain as long as we do not think . . . the second . . . I shall call the Chamber of Maiden-Thought." There "we become intoxicated with the light and the atmosphere, we see nothing but pleasant wonders, and think of delaying there for ever in delight." In other words, this is the first flowering of the mind and imagination, suffusing everything with novelty and wonder. "However among the effects this breathing is father of is that tremendous one of sharpening one's vision into the heart and nature of Man — of convincing one's nerves that the World is full of Misery and Heartbreak, Pain, Sickness and oppression — whereby This Chamber of Maiden Thought becomes gradually darken'd." [8] The inevitable accumulation of experience and knowledge destroys the "Maiden-Thought" state of mind. It may be that some such notion lies behind the symbolism of the steps in *The Fall of Hyperion.* Perhaps the climbing of the steps can be interpreted as more than a demonstration that one is troubled by the "miseries of the world." Rather the suggestion may be that the steps symbolize a gradually increasing awareness of it. The first step is the most painful and difficult; for after starting, one draws warmth and life from the process.

— 4 —

Even if we "imagine . . . happiness carried to an extreme," an unmingled earthly bliss, "what must it end in? — Death — and who could in such a case bear with death — the whole troubles of life which are now frittered away in a

8. *Letters,* I, 280–281.

series of years, would the[n] be accumulated for the last days of a being who instead of hailing its approach, would leave this world as Eve left Paradise." On the other hand, there is no likelihood of the world becoming such a paradise:

The point at which Man may arrive is as far as the paralel state in inanimate nature and no further — For instance suppose a rose to have sensation, it blooms on a beautiful morning it enjoys itself — but there comes a cold wind, a hot sun — it cannot escape it, it cannot destroy its annoyances — they are as native to the world as itself; no more can man be happy in spite, the world[l]y elements will prey upon his nature.

Nothing is more implicit in the poetry of May to September, 1819, than this realization of the inevitability of suffering in a world of process. With this realization, the poet must seek some emotional acceptance of life as it really is. The conception of the world as a "vale of Soul-making" is one such effort; for, continuing the letter already quoted, Keats wrote, "There may be intelligences or sparks of the divinity in millions — but they are not Souls . . . till they acquire identities, till each one is personally itself. I[n]telligences are atoms of perception . . . how then are Souls to be made . . . but by the medium of a world like this? . . . Do you not see how necessary a World of Pains and troubles is to school an Intelligence and make it a soul?" [9] With the exception of such brief moods and fleeting intuitions, however, Keats does not find any securely felt attitude. Perhaps he did not live long enough. But he did occasionally assert that man must turn to the concrete, experiencing it as fully as possible. This, indeed, is the theme of the "Ode on Melancholy" and "To Autumn."

To discuss these odes together is to depart once again from the order of composition, but in this brief six months

9. *Letters,* II, 101–102.

chronological development is less important than the one nexus of doubt from which all of the poems emerge. For if the transcendental idealism serenely expressed in the "Ode to Psyche" marks one extreme position in the self-debate waged from April to September in 1819, "Melancholy" and "To Autumn" stand at the antithetical pole. The three odes indicate the opposing boundaries and range of Keats's mature speculation. None of Keats's lyrics can be regarded as a settlement or resolution of the central uncertainties, and "To Autumn" and "Melancholy" are not exceptions. They are momentary affirmations, but, as with the other odes, the attitudes they express were deep-seated and persistent, and had any final summing up been achieved, these attitudes would also have been represented. In the background of these two odes, though not directly present in them, stands, first of all, Keats's own skeptical, questioning frame of mind which blocked a commitment to vision in the manner of Shelley or Blake. Secondly, there is the analysis of visionary experience worked out in the lyric and narrative poems of this period, leading Keats in the "Nightingale," *Lamia,* and *The Fall of Hyperion* to suggest that the appeal of dreams may be deadly to the dreamer. And finally, there is the moral concern which results in a suspicion that to seek a subjective escape is unworthy or even contemptible. The harsh adjective is justified by the rigor of Apollonius, who speaks for one side of Keats, and by the self-condemnation voiced through Moneta.

"To Autumn" and "Melancholy" are not twin examples. "Melancholy" is rather an anticipation, an earlier exploration of what the flawless ode of four months later so triumphantly embodies. Here, in "Melancholy," as in other poems, the paradise or haven man might desire, would be to experience an immortal intensity in an ecstasy of unmixed pleasure. But among the general themes of the ode are the inevitability of process and the impossibility of what Keats elsewhere calls a "pure wine/ Of happiness." To experience fully inevitably means to know pain or melancholy as well as pleasure. In fact, Melancholy has her "sovran shrine," is most to be felt, in precisely those experiences which are also most happy.

As we have seen, the desire for an immortal fulfillment has as its corollary the wish to escape from process. The very symbols which express the movement into the desired state of mind — wine or death in the "Ode to a Nightingale," for example — become, if the movement is frustrated, symbols of non-experiencing. This theme appears, with more sober colorings, in "La Belle Dame Sans Merci," and also in *Lamia,* where the blocked attempt to rise into a visionary fulfillment really becomes a descent into oblivion. Translating these symbolic apprehensions into the language of exposition, one can see that they rise from the undeniable facts of psychological experience. A persistent habit of envisioning happy situations remote from present, actual circumstances naturally indicates a radical dissatisfaction with things as they are. If the dream or vision grounds itself in impossibility, fact will intrude, spoiling the satisfactions of the dream. In such a case, the alternative to an acceptance of things as they are would be an unconscious endeavor not to perceive or experience, a deadening of sensibility and awareness. At the beginning of the "Ode on Melancholy" the poet may be speaking to the man of "pale forehead" — the "pale warriors" of "La Belle Dame" who, like himself, have been unable to retain the satisfactions of vision — and urging that he should not take the downward course to oblivion ("go not to Lethe"). Thus many of the symbols usually associated with the flight into vision — the wine, the rosary of the religious aspirer, death and Psyche — are here indiscriminately lumped together and marshaled under the heading of Lethe as symbols of forgetfulness, perhaps suggesting that the aspiration to a visionary haven has converted itself into a desire for unawareness.

It may seem, however, that this interpretation is suspiciously pat to the theme I have been tracing, and that it is not fully justified by what is said in the poem. Certainly one does not have to go outside the poem to read the first stanza:

> No, no, go not to Lethe, neither twist
> Wolf's-bane, tight-rooted, for its poisonous wine;
> Nor suffer thy pale forehead to be kiss'd
> By nightshade, ruby grape of Proserpine;
> Make not your rosary of yew-berries,
> Nor let the beetle, nor the death-moth be
> Your mournful Psyche, nor the downy owl
> A partner in your sorrow's mysteries;
> For shade to shade will come too drowsily,
> And drown the wakeful anguish of the soul.

Lethe, the poisonous wine, nightshade, and the like are symbols of death or oblivion in their own right. Moreover, in the first stanza the "death-moth" as a mournful Psyche, the "rosary of yew-berries," or the poisonous wine are also approximate equivalents to the beetle or the downy owl. They are images associated with melancholy. In the case of the "melancholy fit," to turn to such images is to seek what harmonizes with the mood. But things are defined by contrast, and in a universe of melancholy, its essence can scarcely be comprehended or felt. Instead, the "wakeful" perceiving of the soul is drowned. Of course, all these symbols are subsumed by the question of how to take the melancholy fit; for exactly this state can either create a deadened sensitivity or else it can be turned into a sharpened

286

awareness of the concrete. The problem is the human use of it. The answer is not to dodge the melancholy through oblivion, but to experience through it. Against the attitude of the "pale warriors" of "La Belle Dame," the poem urges an unreserved and intense involvement in process. The wakefulness of the soul is to the highest degree prized, even though, in the state of melancholy, the intensity may become anguish. Hence such expressions in the first stanza as "poisonous wine," the "forehead . . . kiss'd/ By nightshade," or the "mournful Psyche" may have a significance that goes beyond what has been mentioned. In the first place, the wine would be poisonous, the "death-moth" a "mournful Psyche," and the like, not only in a literal sense but also because they do suggest an escape, if only into oblivion, and such an escape would be destructive to any possibility of happiness. More than this, however, the phrases bring together opposites — wine and poison, kissing and death — and so prelude or anticipate an important theme in the poem.

The perception that melancholy dwells with Beauty is not, of course, a mere rhetorical toying with antithesis. Neither is it simply the sentimental "Dejection taken up for pleasure's sake," the "sweet desolation-balmy pain" so frequently found in romantic poetry.[10] As recent critics have noticed, the pleasure-pain paradox, the coalescing of joy and sorrow in a single experiencing, runs throughout much of Keats's poetry. In the early verse, perhaps, this attitude to the nature of experience usually appears more as a flourish than as a perception vitally felt. Thus when Keats writes of birds "warbling for very joy mellifluous sorrow," or of bees who "know there is richest juice in poison-flowers," one need not take the expression very seriously. But as he continued

10. *Prelude*, VI, 551; "I Stood Tip-Toe," line 162,

to write, Keats clarified and deepened the content of such phrases. In *Hyperion* Apollo, awaking from a dream, played his lyre, and

> all the vast
> Unwearied ear of the whole universe
> Listen'd in pain and pleasure at the birth
> Of such new tuneful wonder;   (III, 64–67)

and in the "Ode to Psyche" Keats speaks of "branchèd thoughts new grown with pleasant pain." It is true that in this context Keats refers only to creative activity, but then such activity is itself a type or even a metaphor of intense involvement.

The second stanza begins with a metaphor of process:

> But when the melancholy fit shall fall
> Sudden from heaven like a weeping cloud,
> That fosters the droop-headed flowers all,
> And hides the green hill in an April shroud.

At first glance, one might wonder why the metaphor is elaborated, and whether the details relate to the over-all movement of the poem. But it as least suggests that the melancholy fit is not wholly undesirable. The "droop-headed flowers" have a grammatical relation only with the "cloud," but the implication may be that the poet can also be awakened by a melancholy fit, a notion entirely consistent with the theme of the poem. More than that, however, the metaphor defines the conditions of life in a world of process, and implies that melancholy is inevitably a part of it. The "weeping cloud . . . hides the green hill in an April shroud" — a paradoxical phrase since April is the season of budding, the direct antithesis to the shroud or death-time. But at the same time, the cloud, with its suggestion of a temporary death, "fosters the droop-headed flowers," and without it there could be no fulfillment. When the melancholy fit falls one should seek to know it as fully as possible, and at the same time to savor things through the perspective it offers. Hence one should turn to what arouses a massive response in any mood. The morning rose, the "rainbow of the salt sand-wave," the "globèd peonies," and the rich anger of the mistress are all images of fulfillment, of things declaring their identity, revealing their essential being or "inscape," to use Hopkins's word; and the empathic reaction to these things creates the "havens of intenseness" which man would like to preserve. But the fulfillment is evanescent. The rose is a morning rose, its future uncertain as the day proceeds. "Suppose a rose to have sensation," wrote Keats, "it blooms on a beautiful morning it enjoys itself — but there comes a cold wind, a hot sun." [11] The rainbow of the wave is even more fleeting, for it forms as the wave rises to its crest and breaks. The anger of the mistress, one presumes, is equally short-lived. Yet even though these are momentary and fleeting, one can still possess them wholly. One can "glut" sorrow on a rose, "feed deep" upon the eyes of the mistress, and these images, presenting the sense of sight in terms of taste, suggest the intensity of the empathic response. Similarly, as W. J. Bate and others have pointed out, the phrase "globèd peonies" suggests the hand cupping the flowers in a full relish of their identity. At the same time, such expressions as "glut," or "feed deep, deep" imply a prolonging of the experience as it occurs. To become glutted takes a while, and the reiteration of "deep" draws out the feeding. The word "emprison" has a similar force, bespeaking a desire to arrest and hold immobile the momentary intensity. Thus as I said earlier, while these lines suggest the evanescence of the fulfillment, they also express the paradox of empathy — the unawareness of time at the height of intense experience.

11. *Letters*, II, 101.

But because these beautiful objects quickly fade, to turn to them is also to nourish the melancholy fit, and the last stanza generalizes the theme. Previously the poet had implied that melancholy is not simply a fit or mood, but something inextricably present in human life and experience. Now it is recognized that melancholy "dwells with Beauty" because beauty must die, and with Joy that is ever "bidding adieu." In pleasure so intense that it is "nigh" or almost aching — an emotion which becomes not simply pleasure but the full reaction of the whole being — melancholy resides, just as while the "bee-mouth sips" — an intoxicating image of delicate and intense pleasure — the nectar turns to poison in the bee's body. The metaphor perfectly expresses pleasure and pain slipping into each other and becoming one complex reaction in the organic processes of mind. In the "temple of delight" is the "sovran shrine" of Melancholy. But only the man who experiences most fully, the man of "strenuous tongue" and "palate fine," tastes the sadness at the core of "Joy's grape." Thus *Lamia, The Fall of Hyperion,* and the "Ode on Melancholy" can be seen as extending and clarifying a mood or attitude implied in most of Keats's major poems of 1819. In human life moments of intense experience decay as inevitably as they grow, and happiness cannot be disengaged from sorrow. To abstract materials from concrete life and build a visionary home leads to delusion and disappointment, and the hope to find some visionary reconciliation with process may vanish before accumulated experience and awareness.

— 5 —

Of the ode "To Autumn," Allen Tate has said that it "is a very nearly perfect piece of style but it has little to say," and this opinion seems to be widely held.[12] But within the framework of Keats's habitual symbols and general attitudes, the ode seems to me unusually significant. Even more than Keats's other odes, "To Autumn" is objective, oblique, and impersonal, carried scarcely at all by direct statement that involves the poet.[13] Like that of the "Grecian Urn" or the "Nightingale," its expression is concrete and symbolic, and as in these other odes, the symbol adopted had been previously established in Keats's poetry. Something has already been said about his use of the seasons. Generally it is rather conventional: spring is the time of budding, summer of fulfillment, and winter of death. The poem, "The Human Seasons" (March 1818), is typical as it runs through the "four seasons in the mind of man." In spring, the period of "youthful thought," man's growing faculties take in "all beauty with an easy span." Summer is the time of "luxuriously" enjoying or ruminating what was culled in the spring. Man "has his winter too of pale misfeature,/ Or else he would forgo his mortal nature." Autumn, coming between summer and winter, can be seen as the intensifying and prolonging of summer. In other words, autumn suggests precisely that lengthening out of fulfillment as its crest or climax which Keats had desired to find in the concrete world. So the poet,

12. "A Reading of Keats," *American Scholar*, XV (Spring 1946), p. 58.
13. Leonard Unger, "Keats and the Music of Autumn," *Western Review*, XIV (Spring 1950), pp. 279–280, makes the point very well: "Whereas in 'Ode to Melancholy' the theme . . . is the immediate subject, in 'To Autumn' the season is the subject and the details which describe and thus present the subject are also the medium by which the theme is explored. . . . For example, Herrick's 'To Daffodils' has a theme which is at least superficially similar to Keats'. But in Herrick's poem the theme is openly stated, and it is, in fact, the subject, which is illustrated by logical analogy with the daffodils. In 'To Autumn,' however . . . the theme inheres in the subject, and is at no point stated in other terms."

turning to the concrete, to process, can contemplate it with serenity.

Autumn, accordingly, is described as a season of "mellow fruitfulness." The sun is ripening or "maturing" the earth, "conspiring" to load the vines and bend the apple trees, to "swell the gourd, and plump the hazel shells." In such verbs as "load" and "bend" there is a sense of strain. The season fills "all fruit with ripeness to the core"; and these images of full, inward ripeness and of strain suggest that the maturing can go no further, that the fulfillment has reached its climax. Even the cells of the bees are "o'er-brimm'd." Yet the ripening continues, "budding more,/ And still more, later flowers." The bees — and the reader only partially identifies himself with them — "think warm days will never cease." Thus through the imagery the poem suggests an intensity of fulfillment prolonged and almost seeming to be immortal. At the same time, however, there are indirect images of aging. For the sun is maturing — it is not only ripening things, but it is also growing older. So also, one presumes, is autumn itself, the "close bosom-friend" of the sun. Process is taking place, and the season is drawing to a close, however slowly and unnoticed.

The second stanza picks up and continues the imagery of arrested motion in the first.[14] Autumn is here personified in a variety of attitudes; but the dominant image is of autumn as the harvester — and a harvester that is in a sense another reaper, death itself. Instead of harvesting, however, autumn is motionless, death being momentarily held off as the ripening still continues. First autumn appears "sitting careless on a granary floor." The granary is where the harvest

14. For this and other points in my discussion of "To Autumn," I am indebted to the admirable analysis of the poem's imagery by Reuben A. Brower, *The Fields of Light* (New York, 1951), pp. 39–41.

would be stored, but autumn is not bringing in the grain. The assonance and alliteration of the line, "Thy hair soft-lifted by the winnowing wind," leads into the image of autumn "drows'd" or "asleep" on a "half-reap'd furrow" — again the harvest arrested — "while thy hook/ Spares the next swath and all its twinèd flowers." Finally autumn is seen by a cider press where it watches "the last oozings hours by hours." This is one of the two images suggesting activity (the other being the gleaner with "laden head" crossing a brook), but the motion is so slow that the reader takes the cider press almost as a repetition of the "half-reap'd furrow." But, of course, these are the "last oozings," and the harvest is drawing to a close. The notion of death is present to emerge more nakedly in the third stanza.

As with the "rainbow of the salt sand-wave" or the night-ingale "pouring forth" its soul, things reveal their essential being or identity most intensely at the moment of dying or readiness to die. So the last stanza begins with the one comment the poet offers in his own person: "Where are the songs of Spring?" In the "Ode on a Grecian Urn" the same contrast between spring and the close of process was felt:

> Ah, happy, happy boughs! that cannot shed
> Your leaves, nor ever bid the Spring adieu.

In the "Ode on a Grecian Urn" the contrast leads or per-mits the poet to rebel against process in the wish to hold the spring forever. This rebellion, however, is now explicitly denied — "Ay, where are they?/ Think not of them, thou hast thy music too." There follows an image of the day, which, like autumn, is "soft-dying," and the death is ac-companied by a fulfillment; for as it dies the day blooms or flowers ("While barrèd clouds bloom the soft-dying day," and "touch the stubble-plains" with the warm color of the rose). The stanza proceeds with images of death or withdrawal, and of song, and the songs are a funeral dirge for the dying year. The "small gnats mourn" in a "wailful choir"; the wind "lives or dies"; "full-grown lambs loud bleat"; "hedge-crickets sing"; the "redbreast whistles"; and the swallows which are gathering for departure "twitter in the skies." At the same time the repeated suggestions of gentleness or softness — "small gnats," "light wind," "lambs," "treble soft," "twitter" — suffuse the stanza with a tone of tenderness; and the objectivity of the last few lines suggests an acceptance which includes even the fact of death. But death here is neither a pining for an "easeful" escape nor is it an intensity, a blind, climactic outpouring and release analogous to the song of the nightingale. Rather it is recognized as something inwoven in the course of things, the condition and price of all fulfillment, having like the spring and summer of life its own distinctive character or "music" which is also to be prized and relished. In the last analysis, perhaps, the serenity and acceptance here expressed are aesthetic. The ode is, after all, a poem of contemplation. The symbol of autumn compels that attitude. The poet's own fears, ambitions, and passions are not directly engaged, and hence he can be relatively withdrawn. And because spring is also subsumed in the context, he can seem to suggest that life in all its stages has a certain identity and beauty which man can appreciate by disengaging his own ego. Thus the symbol permits, and the poem as a whole expresses, an emotional reconciliation to the human experience of process.

— 6 —

More than that of most poets in the last century and a half, the poetic career of Keats has in itself possessed a power of kindling the imagination. It is not simply that he died with so much potentiality, as we suppose, unfulfilled. It is also that he developed so suddenly. And his remarkable evolution in stylistic variety and control was accompanied by a growth which was, in a large sense of the word, moral — illustrating that "grave moral concern" Taine thought a national defect in the English. The modern reader is not more satisfied with *Endymion* than Keats was, and he may feel, with Keats himself, that the greater technical control of "The Eve of St. Agnes" only obscures and makes less "glaring" a "simplicity of knowledge." [15] But Keats's more mature poetry shows him exploring a range of concern which subsumes much of Wordsworth and almost all of Shelley, and which, at least in some directions, may have carried him further than either Wordsworth or Shelley were able to go. For if he shared with Wordsworth and Shelley their hope that through the imagination man may discover and, at least for the moment, unite himself with a permanence answering to the heart's desire, he also, like Wordsworth, abandoned this hope. And the "Ode on Melancholy" shows him denying the final Wordsworthian bid for a repose achieved through suppression of feeling.

None of the romantic poets was able to achieve a serene affirmation of the conditions of human life, a sense that "ripeness is all." Keats was no exception. Yet throughout his career Keats sought a basis for such an affirmation. Of course, one may feel that the "Ode on Melancholy" views the decay and loss inevitable in process with some serenity; for the consciousness that the flashing out of beauty is momentary sharpens the experience of it. The reconciliation here, as in "To Autumn," is, perhaps, ultimately aesthetic. The noble view of the world as a "vale of Soul-making"

15. *Letters,* II, 174.

in which individual identities or souls are carved from human potentiality by the struggle with circumstance is another effort to achieve some emotional acceptance of process. It is a myth, and like any successful myth it has scope and immediacy, transmuting conception to feeling, and capturing an acquiescence which logic or "consequitive reasoning," as Keats himself said, could never obtain. But the myth of the "vale of Soul-making," dazzling in imaginative impact as it is, was not further developed by Keats before he died.

What remains from this prolonged, brilliant, and interrupted exploration is, perhaps, only a bravery in confronting life in a world of process filled with suffering and uncertainty. Yet the varied speculations which underlie Keats's poetry from "La Belle Dame" to the ode "To Autumn" may potentially include a rejection of the romantic quest for permanence. This, in fact, is an important aspect of the Negative Capability which critics have rightly stressed as a central theme both in his poetic procedure and in his more general approach to life; for he expands the phrase, in describing the quality that goes "to form a Man of Achievement especially in literature," by adding: "that is when a man is capable of being in uncertainties, Mysteries, doubts, without any irritable reaching after fact & reason." [16] What is involved, of course, is more than a willingness to accept insecurity for its own sake. In *Hyperion,* the speech of Oceanus implies that in the "sullen ferment" of an evolving universe the consolation for loss must be, among other things, the perception of what Mnemosyne calls "loveliness new born." The notion may be that the uncertainty experienced in every kind of human endeavor can be prized as a source of novelty, interest, and creative effort.

16. *Letters,* I, 193.

This, however, was only one of Keats's many speculations. What remains as an undeniable fact is his own uncertainty and self-division during the period of his greatest poetry. Here, indeed, we may be noticing an additional reason for the appeal of Keats to our own time. Though the centers of doubt may be somewhat changed, the contemporary poet is likely to be equally divided, and the problem, in our own day as for Keats, is how in this state of mind can poetry be made. The answer, for Keats as for Shakespeare, and, perhaps, for any poet in a similar dilemma, lies in drama. It is significant that *Lamia* and *The Fall of Hyperion,* where Keats abandons drama, especially illustrate the need for it. Radically conflicting impulses may be a fertile soil for some kinds of poetry, but it is doubtful whether they can make for entire success in a narrative mode. Certainly this is true when the narratives are modeled on Dryden and Milton and intended to make a statement. Both Dryden and Milton, after all, knew what they wanted to say, at least in comparison with the youthful Keats, and they derived from the inward settlement a firmer control of their materials. Keats did not; and hence despite potentialities that "The Eve of St. Agnes" shows, he may not have been ready in 1819 to write narrative verse. It is significant that neither version of *Hyperion* was finished.[17] At least one of the obstacles may have been the centrifugal character of Keats's sympathies, which would make it difficult for him to achieve a clear and stable point of view. *Lamia* is equally revealing. That none of the characters

17. D. G. James, *The Romantic Comedy* (London, 1948), pp. 137-138, has said that Keats failed to complete these epics because his sympathies were wholly on the side of Apollo and the new divinities. The epic mode, that is, demanded a conflict, but there was no conflict in Keats's own mind, and hence it was difficult for him to manage an epic form. The argument, as James presents it, certainly seems persuasive; yet it is weakened when James goes on to imply that Milton could portray a conflict because his sympathies were divided.

represents a reasonably acceptable ideal perhaps indicates Keats's own inability to make a commitment. And more than that, the intention often seems confused. There is, for example, the passage denouncing abstract science ("Philosophy will clip an Angel's wing") which calls attention to itself as though it were a key to interpret the poem; yet it seems hardly more than an unnecessary digression. And Keats could not maintain a firm attitude to Lamia herself. One can turn to *Paradise Lost* for a contrast. It was a common romantic assumption, of course, that Milton, being a rebel, was partially identified with Satan, and hence that the poem reflects a conflict in Milton himself. But the reverse is more probable. Because there was no personal involvement or sympathy, Milton, for the sake of his poem, could grant Satan a certain magnificence. Writers, like other people, can afford to be generous to the extent that they are secure. To Keats, however, what Lamia represents was an attraction and hence a threat. He could not be generous without becoming committed. Thus the poem initially presents Lamia with mockery, seems intent on exposing her, but goes on to treat her with a certain tenderness and sympathy. This is not to suggest that *Lamia* or *The Fall of Hyperion* are not remarkable achievements. Keats's talent could easily compensate for a form selected with less than perfect tact. The point is only the embarrassments of narrative for a poet with Keats's skeptical, uncommitted habit of mind.

The five great odes of Keats would serve to demonstrate that on any complicated question an unqualified position is also likely to be a more shallow one. From this point of view, "to Psyche," "Melancholy," and "To Autumn" can be considered together and contrasted with the "Grecian Urn" and the "Nightingale." Of course, the three odes still rise far above the mean of lyric expression. But they lack

298

the complexity, the passion, and the sweep of the other two. It is significant, then, that each of the three, presenting only one side of the conflict dramatically fought out in the "Grecian Urn" or "Nightingale," are relatively assured statements. In other words, Keats was not able to project as much of himself into them. Hence there may be a further significance in the fact that neither "Psyche," "Melancholy," or "Autumn" makes use of a central symbol in the same way as the other two odes. In "Melancholy," a symbol is almost totally lacking as an organizing factor. In "Psyche" and "Autumn," there is a rudimentary conceptual presence — the goddess or the season of the year — but it is so general, so open to varied interpretation, that it still compels the writer to impose attitudes more than to discover them. Only in the "Grecian Urn" and the "Nightingale" is there a central object possessing a specific and limited identity. Nothing, then, may demonstrate Keats's need for symbol more concretely than the greater scope and success of these two odes. There is, first of all, a sharp focus achieved by excluding whatever is not relevant to the symbol contemplated. The symbol, moreover, becomes an actor or participant separate from the speaker, thus allowing dramatic interplay and progression. Finally, the poet need not unify his attitudes before writing the poem. If he himself remains perplexed and divided, the central symbol may hold the poem together and permit a temporary, *ad hoc* resolution.

Thus the "Ode on a Grecian Urn" and the "Ode to a Nightingale" can be described as a poetry of symbolic debate. While there is no intent to suggest that Keats has been a model, it is certainly true that many contemporary poets, notably Yeats, have followed a similar practice, using a symbol to organize a poem and yet within the poem embodying different attitudes to it. The conflict may be expressed in the Janus-like qualities of the symbol itself, as in the "Ode on a Grecian Urn," and then the poem is likely to be unusually compressed, every word, ideally speaking, contributing to the conflict. Or it may be presented by shifting attitudes toward the symbol in the course of the poem, as in "Bright Star" or the "Ode to a Nightingale," though, of course, both methods are employed to some extent in each of the two odes. Despite these similarities, there are naturally many ways in which contemporary poets do not resemble Keats in their use of symbol. One of the leading distinctions — and here I am thinking of the more successful contemporary efforts — is that a poet today is likely to seem more objective — if, by "objective," we mean the use of details and inferences (with something analogous to a neoclassic conception of "decorum" or "propriety") restricted solely to the implications of the symbol. At the end of the "Ode on a Grecian Urn," as in "Bright Star," Keats goes beyond or even contrary to the implications of the symbol in order to make what could be called an "assertion." As with the conclusion of Wordsworth's "Intimations of Immortality," the assertion is even made, in one sense, because it is what the poet — in fact, human nature generally — would like to believe, the difference being that, with Keats, the symbol has made the occasion more specific and limited. The form of the drama, as with Yeats and Eliot so often, is in the growing reaction to the symbol. But the drama, thus released, is not for that reason really apart from the symbol. It reacts from the symbol and focuses back upon it.

The organic view of nature, which the romantics proclaimed with such a sense of discovery, imposed a heavy burden in encouraging the use of symbol while at the same time frustrating it. In "The Circus Animals' Desertion," Yeats, as

Auden remarks, put the situation of the modern poet exactly: symbols help as "ladders," but ultimately they seem only "shows," and the poet is forced to go back to

> where all the ladders start,
> In the foul rag-and-bone shop of the heart.[18]

A relentless ideal of naked personal sincerity (an ideal that most poets before the romantics would not have understood) has been in constant conflict with the attempt by poets, since Wordsworth, to create a symbolic art. Perhaps the resolution is only in drama. But a further burden on the romantics was to have sensed this, and to have had in mind the great and intimidating example of Shakespeare (whom Goethe was grateful that he lacked as a predecessor in his own language). The problem, perhaps, was to find whether there could be another way of exploiting the perennial strengths of drama, while assimilating the self-consciousness — the thinking "into the heart" — that, as Keats saw, was putting new barriers and challenges before poetry. The "Chamber of Maiden Thought," he goes on, is becoming "gradually darken'd and at the same time on all sides of it many doors are set open — but all dark — all leading to dark passages . . . To this point was Wordsworth come . . . Now if we live, and go on thinking, we too shall explore them." [19] Implicit in this is the fact that, with Keats, we are dealing with a talent, indeed an entire approach to poetry, in which symbol, however necessary, may possibly not satisfy as the principal concern of poetry, any more than it could with Shakespeare, but is rather an element in the poetry and drama of human reactions.

18. *Collected Poems,* p. 336.
19. *Letters,* I, 281–282.

INDEX

303